CW01239452

RAILS ACROSS THE PLAIN

THE AMESBURY & BULFORD BRANCH
THE LARKHILL MILITARY RAILWAY

JEFFERY GRAYER

WITH FOREWORD BY MAJOR W. G. CLARKE

NOODLE BOOKS

© Kevin Robertson (Noodle Books) and Jeffery Grayer 2011

ISBN 978-1-906419-51-6.

Printed in England by Ian Allan Printing Ltd.

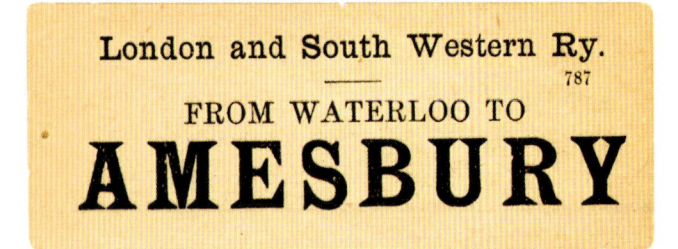

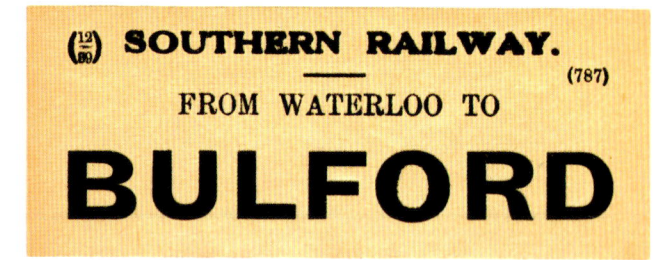

London and South Western Ry.
787
FROM WATERLOO TO
AMESBURY

(12/60) SOUTHERN RAILWAY.
(787)
FROM WATERLOO TO
BULFORD

First published in 2011 by Kevin Robertson under the **NOODLE BOOKS** imprint

PO Box 279, Corhampton, Southampton, SO32 3ZX
www.noodlebooks.co.uk

The publisher and author hereby give full notice that all rights to this work are reserved. Aside from brief passages for the purpose of review, no part of this work may be reproduced, copied by electronic or other means, or otherwise stored in any information storage or retrieval system without written permission from the Publisher. This includes the illustrations herein which shall remain the copyright of the author unless otherwise stated.

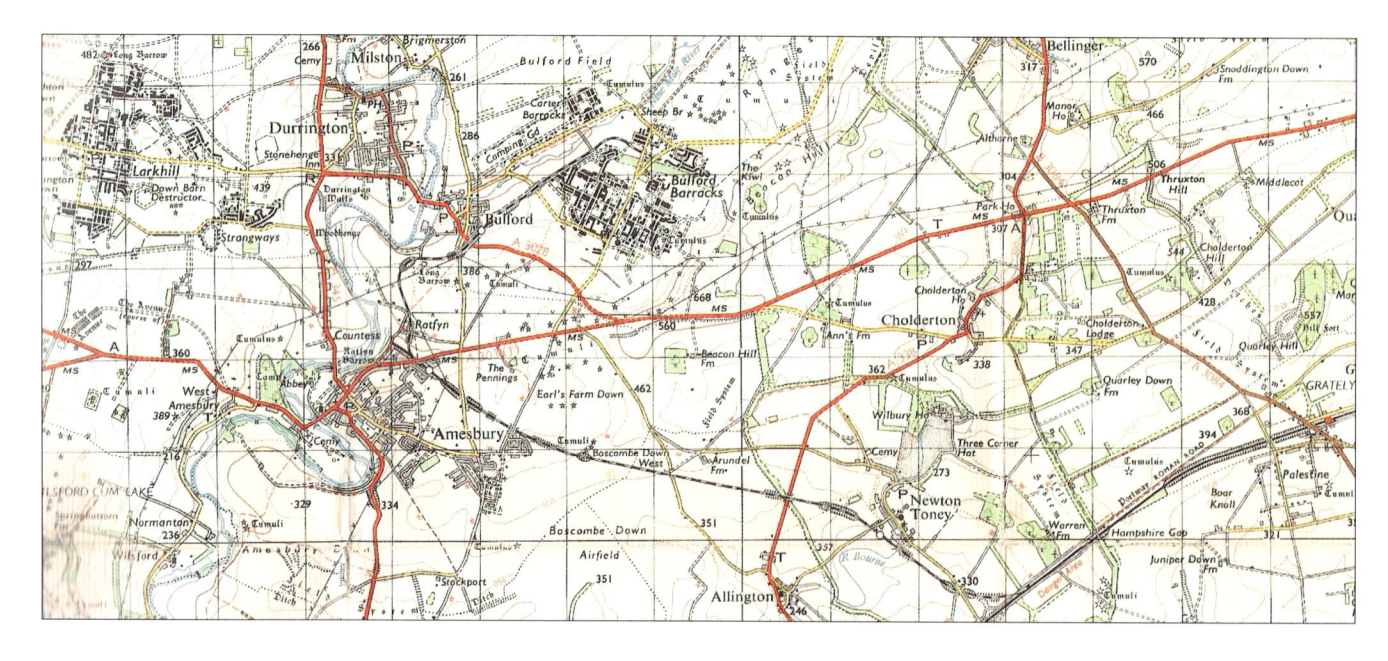

This Page - Route of the line from Grateley to Amesbury and Bulford. Reproduced from a 1960 Ordnance Survey map. (With the kind permission of Ordnance Survey)

Front Cover - The "Rambling Rose" railtour of March 23 1963, the final passenger train to traverse the branch was headed by Drummond M7 tank No. 30108 seen here shunting back into the up platform at Amesbury. (Unknown)

Frontispiece - Hard to believe today that this tranquil bucolic sylvan setting, beneath an overbridge to the south of Newton Tony, once echoed to the rumble of lengthy troop trains taking men to the carnage of the Western Front. (Jeffery Grayer)

CONTENTS PAGE

FOREWORD 4

INTRODUCTION 5

1. SALISBURY PLAIN 7
The Plain......The Military......Railways Skirt The Plain.....Failed Plans

2. A BREACH IS MADE 15
Initial Proposals.....Construction.....Revised Junction Arrangements.....Extension

3. OPERATION 45
Improvements...Timetables...Military Traffic...Accidents...Signalling.....Motive Power...Coaching Stock

4. THE LARKHILL MILITARY RAILWAY 57
Origins....Construction....The Route Described....Closure....Tank Practice Railway

5. DECLINE 81
Retrenchment....Passenger Closure....Goods Services....Total Closure.....Demolition and Remains

6. ICON OF THE PLAIN 102

APPENDICES

I.	Chronology	112
II.	Track Diagrams	113
III.	Plans and Drawings	116
IV.	Timetables	123
V.	Gradient profiles Amesbury & Military Camp Railway	124
VI.	Working Timetable Appendices 1934 and working arrangements	125
VII.	Proposed and constructed lines in the vicinity of Stonehenge	128
VIII.	Rateable values	130
IX.	Estimate of Expenses, Amesbury & Military Camp Railway, Newton Tony Curve	133
X.	Envoi, Bibliography and Acknowledgements	135

FOREWORD

It has given me enormous pleasure to read Jeffery Grayer's manuscript of 'Rails Across The Plain'. In asking me to write the Foreword to his work he is acknowledging the research that I too have carried out on the history of the Army on Salisbury Plain. Although the book essentially tells the story of the railways that were built on the Plain during the last century, it also encompasses much of the social and military history of the area and the effect that the railways had upon the Plain and its inhabitants.

It is hard for people to imagine today just how busy and large was the presence of the Army in this part of south Wiltshire during both world wars and for many years afterwards, indeed, until successive defence reviews and the 'Beeching Axe' finally reduced the Army and the railways and to the pitifully small organisations they have now become. At its peak there were 34 hutted camps at Larkhill and Rollestone each large enough to house an infantry battalion or an artillery brigade. In addition there were the camps at Bulford and Tidworth, the aerodrome at Stonehenge and the camp at Druids Lodge, all in their time served by various railway spurs.

In their heyday the Amesbury & Bulford Railway and the Larkhill Military Railway made the occupation of the Plain by the Army a viable proposition and in so doing contributed greatly to the efficient training of many tens of thousands of soldiers from Britain and the Empire, as well as those from many allied armies. Although none of the lines remain, it is still possible to see much of the route where they once existed. Some have now become well-worn footpaths.

This admirable archive therefore records the story of more than one hundred years of railway and military history on Salisbury Plain and it complements the many other books published on these two subjects over the years. It also highlights perfectly the shared history of the railways, the Army and Salisbury Plain.

Major W G Clarke

Garrison Staff Officer, Royal Artillery, Larkhill.

May 2011

Above - The view over Bulford Camp looking north from Beacon Hill. (Unknown)

Opposite - Aerial view taken in the 1930s showing the approach cutting to Amesbury station (1), the spur leading ahead to Shrewton (2), and the Bulford extension curving away to the right (3). In the foreground is the overbridge (4) featured on page 108.

INTRODUCTION

The former branchline from the erstwhile LSWR mainline near Grateley to Amesbury, Bulford and Bulford Camp, together with the associated Larkhill Military Railway, have received scant attention over the years from transport publishers. Twenty years ago a short privately published booklet, now out of print, appeared relating the significant features of the story of the rise and fall of this line and shortly after a further mainly pictorial album, now also out of print, provided a selection of views of the route although the title was primarily concerned with the mainline from Basingstoke to Salisbury. Whilst the majority of the railway lines in the south of England have benefitted from full surveys in their own right, these lines on Salisbury Plain have remained largely disregarded by the railway historian and have merited only a passing mention in various publications dealing with Wiltshire's railways as a whole.

This shortcoming has now been remedied in this new volume, lavishly illustrated with many views not published before, which not only tells the history of this group of lines but sets them in the context both of Salisbury Plain and of the related military activities which they did so much to facilitate, not merely in two World Wars, but for more than 60 years until final closure in 1963.

Numerous interesting facets of the line, together with substantial background on some of the more noteworthy characters and events at locations bordering the route, have been collected together by the author and these combine to give this fascinating story a wide appeal outside the confines of a book of interest purely to railway enthusiasts. The importance of Stonehenge in the history of railways in the area is not overlooked and the story is brought right up to date by consideration of alternative public transport schemes to improve the local environment at the stones by reducing the impact of the car upon this World Heritage site.

Kevin Robertson

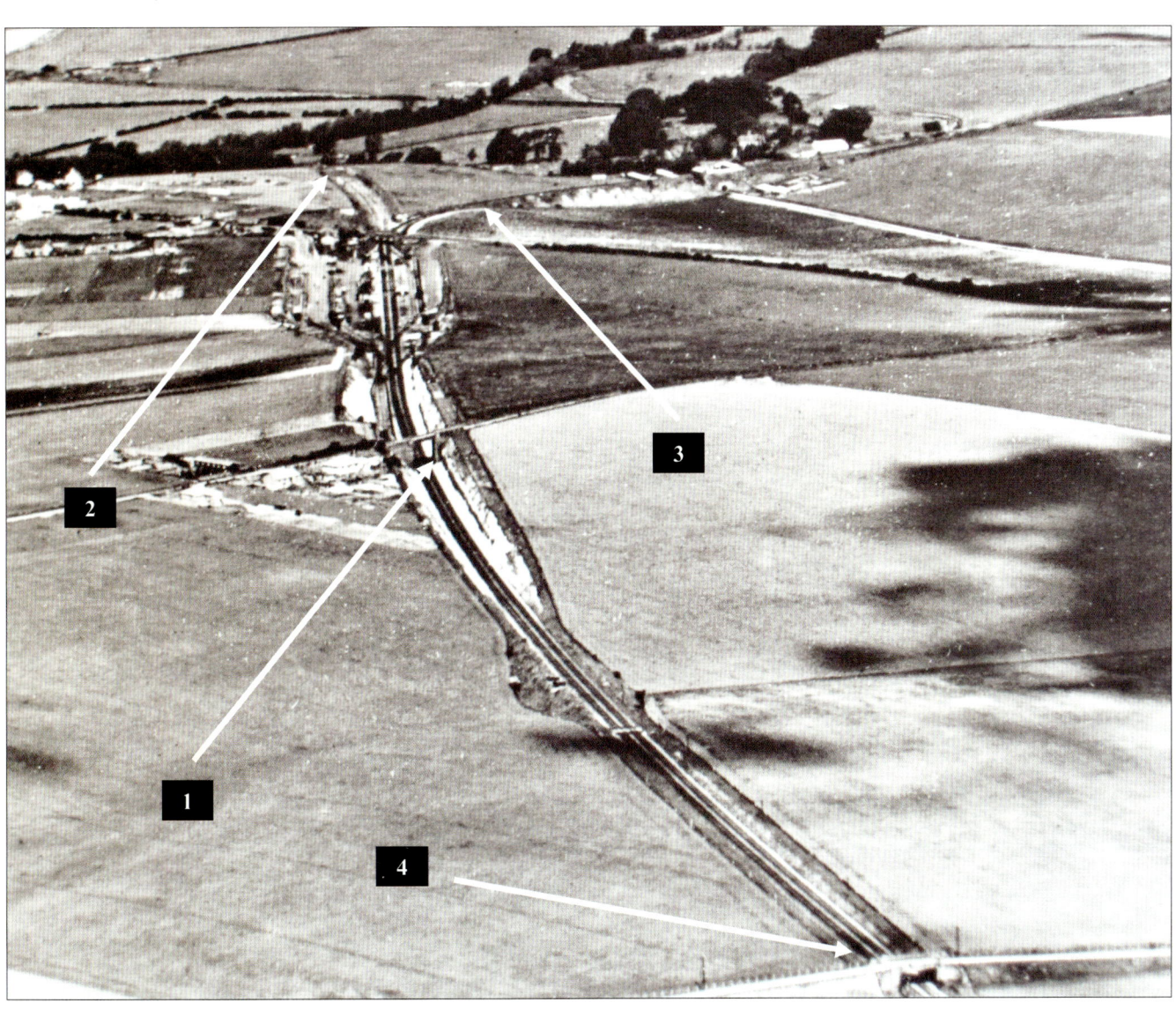

The troubled west was red with stormy fire,
O'er Sarum's plain the traveller with a sigh
Measured each painful step, the distant spire
That fixed at every turn his backward eye
Was lost, tho' still he turned, in the blank sky.
By thirst and hunger pressed he gazed around
And scarce could any trace of man descry,
Save wastes of corn that stretched without a bound,
But where the sower dwelt was nowhere to be found.

No shade was there, no meads of pleasant green,
No brook to wet his lips or soothe his ear,
Huge piles of corn-stack here and there were seen
But thence no smoke upwreathed his sight to cheer;
And see the homeward shepherd dim appear
Far off - He stops his feeble voice to strain;
No sound replies but winds that whistling near
Sweep the thin grass and passing, wildly plain;
Or desert lark that pours on high a wasted strain.

Salisbury Plain

1. SALISBURY PLAIN

THE PLAIN......THE MILITARY......RAILWAYS SKIRT THE PLAIN.....FAILED PLANS

THE PLAIN

The lines opposite, taken from a poem composed by William Wordsworth as he made his way from the Isle of Wight to North Wales via Salisbury and the Wye Valley between late July and September 1793, perfectly capture the essence of that barren tract of land known as Salisbury Plain. Whilst journeying north from Salisbury, Wordsworth and his travelling companion William Calvert were involved in an accident that destroyed their carriage. Miraculously unharmed, the pair decided to split up, with Calvert heading north and Wordsworth west, towards Wales. For two or three days, the poet wandered the bleak Plain, composing as he went the first version of the poem.

The boundaries of the Plain have always been open to interpretation there being some difference of opinion as to its exact area. It is generally recognised as being that undulating tract of chalky downland covering an area some twenty miles long and sixteen miles wide in the south-east corner of Wiltshire lying between Salisbury in the south and Devizes in the north. The river valleys surrounding it, and the downs and plains beyond them loosely define its boundaries. To the north the edge of the plain overlooks Pewsey Vale and to the northwest the valley of the Bristol Avon. The River Wylye runs along the south west side of the Plain, and the River Bourne to the east. The Hampshire Avon flows through the eastern half and to the south the Plain peters out as the river valleys come together before meeting at Salisbury. The Hampshire Downs and the Berkshire Downs are areas of chalk downland to the east and north of Salisbury Plain, and the Dorset Downs and Cranborne Chase lie to the south west. The Plain is a country of limey soil spread thinly over more than a thousand feet of pure soft white limestone consisting almost entirely of the fossils of minute animals and sea-plants, which lived between seventy and one hundred million years ago when the Plain formed the bed of a comparatively shallow sea. Even today, as in Wordsworth's time, the area is largely devoid of significant habitation. Amesbury is considered to be the largest settlement though there are a number of small villages, such as Tilshead, Shrewton and Chitterne in the middle of the Plain, as well as various hamlets and army camps.

It is difficult for 21st. Century man to imagine what the Plain was like in the latter years of the nineteenth century, when all lines of communication, save for the few principal turnpike roads which crossed the area, were little more than narrow tracks, chokingly dust-bound in summer and morasses of clinging mud in winter. The area was generally devoid of any human presence except for the occasional shepherd or lone traveller making his way on foot. A personal reminiscence of a commentator crossing the Plain by bicycle in the late 1890s speaks of *"a lonely and very beautiful place with hardly any traffic on the tracks that served for roads. Somewhere around Shrewton a shepherd*

Salisbury Plain encircled by public railways but only breached in a couple of isolated instances (Ian Allan)

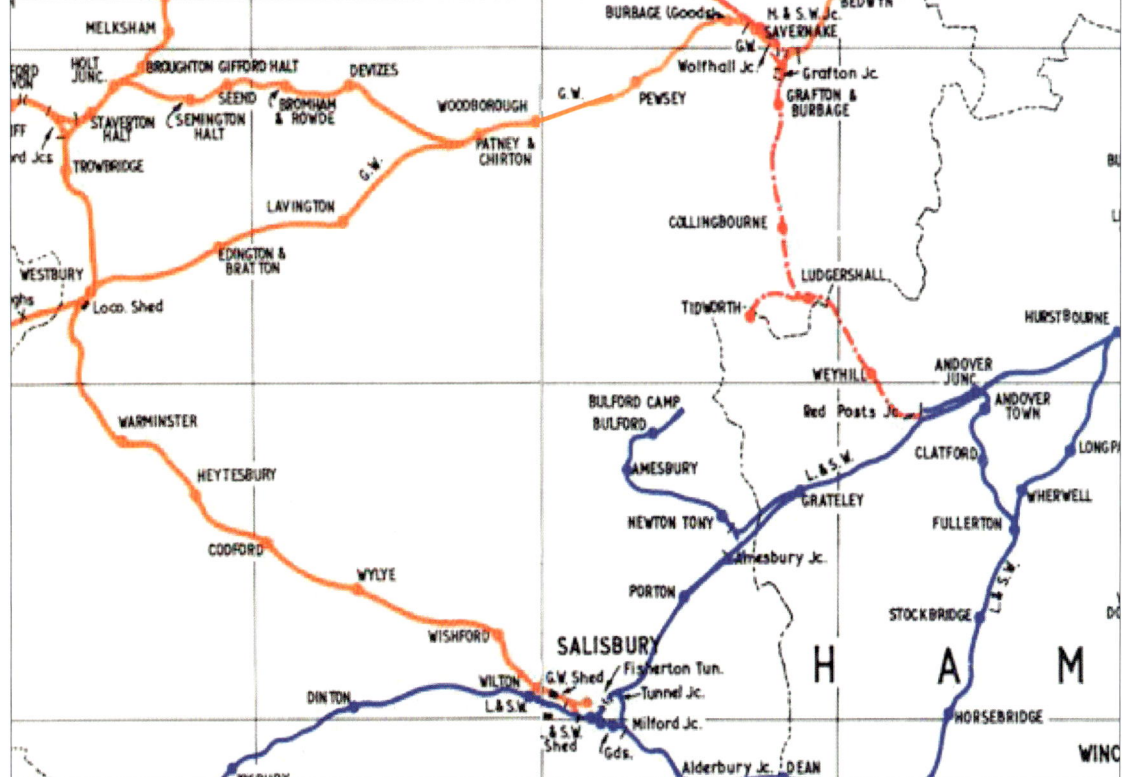

The Autumn Campaign: The March Past at Beacon Hill Amesbury (The Illustrated London News)

came running across to pass the time of day, saying that I was the first living person he had seen for the past two days". On the face of it this was not an area likely to appeal to railway builders even in the wildest dreams of the most optimistic of speculators and it is no surprise that although the Plain was skirted by a number of routes in only two instances was the area penetrated by relatively short branchlines.

THE MILITARY

The expanse of Salisbury Plain is sometimes erroneously confused with the extent of the military training area to which it plays host. In fact the MOD lands only cover approximately half the geological extent of the plain but the area of MOD ownership does make it the largest military training area in the UK. Today the estate totals approximately 92,000 acres (143.75 sq. miles), stretching from Ludgershall in the east to Warminster in the west and, at its extremities, measures 27 miles by 10 miles. It contains about one-ninth of the whole county of Wiltshire. Of the total, around 39 square miles (100 km^2) are permanently closed to the public with access being severely restricted in other areas. In the last decade of the 19th.C military interest in the Plain began to develop at the national level. Military training had been conducted on the downs before this time on an ad hoc basis, particularly for large set-piece manoeuvres most notably those of 1872 which were centred around Beacon Hill and a site which is now Bulford Camp, and for smaller exercises arranged by the local yeomanry with the local landowners who were themselves often members of the yeomanry regiments. An engraving of the 1872 "*Autumn Campaign – Marchpast at Beacon Hill Amesbury*" was featured in the Illustrated London News in September of that year. Providing such exercises were restricted to the period between harvest and the start of the shooting season they would have interfered little with normal farming activities. However, three factors came together in the 1890s to bring about the transformation of the Plain from sheep pasture to battleground. The growing professionalism of army training demanded large, permanent areas for practice, and by the 1870s this demand was outstripping the availability of the heathland around Aldershot, the traditional home of the British Army, which had been purchased in 1854. The collapse of the old sheep and corn farming regime and agricultural depression generally meant that downland areas of Salisbury Plain could be purchased relatively cheaply and lastly legislation passed in 1892, as the Boer War loomed, enabled the War Office to purchase land for training more easily than previously.

The first purchase was made on 25th March 1897 comprising 750 acres at Bulford from Miss J.M. Seymour of East Knoyle at a price of £7,500. On this site now stands Bulford Camp. In the following month, Lord Lansdowne, Secretary of State for War, set up a War Office Salisbury Plain Committee (WOSPC), consisting of the Parliamentary Under-Secretary of State, the Finance Secretary, the Adjutant-General, the Quartermaster-General and the Inspector-General of Fortifications, to deal with the problems involved in the acquisition of further land for military purposes. By the time the Committee was dissolved on 1st May 1902, some 42,000 acres had been bought at a cost of over £550,000, the most notable purchase being the Tidworth Estate of Sir John William Kelk for £95,000. The first acquisitions were manors and farms mainly at the eastern end of the Plain; their purchasing continued until 1912. No further purchases were made until the period 1927-1933 when numerous acquisitions were made in the Warminster area. The village of Imber was bought during this period but the farming community was not totally dispossessed until after the outbreak of the Second World War. Shortly before 1939 the War Department acquired a further 3,000 acres at Everleigh and Collingbourne Ducis at a cost of £46,850 and as late as 1954 the 1,100 acre Everleigh Manor Estate was purchased for £21,000. However, not quite everything within this area is MOD property there being a number of houses and cottages in the Avon Valley which remain privately owned as is the Coombe Estate, which extends from Coombe towards Everleigh. To be on the safe side, the WOSPC decided to postpone all negotiations for land purchase on the Tidworth side of the River Avon whilst the GWR were floating plans for a line through the valley. In the event, as we shall see, the railway was not built but negotiations to purchase the Coombe Estate were never resumed and ever since it has remained an obstacle hampering north-south movement on tactical exercises.

RAILWAYS SKIRT THE PLAIN

Rails had progressively skirted the Plain, as detailed in the Chronology at Appendix 1 and as shown on page 7, beginning with the extension of the Wilts, Somerset & Weymouth line from Warminster, which had been reached from Westbury in 1851, to Salisbury opening in 1856. This was closely followed by the arrival at Salisbury of the LSWR line from Andover the following year. The Berks & Hants Extension line from Devizes through Pewsey to

The potential importance of Upavon is apparent with lines to Pewsey, Marlborough and Fairford to the north east and to Woodborough, Calne, Malmesbury, Tetbury and Stroud to the north west with the line continuing to Amesbury and Porton to the south. There was also a plan for a line from Upavon to Ludgershall. In the event rails never penetrated this part of the Avon valley.

(Wiltshire & Swindon Archives [WSA])

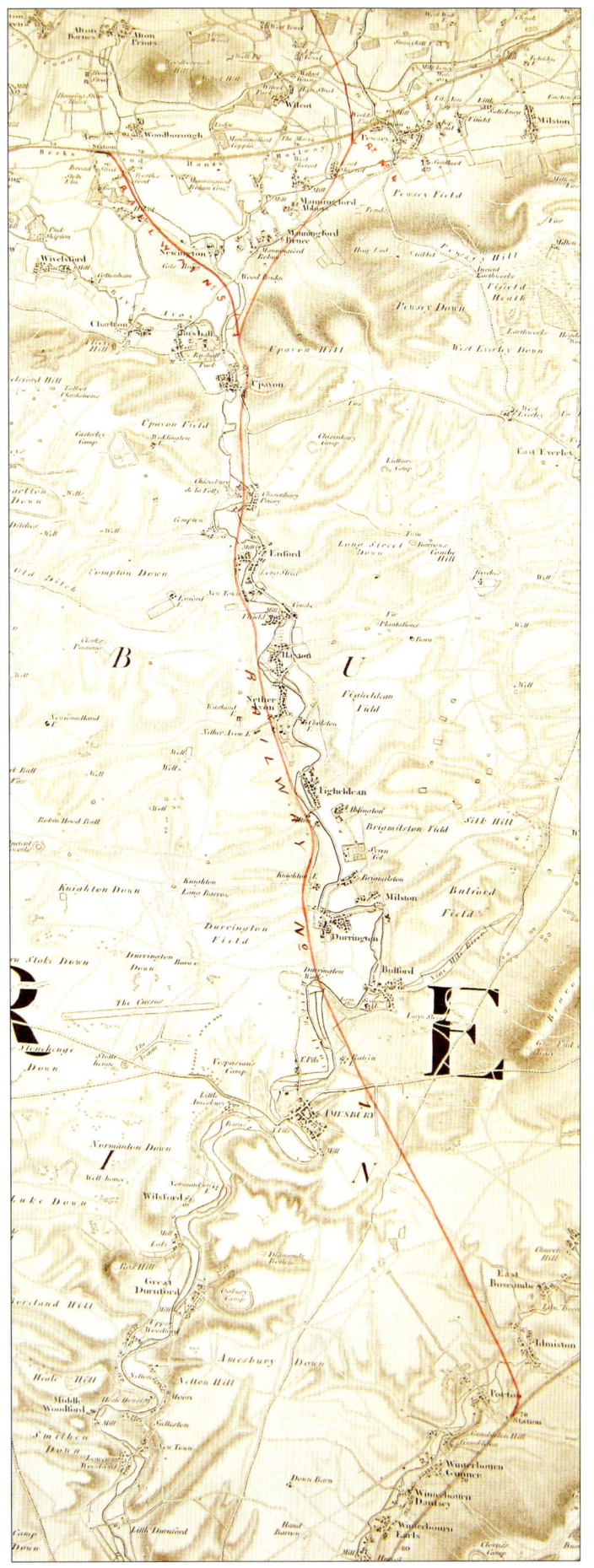

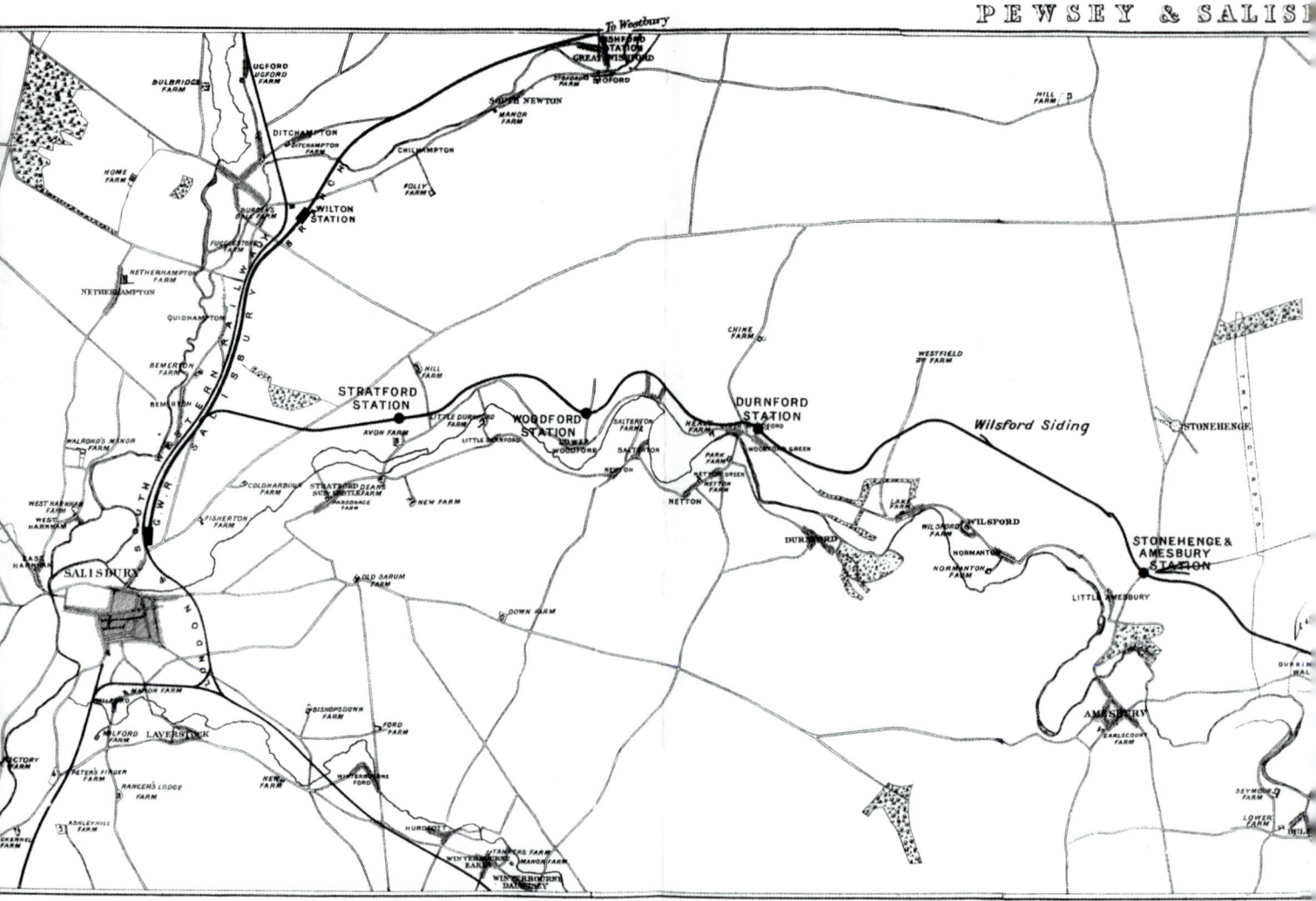

Savernake and Newbury was completed in 1862 and 20 years later the Swindon, Marlborough & Andover (latterly MSWJR) line from Savernake reached Andover. Completing the encirclement of the Plain was the GWR extension of 1900 from Patney & Chirton to Westbury.

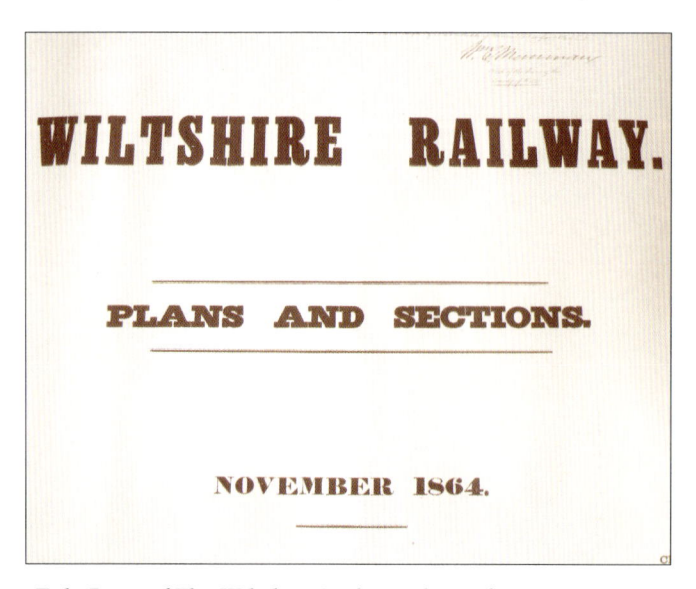

Title Page of The Wiltshire Railway plans of 1864. (WSA)

FAILED PLANS

From the mid 1840s, the period of the "Railway Mania", and for the next 60 years or so there were several proposals for lines across the Plain with an eye on long distance rather than local traffic. In 1846 the Manchester & Poole Railway scheme, whose engineers included Robert Stephenson, envisaged a route from Poole via Breamore, Downton, Laverstock, Idmiston, Newton Tony, Grateley and Thruxton to a junction near Ludgershall with the proposed Manchester & Southampton Railway which connected with the Birmingham & Gloucester line at Cheltenham reached via Marlborough, Swindon and Cirencester. Not unnaturally strong opposition from both the GWR and LSWR killed this bill off at the Committee stage although much of the route north of Marlborough was subsequently incorporated into the later M&SWJR line. The Wiltshire & Gloucestershire Railway, authorized in July 1864, was sponsored by the Midland Railway in an attempt to invade G.W.R. territory with a line from Stroud via Tetbury and Malmesbury to Christian Malford near Chippenham, but its designs were frustrated in 1864 by Board of Trade arbitration on appeal from the GWR. An extension of this proposed line from Christian Malford via Calne to a junction with the GWR at Woodborough near Pewsey was to be known as the North &

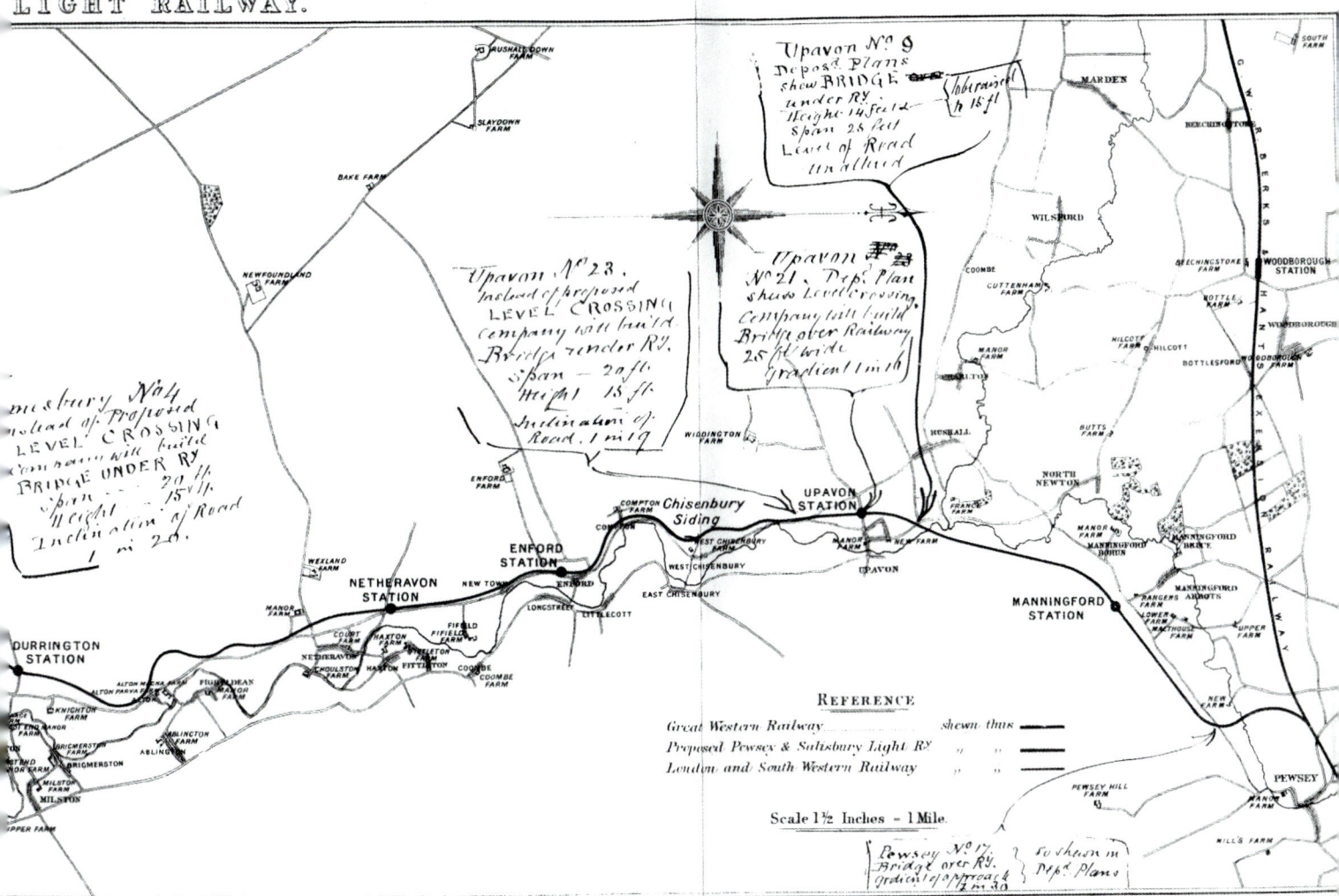

South Wiltshire Junction Railway and the Wiltshire Railway proposed a line from Woodborough via Upavon, Durrington and Amesbury to Porton on the LSWR mainline with a spur from Upavon to Pewsey continuing on to Fairford via Marlborough, Ogbourne, Chiseldon and Stratton St. Margaret, the schemes securing Acts of Parliament in July 1865. All three companies allowed their powers to lapse however, and were wound up. Also in 1865 came the stillborn Upavon & Andover railway proposing a spur from Upavon to Ludgershall and on to Andover. These plans would have seen four lines converge upon Upavon making it an important railway junction.

The LSWR entered the fray in 1882 with the Bristol & LSW Junction Railway which was a blatant attempt to draw London - Bristol traffic away from the GWR by routing it via Basingstoke, a branch 2.25 miles west of Grateley to Amesbury, thence passing very close to Stonehenge onwards to Shrewton, Imber, Bratton and Westbury thence to Bristol either via the S&DJR by a north facing spur near Foxcote outside Radstock or via the North Somerset line via a junction in Radstock. In March 1883 a deviation was proposed taking the line further away from the monument in response to Sir John Lubbock, the chief parliamentary spokesman for archaeology and president of the Society for Promoting the Preservation of the Ancient Monuments of England, who called for the line to be diverted away from the stones. Although this ancient monument was afforded much less protection in the last few years of the 19th.C with the military using it for manoeuvres for example than it is today, "The Guardian" of the day was concerned enough to

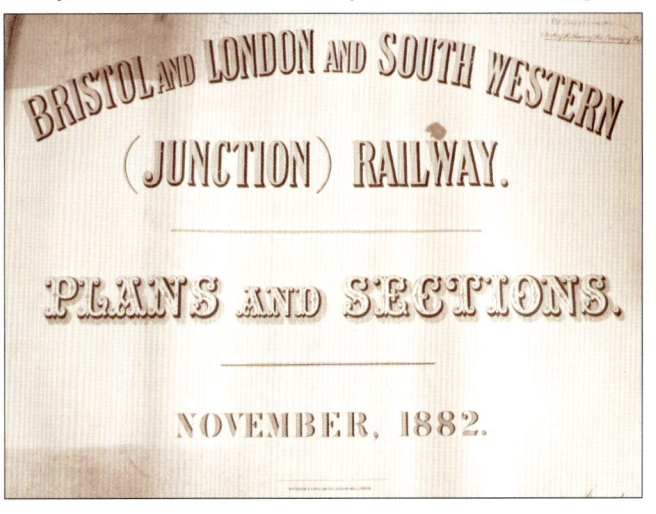

Title Page of Bristol & London & South Western (Junction) Railway plans of 1882. (WSA)

A topical cartoon of the day graphically illustrating the failure of the Bristol and LSW Junction Railway proposal. (Courtesy Bristol Record Office)

report that "*the sound of chiselling and hammering could be heard all day long as tourists seek either to leave their mark upon the stones or to take a piece home with them !*" The GWR's Daniel Gooch became involved writing to the press that "*The Wiltshire people and many others interested in the preservation of ancient monuments are much exercised by the destruction that will be caused to Stonehenge by a railway scheme which is promoted under the name of the Bristol & LSW Junction Railway.*" The promoters responded with "*Sir Daniel Gooch, we think, has gone too far in the statement that the proposed line will, if carried out, cause "destruction" to Stonehenge. Quite half a mile of space will, we are assured, intervene between Stonehenge and the rail added to which may be mentioned the fact that the line will be at the bottom of an incline, and very much below the level of the stones. It is a fact that while hundreds of the owners and occupiers of property in the county have petitioned Parliament in favour of the bill only four or five have been found to sign the petition against it.*" When presenting their case to parliament much play was made of the fact that "*anybody wishing to visit that natural monument has to drive 12 miles at present, whereas we shall deposit him tolerably close to it.*"

In spite of the proposed deviation at Stonehenge needless to say the GWR voiced strong opposition to the proposal and the bill was defeated the following year. Ironically one had to wait until rail privatisation at the end of the 20th.C before a service from Bristol to London Waterloo was introduced, South West Trains currently operating services via Bath, Warminster, Salisbury, Andover and the former LSWR mainline to London. The GWR responded with a provocative scheme of its own from Pewsey to Salisbury then on to Southampton. The line would make its own way out of Salisbury, paralleling the LSWR route to Romsey near Alderbury and branching off the Salisbury - Bournemouth line to the south east of Alderbury village, thence through Redlynch to the south of Landford reaching the outskirts of Southampton near Shirley. Naturally this incursion into "home territory" was strongly opposed by the LSWR who succeeded in having the line rejected although an act of 26th July 1883 covering the section from Pewsey to Salisbury was authorised. However, as we shall see this line was never constructed. In 1887 came the bizarre Collingbourne & Avon Valley railway for a line 7 miles 2 furlongs and 6 chains in length from Collingbourne Ducis on the MSWJR route across to the valley of the River Avon terminating in a field in the parish of Fittleton near Netheravon. This proved to be another non-starter.

Another long distance route which was planned to cross the Plain was that of 1893 for a line from Swansea to London via Thornbury, Yate, Bath and Salisbury Plain to the LSWR at Andover. This was one of many schemes designed to break the GWR monopoly of London traffic from South Wales. Although the route via Salisbury Plain was subsequently amended to run via Dursley, Tetbury, Malmesbury and Hungerford to the LSWR at Basingstoke, the GWR countered the proposals with the Wootton Bassett to Patchway cut off and this sealed the fate of the South Wales project. In the view of the Railway Times of November 9th. 1895, this action on the part of the GWR effectively prevented the South Wales Railway, "*an utterly unnecessary railway*", from becoming law. The Railway Times went on to say of these schemes "*At one moment it is proposed to invade the peaceful solitudes of Salisbury Plain and force the South Western into an unholy alliance, at another to construct a new line in such wise as to benefit the racehorses of Lambourn or the undergraduates of Oxford.*" By January 1896 the South Wales scheme had been laid to rest.

Of course, all this military activity at the end of the 19th.C naturally interested railway promoters who could now see considerable benefits in penetrating the Plain to serve this

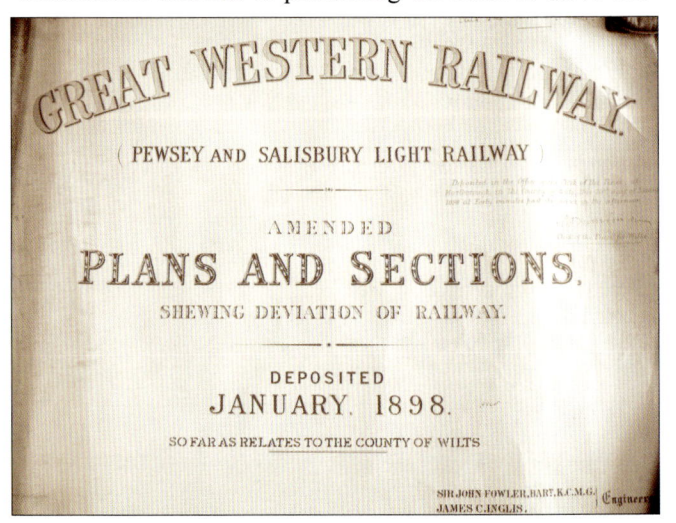

Title Page of Pewsey & Salisbury Light Railway plans of 1898. (WSA)

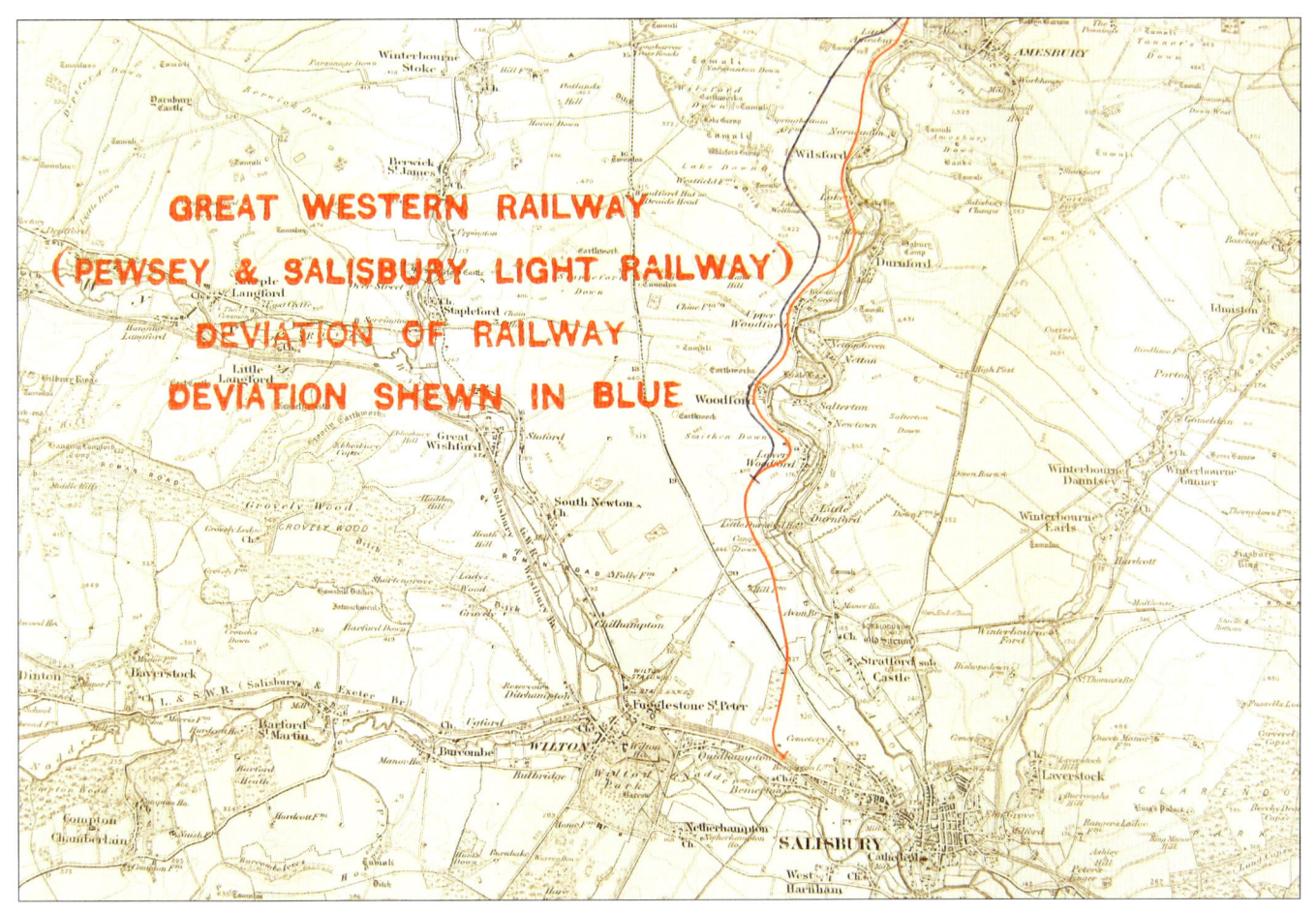

The southern end of the 1898 Pewsey & Salisbury Light Railway scheme proposed by the Great Western Railway, showing the amended track deviation. (WSA)

rapidly expanding local military presence rather than focussing on the longer distance traffic potential of purely through routes. The arrangements whereby troops would leave their trains at Porton, the nearest railway station to the ranges, and march with their equipment to their quarters over six miles of country roads to Bulford or eight miles to Larkhill, were clearly unsatisfactory. Even though the distance from Ludgershall station to Tidworth Camp was only two miles the road out of Ludgershall climbed 145 feet in just a mile and was a severe test for horse drawn wagons loaded with equipment especially in inclement weather. When reviews of the troops took place, upwards of 50,000 men would be in the area to take part in the parade, travelling on foot from their assembly point which may have been some miles distant. For the annual manoeuvres on the Plain in August/September 1898 Grateley, for example, received 8 special trains carrying spectators on 8th. September, the day of the Grand Review. The following year "The Times" of August 1899 reported on the arrival of volunteer troops on the Plain by rail –

"For the first time since the acquisition by the Government of Salisbury Plain as a military training ground the Volunteers are this year using it for the purposes of an encampment and the initiative step in this direction was taken yesterday when there arrived the Staffordshire Volunteer Brigade which is to go under canvas for a week at Bulford. In consequence there was a busy time at Ludgershall station, on the M&SWJR where the principal part of the detraining was undertaken. The men of the 2nd. and 3rd. Battalions South Stafford and the 1st. And 2nd. Battalions North Stafford started in the early hours of Sunday morning from their several headquarters in Staffordshire and travelling through were transferred to the M&SWJR at Cheltenham and proceeded to Ludgershall. The arrangements for receiving the special trains were expeditiously carried out. The men created a very favourable impression by their smart appearance but a long march was necessary before they arrived at Bulford the distance from Ludgershall to the camp being fully 8 miles. The heat was very trying and the roads dusty. Altogether 8 special trains arrived at Ludgershall while 2 conveying the 1st. Battalion of the South Staffordshire proceeded to Grateley station on the LSWR and the men there had a march of over 6 miles to Bulford."

The first mention of an LSWR line to serve Amesbury comes in the LSWR Traffic Committee minutes of 24th. July 1895 following receipt of a letter from Lt. Col. Henry Wales regarding a proposed tramway or light railway to Amesbury or Stonehenge. A junction was proposed with the LSWR mainline between Porton and Grateley, and at that time a new station at the physical junction was envisaged, the LSWR undertaking to construct a new station and exchange sidings here to handle the military traffic.

The passing of the Light Railways Act in 1896, which was designed to encourage the development of the network by permitting more basic railways using minimal construction and operating techniques without the necessity and expense of going before Parliament, was an added incentive. A line built to "light" standards was however, probably going to be unsuitable for the heavy traffic envisaged by the military. First off the mark, as they so often were, was the Great Western. Their initial proposal, put forward under the guise of the Pewsey and Salisbury Light Railway envisaged a route, very similar to that of their 1883 proposal, diverging from the mainline west of Pewsey following the course of the Avon valley to join the Warminster – Salisbury line ¾ mile west of the city at Bemerton, now a suburb of Salisbury. Nine stations were envisaged serving Manningford, Upavon, Enford, Netheravon, Durrington, Stonehenge & Amesbury, Durnford, Woodford and Stratford. That at Stonehenge & Amesbury was sited to tap the tourist potential close to the road from Amesbury to the monument just under a mile from the stones themselves. This proposal was placed before the initial meeting of the WOSPC on 11 May 1897 who agreed to examine it in detail. However, by the time of the next meeting just a fortnight later it was decreed that not only was the proposal of no value to the military it would positively interfere with its interests, because *"construction of this railway will neutralise, if not entirely destroy, the instructional value, in a military sense, of the River Avon. There is no military operation which can be more usefully practised than the crossing of a river in the face of opposition. This practice the Avon will give, but if a railway is to be made alongside the river, the defiles over or under that railway will not, as a rule, coincide with those over the river, and a situation will be produced which will practically prevent instruction being afforded."*

In view of this it was felt that the plan should be opposed *"lock, stock and barrel"*. As an added insult to the GWR reference was made to a contemporary proposal by the LSWR for a line *"which would be much more suitable from our point of view."* Never content to take no for an answer the GWR pursued the matter and obtained an enquiry which was held at Salisbury on 25th October 1897. As the WOSPC had such strong views on the route it was decided to refer the matter to Parliament for a final decision. In January 1898 a slightly amended route was proposed from just north of Amesbury to just south of Woodford taking the line of the railway further from the river. A decision from Parliament in the end became unnecessary as on April 28th. 1898 the Board of Trade refused to grant any powers to construct the line on land belonging to the WD, some 4.5 miles of the proposed route doing just this. The following month the GWR, despite these objections from the WD, wrote to the LSWR, whose own proposal for a line to Amesbury and Shrewton was being looked upon favourably by the WD at this time, with a proposal that the Companies make a connection between the proposed lines at a point near Amesbury and that the Amesbury to Shrewton section be operated as a joint line between the Companies. Possibly this idea originated with the Light Railway Commissioners and the notion of joint ownership of this section of the line was in fact accepted by the LSWR as an agreement was reached in August 1898 to construct this section at joint expense. However the eventual enforced abandonment of the GW route rendered any such plan stillborn.

One final scheme that envisaged rails crossing the northern part of the Plain needs to be mentioned; this was the grandly titled Bristol, London & Southern Counties Railway of 1903. This, one of the final proposals for connecting the port of Avonmouth with London, proposed a line from Avonmouth with a spur to serve central Bristol, the terminus being located just off The Centre near Lewins Mead, then passing by way of a third track along the Avon valley between the GWR and MR lines to Bath, tunnelling under part of the Georgian city to emerge near Monkton Combe thence by way of Trowbridge, Potterne and Urchfont to Upavon, which as previously related was to have been served by the stillborn Pewsey – Salisbury line. From here the line ran east to make connection with the MSWJR north of Ludgershall and continued eastwards until a junction near Overton was made with the LSWR mainline. The scale of property demolition envisaged in both Bristol and Bath was extremely large so on these grounds alone it is not surprising that, together with opposition from the established railway companies, this route was a non-starter.

King George V accompanied by Queen Mary inspecting military huts on Salisbury Plain.

2. A BREACH IS MADE

INITIAL PROPOSALS…...CONSTRUCTION…...
REVISED JUNCTION ARRANGEMENTS…...EXTENSION

INITIAL PROPOSALS

The proposal from the LSWR, contemporary with that of the GWR, which came before the WOSPC on 24th May 1897 envisaged a line from a junction near Grateley to Amesbury and Shrewton. The "Railway Magazine", describing the opening of this new line four years later, made great play of the fact that the LSWR Directors - *"with that regard for the efficiency of our national defence and the convenience of the military authorities that have always characterised their policy at once determined upon constructing a line of railway to connect the new military establishment with the LSWR which, as readers of the Railway Magazine know, in consequence of its connection with Aldershot, Portsmouth and Southampton forms the chief means of inland transport between various important military and naval centres and ports."*

The LSWR had built up a reputation as *"the military line"* and had accumulated a great deal of experience in handling large troop movements. Six months later a draft order of the "Amesbury & Military Camp Light Railway" (A&MLR) was presented to the committee. This was unanimously approved and hopes were expressed that in time the LSWR would be *"ready to extend the line from Shrewton to Tilshead."*

Hard on the heels of this came another proposal, this time from the MSWJR, for a route from Ludgershall to Salisbury but at a meeting on 23rd September 1897 the WOSPC decided that *"the proposed line would not suit the purposes of the WD in any way and that the other line proposed by the LSWR was far preferable."* Not disheartened the MSWJR submitted a fresh proposal for a line from Ludgershall to Amesbury via Cholderton, 10 miles 7 furlongs in length at an estimated cost of £49,928, with a spur to Bulford, 1 mile 7 furlongs in length at an estimated cost of £10,034, to be known as the Ludgershall & Military Camps Light Railway. In the prospectus the gauge of the railway was given as the usual four feet eight and a half

Above - Title page of the Amesbury & Military Camp Light Railway Plans. (WSA)
Below - The originally proposed route of 1897 for the Amesbury & Military Camp Light Railway to Shrewton. (WSA)

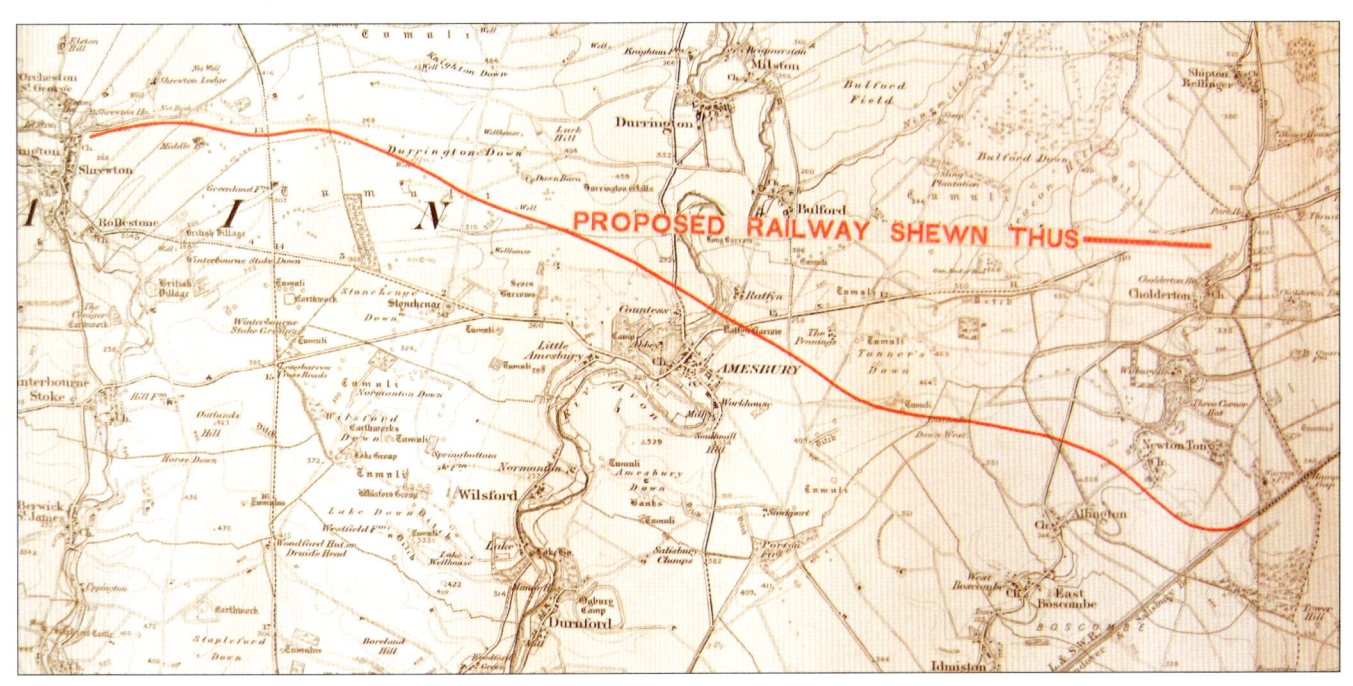

inches but interestingly enough the motive power "*shall be steam or electricity*" rather than the more usual mention of steam only. Again the WD initially disapproved ostensibly on the grounds that it crossed WD property. In fact this proved not be to the case and at a meeting of 11th March 1898 it was stated that there would be no objection to the plan as "*the proposed line ran entirely outside the boundaries of the WD's property.*" Simultaneously however, it was pointed out that the line "*must run in with the proposed line to be constructed by the LSWR from Grateley to Shrewton.*" What scuppered this proposal initially was opposition from the LSWR and from several landowners on the proposed route and a lack of support from the population of the district through which the line was to pass. At an inquiry held at the Star & Garter Hotel in Andover on 24th. June 1898 the Light Railway Commissioners, headed by The Rt. Hon. The Earl of Jersey, stated that in view of the fact that "*three of the landowners owning land for something like six or seven miles on the line are against it*" they felt unable to recommend the scheme unless" *the company could show that there was a counter-balancing feeling in the district that will justify us over-riding that opposition*". With his tail between his legs the

Above - Contractors special on the MSWJ / War Department Tidworth branch around the time of opening. The wagons and second locomotive are labelled as H L Lovatt. The branch to Tidworth was destined to be the only incursion by the MSWJ on to Salisbury Plain.
Opposite page - The Midland & South Western Junction Railway route of the proposed Ludgershall & Military Camps Light Railway from Ludgershall with separate branches to Amesbury and Bulford. (WSA)

representative of the MSWJR, one Mr. Dawes, said in conclusion *"then we shall have to put our house in order and come before you again to consider if we have not made out a fair case."* The scheme was ultimately rejected however, as *'the route was at no point more than 3 miles from an existing or sanctioned station'*.

WD contractors did however construct a branch from Ludgershall to Tidworth originally as a military siding for the conveyance of military personnel, stores and workmen engaged in the construction of Tidworth barracks. This route was completed on 8th. July 1901 making it the first line, by a short head, to penetrate the Plain. The MSWJR took over operation of the line, which opened to goods traffic on 1st. July 1902 and to passengers on 1st. October 1902, forming an integral part of that company's operations although remaining the property of the WD. It was a wise move as it turned out, Tidworth becoming the MSWJR's principal revenue generator with income exceeding the combined total of all other stations on the line !

Given the green light by the WD the LSWR proceeded with their own proposal and it was reported in November 1897 that surveys and plans were in progress. A capital figure of £50,000 with £15,000 borrowing powers was announced on the 9th November. These figures were later amended to £60,000 and £20,000 respectively. The application for the Light Railway Order was, however, not entirely straightforward. It came before the Light Railway Commissioners in January 1898 but various difficulties with the settlement of a road bridge and the requirement for cattle guards at various level crossings delayed matters until July. An LRO was finally authorised by the Board of Trade on 24th. September. The LSWR reported to Directors in October 1898 that Land Plans were in preparation and that the Company had precedence to enable the work to commence *"as soon as possible"*.

CONSTRUCTION

The Company Engineer was keen to progress matters and he met with the well respected firm of J. T. Firbank of London in January 1899 with a view to them undertaking the construction of the line. Joseph Firbank's first large contract had been with the Monmouthshire Railway and Canal Company in 1854 and he had subsequently been employed in South Wales for thirty years. In 1856 Firbank undertook a contract for widening the LNWR near London, and from 1859 to 1866 was engaged upon a number of contracts for the LB&SCR. He was occupied with the Midland's London extension from 1864 until 1868 and in 1866, the height of his construction activity, he was employing 2000 men. In 1870 Firbank was engaged as contractor on the Smardale to Newbiggin section of the Settle and Carlisle extension of the Midland Railway, a stretch of line noted for its impressive physical features and isolation. His last contract was for the Bournemouth direct line from Brockenhurst to Christchurch and in total some 49 lines were constructed by Firbank from 1846 to 1886. By April 1899 an agreement had been concluded with Firbank, the firm already being involved with other schemes in the locality including the nearby Basingstoke & Alton Light Railway, to commence construction at an estimated cost of £62,517.

The cost was considerable at around £6,000 per mile for a line of 10 miles 6 furlongs in length. *"A most expensive line really in the sense of a light railway"* observed the Light Railway Commissioners and Sir Courtenay Boyle of the Board of Trade was even less reticent when looking at a number of Light Railway Order applications currently being considered, observing cynically *"the Board has doubt whether some of these schemes are light railways at all"*. Indeed it was a "light railway" in name only for it was laid with 87lb/yard (not the 60lb/yard allowed for in the LRO) bull head rail rather than the lighter flat bottomed type and the formation, both embankments and cuttings, was presciently in the light of future doubling, made wide enough to take two sets of rails. Cuttings were considerable ranging from 8 - 38 feet in depth whilst embankments were up to 35 feet high in places. The "Railway Magazine" concluded that *"having in view the importance, from a national point of view, of the undertaking the LSWR incurred considerable expense in connection with the new railway."* The principal items of expenditure were 275,000 cubic yards of cuttings, at an estimated cost of £13,780, permanent way including fencing, at an estimated cost of £21,974. (See Appendix 1X)

To give a brief flavour of the line it is perhaps worth quoting from the LRO which set out –

"A railway 10 miles 6 furlongs commencing at milepost 75 on the main line terminating in the parish of Shrewton. The permanent way will consist of rails of at least 60lbs per yard. The radius of any curve less than 9 chains to have check rails. After leaving the LSWR line half-way between Grateley and Porton, the railway crosses over an old Roman Road (the Portway, running from Old Sarum to Silchester, which paralleled the mainline for some 12 miles) on the level. This is a grass track used for moving sheep. The railway then falls by gradients of 1 in 60 and 1 in 97 for a mile, then passes just south of the village of Newton Toney, over a small valley, then rises at 1 in 51 for half a mile to level out and cross the main road from Allington to Cholderton. Then a long rising gradient of 1 in 93 for a mile then levelling at about 56 feet above the point of the junction. Crossing two sheep tracks on the level, a bridge is to be built in a cutting at 3 miles 4 furlongs asked for by Amesbury District Council. The line falls at 1 in 60 for one and a half miles to Amesbury Village where the Andover Road is to be raised 4 feet 9 inches so the railway can pass under it. The line continues at 1 in 50 to cross the valley on the level and under the main road north of Countess Farm road. This is to be raised 5 feet 3 inches. At 6 miles 3 chains the line will pass under the GWR Pewsey and Salisbury line (never of course built). Passing by way of Durrington Down by easy gradients, at 7 miles 2 furlongs a bridge is to be made requiring the railway to be lowered by 5 feet from the original plans. The road to be crossed is to be raised by eleven feet. The terminus is reached at 10 miles 62 chains on the eastern side of the village of Shrewton".

The sharpest curve was to have a radius of 32 chains with flange rails of 60lbs per yard. Not unexpectedly, given the lack of habitation en route, no houses required to be demolished on the planned line of the railway.

Even with the obviously close harmony existing between the WD and its favoured railway company, the LSWR did not enjoy plain sailing in the execution of the work. On 22nd. November 1899 the War Office suddenly wrote to the LWSR asking them to alter the route of part of the proposed line from Amesbury to Shrewton. Although just outside the WD boundary it seems the change of mind was occasioned by second thoughts that a railway line might prove a potential impediment to military movements, as had been the case with the earlier GWR proposal, the WD stating that *"it is essential that no obstacle be placed in the way of manoeuvres."* There were also concerns that possible further expansion of training land might be inhibited by the presence of the line and worries were even expressed at the proposed line's proximity to the monument at Stonehenge, the route passing within ¾ mile of the stones. However, on this latter point it was to be only a few years later when the Royal Flying Corps, then occupying Stonehenge airfield, wrote to the MOD requesting that the ancient monument be moved as it was interfering with flying activities !

Left - *Who put those stones in the flightpath ! A close thing as an aircraft swoops low over Stonehenge. (Fuller of Amesbury)*

Opposite - *One of the early aircraft to fly at Larkhill was the Bristol Prier high wing, wire-braced monoplane which made its first flight in 1911, some 34 being constructed in both one and two seat variations. It was powered by a Gnome rotary 50hp engine. The Prier monoplanes were mainly used for training and racing although some were purchased for military use. "Flight" magazine for 30 September 1911 introduced the new plane to its readers commenting that "The machine, itself, is undoubtedly the centre of many thoughts, but its comparative inaccessibility on Salisbury Plain does not contribute much to the general fixing of ideas as to its leading characteristics." Pierre Prier, a one-time Louis Bleriot pupil, was instrumental in its design. The rather rudimentary facilities available to the Bristol Flying School at Larkhill are evident in the shape of the hut seen in the background. (Original M Bennett Bulford Camp Studio Courtesy M J Tozer Collection)*

Having examined whether there was a practicable diversion available to them between Amesbury and Shrewton, the LSWR, possibly taking umbrage at having their plans changed at short notice, decided that there was not, or at least only at greatly increased cost, and sought powers to abandon the Shrewton extension. In the event the official abandonment order for this section was not forthcoming until July 1901 and was doubtless a reflection of the WOSPC having been informed in January 1901 that *"there was no immediate prospect of funds becoming available for large additional purchases" (of training land) thus rendering the utility of any railway extension beyond Amesbury questionable"*. This reduced the total length of the line to just 4 miles 78 chains. As work had already commenced on the Shrewton extension at Amesbury the now redundant earthworks on the far side of Amesbury station were utilised as additional sidings, and the LSWR received compensation from the taxpayer for its abortive work. The contractor was compensated through a financial settlement and an offer of work elsewhere on their system, mainly it appears on station reconstruction and widening work at Basingstoke. Firbank's claim for the abortive work incurred amounted to £5,110, the matter being finally settled in October 1901. Changes were required to the layout of Amesbury station, as a result of the curtailment of the extension to Shrewton, involving additional sidings and a water tank at an estimated cost of £9,000. Lasting legacies of the curtailed extension were two levers in the signal box at Amesbury marked "Shrewton Box 1" and "Shrewton Box 2" which survived unused until demolition of the line in the mid 1960s. Four levers in the Amesbury ground frame were also marked "Shrewton Siding No.1 Release", "Shrewton Siding No. 1 Points", "Shrewton Siding No. 2 Release" and "Shrewton Siding No. 2 Points".

Construction of the now shortened branch continued at a good rate and by October 1900 the LSWR Engineer was able to report that *"seven cuttings are now completed, also six banks,*

The Amesbury Ground Frame with levers marked Shrewton.
(Estate of the late Austin Underwood)

CONTRACTORS LOCOMOTIVES

The following contractors locomotives are recorded as being used on the construction.

J T Firbank

Name	Type	Builder	Date	Works. No.	Notes
'Amesbury'*	0-6-0ST	Manning Wardle	1890	1190	Ex Logan & Hemingway
'Amersham'	0-6-0ST	Manning Wardle	1864	129	Ex Kelk & Lucas
'Bradford'					
'Ely'					
'Lively'	0-6-0ST	Manning Wardle	1870	291	
'Wellington'	0-6-0ST	Hunslet	1870	72	
'Ventnor'	0-6-0ST	Manning Wardle			Ex Logan & Hemingway

Some of the above may also have been subsequently used on construction from Amesbury to Bulford.

Sir John Jackson - reported as responsible for construction of the actual camps at Bulford and Larkhill and also for the Larkhill Military Railway.

Name	Type	Builder	Date	Works. No.
'Bulford'	0-4-0ST	Hudswell Clarke	1914	1045
'Chester'	0-6-0T	Kitson	1888	3075
'Devonport'	0-6-0T	Hunslet	1886	401
'Northumbria'	0-6-0T	Hawthorn Leslie		
'Queen Mary'	0-4-0ST	Peckett		
'Salisbury'	0-6-0T	Hudswell Clarke	1914	1069
'Westminster'	0-6-0ST	Peckett		
'Yorkshire'	0-6-0T	Hudswell Clarke	1914	1070

Contemporary with the above, Messrs H E Lovatt (see illustration page 17) were reported as operating an 0-6-0ST of Hunslet build bearing the name 'Amesbury', this was works No. 869. There is some confusion that this may have been replaced by a second engine on to which the same name was transferred. To conclude the debate it is possible an engine bearing this name was at some stage passed to or operated in the area by the War Department.

Note* - It was common practice for contractors to name locomotives at this time, often using these instead of numbers. As will be gathered, locomotives were often named after the area in which they worked, sometimes these names changed upon removal to a new site of work / new owner.

A poor reproduction of the 0-6-0ST 'Lively' engaged in construction. This is taken from the 1974 publication 'Wiltshire Industrial Archaeology', in a piece entitled 'Railway Reveries' by Dennis Thody. The same article also depicts a 'steam navvy' (steam shovel) at work in a cutting between Allington and Amesbury. The name of one other steam locomotive is known which may have been involved in the building. This was 'Sharpness' a Sharp Stewart design but about which no other details are known.

Of slightly less than perfect quality, but fascinating as it shows what was reported to be 'The first train at Amesbury'. Assuming this to be the case, then the date is 26 April 1902. (Military traffic was reported as having commenced from 1 October 1901.) At this stage Amesbury was the terminus of the line. Of the two locomotives one may be identified as of the '395' class. The new line first appeared in the LSWR summer (working) timetable for 1 June to 30 September 1901 although at this stage just as locations without any train times indicated.

and one bank is now being widened. The bottom ballast is now laid for 3 miles 18 chains and the permanent way is laid for 3 miles 10 chains. At Newton Toney the platforms are made and the buildings erected. The Station Master's house is being slated and the slating to the cottages is finished. At Amesbury the rafters are being fixed to the roof of the Station Master's house. The line is fenced and is practically complete. A temporary bridge has been constructed to carry the public road at Grateley". The permanent way was described in the same report as being *"of the LSW heavy standard type laid at an estimated cost of £1997 per mile"*. The contractor used a variety of locomotives during construction of the line including a number of 0-6-0 Manning Wardle tanks named *"Ventnor"*, *"Ely"*, *"Bradford"*, *"Amersham"*, and appropriately one named *"Amesbury"*. Hunslet 0-6-0ST *"Wellington"* is also known to have been used during this period.

In view of the pressing military situation, with the Boer War raging in South Africa, it was felt vital to open the line at the earliest opportunity and there are some unconfirmed reports that it opened as early as 1st. October 1901 for military traffic only. However, a minute of the LSWR Traffic Committee of 4th. December 1901 mentions that *"the War Office want to occupy quarters at Bulford Camp during the winter months and ask if the new line to Amesbury will be opened at an early date. The line may be used at any time for military purposes"* thus indicating that this October 1st. date may be a little premature. A similar situation obtained with the nearby Tidworth branch from Ludgershall which also came into use for military traffic in 1901. After an inspection by Major Pringle on 28th. February 1902, it was not in fact until 5th March 1902 that LSWR directors were advised that notice had been given to the Board of Trade of the intended opening of the Amesbury line and it was not until their issue of March 29th. that the Salisbury & Winchester Journal reported the "unofficial opening" –

AMESBURY, THE NEW RAILWAY - What might be termed an informal opening of the new railway occurred on the 21st. inst. When the 3rd. Battalion Lincolnshire Regiment and the 3rd. Battalion East Yorkshire Regiment entrained at Amesbury station to begin their long journey to South Africa. A large number of persons assembled to witness their departure and as the two long trains steamed out of the station hearty cheers were given for the departing troops, which were warmly returned by the men.

The line opened for general goods traffic on 26th. April 1902 with the official opening for passengers scheduled for June 2nd. although no ceremonial opening train was laid on. There were similar delays in formally opening the Tidworth branch which accepted goods on 1st. July 1902 and passengers on 1st. October. Ironically, in view of all the haste with which these lines were constructed and opened, the first service to arrive at Amesbury brought the morning newspapers announcing the end of the Boer War following the signing of the Treaty of Vereeniging the previous month. The local news reported the opening –

AMESBURY - OPENING OF THE NEW LIGHT RAILWAY – Without any formal ceremony whatever the new line from Grateley to Amesbury was opened for public use on Monday morning. A few spectators had assembled to see the first train arrive at 8:32 which brought some 15 or 16 passengers, and, what was a noticeable fact, it also brought the morning papers containing the good news that the war

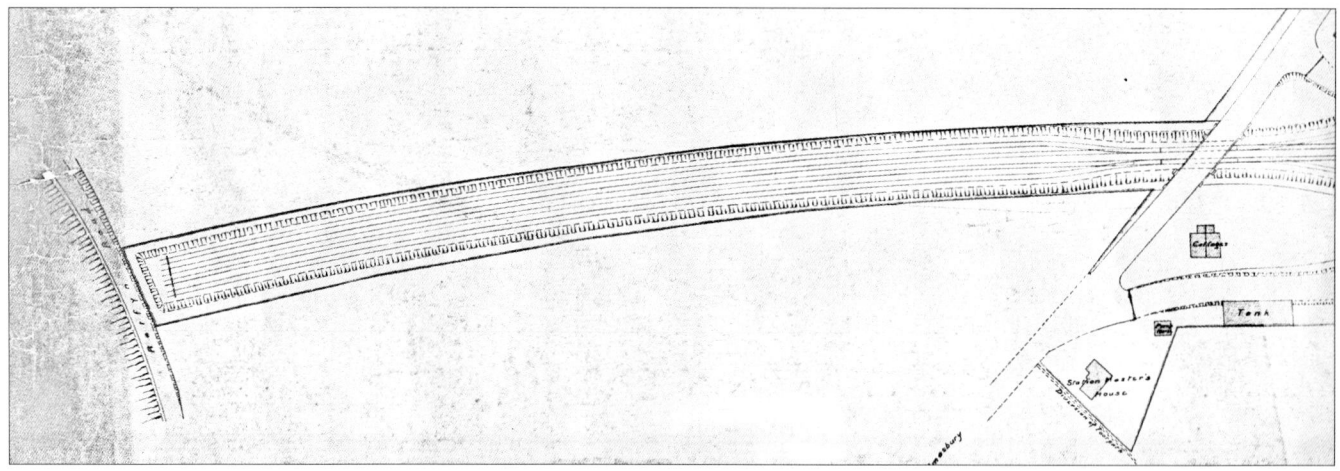

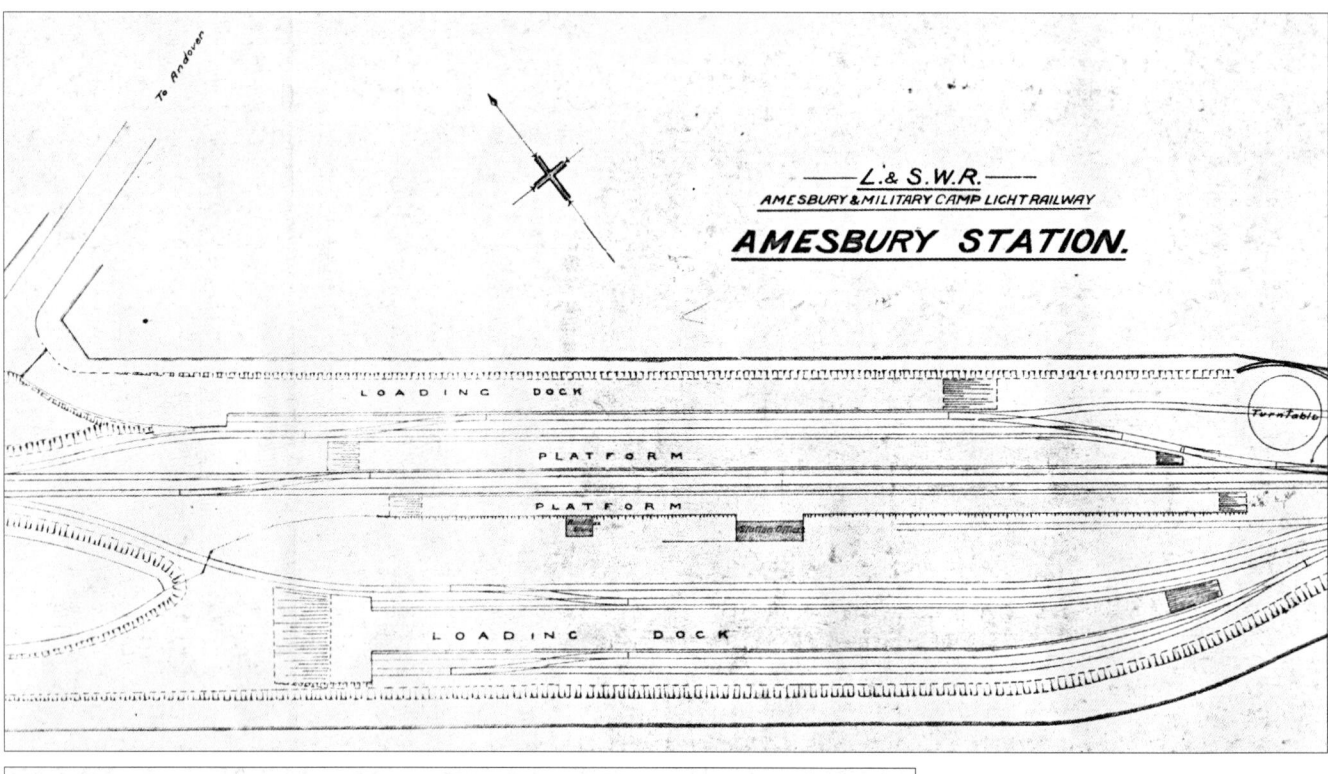

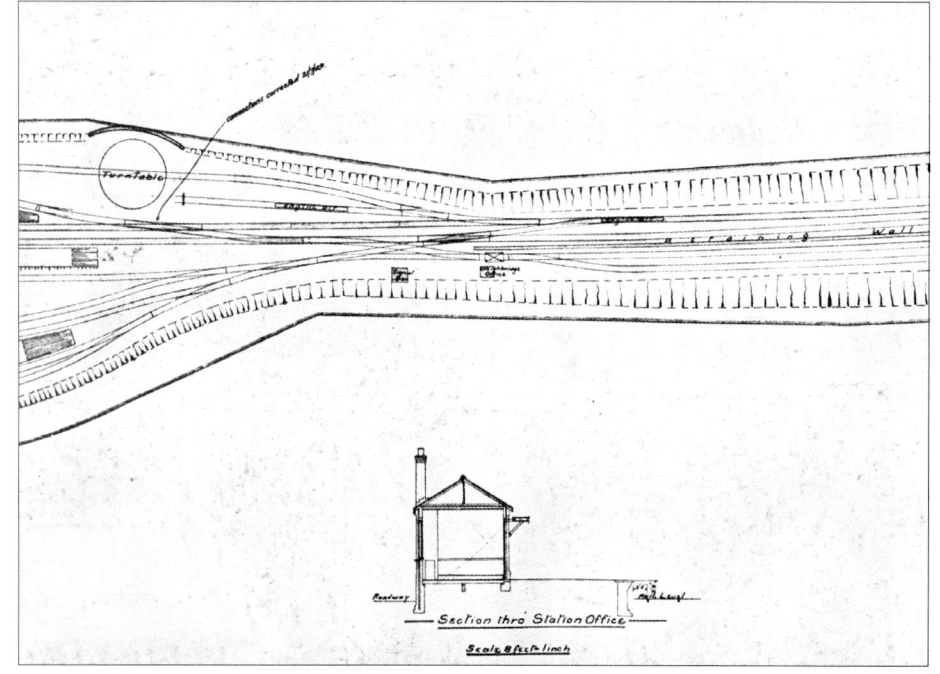

The original track layout at the Amesbury terminus: reproduced in three parts - left to right / top to bottom. Originally dated 1901, the obvious omission is the extension to Bulford which would diverge west of the Andover to Salisbury road overbridge. The dead end set of sidings terminating at the Ratfyn Road were officially referred to as Shrewton Sidings.

The Amesbury and Military Camp Light Railway (Amendment) Order of 1901, made under the Light Railways Act of 1896. This Order authorised the abandonment of the Shrewton extension.

was over and that peace was assured. A hearty cheer was raised by those on the platform. A fair number of passengers travelled by the first "up" train at 8:55. Some of them merely took a short trip to Newton Tony or Grateley by way of "inaugurating" the new line. The Company are running six trains each way daily and there are no Sunday trains. Communication with Salisbury will, unfortunately, be little improved by the present arrangements the distance via Grateley being 17 ½ miles and the 3rd. Class fare 5 ½d. It is much to be desired that the directors may see their way to a reduction of fares at any rate on one or two days in the week and an earlier up train and a later down train would be a great convenience to Amesbury and the neighbourhood. At present the first up train leaving at 8:55 reaches Waterloo at 12, and the last down train leaves Waterloo at 3:45 and reaches Amesbury at 7:04.

It was perceptive of the local news to spot major weaknesses in the ability of the new line to attract local traffic. Two problems, that of connections to London and the running of trains earlier and later in the day were later addressed through timetabling adjustments but the obvious drawback of making Amesbury residents reach their preferred market town of Salisbury by a very roundabout route via Grateley was readily apparent in a comparison of the distance by rail, 17½ miles, as opposed to the distance by road of just 8

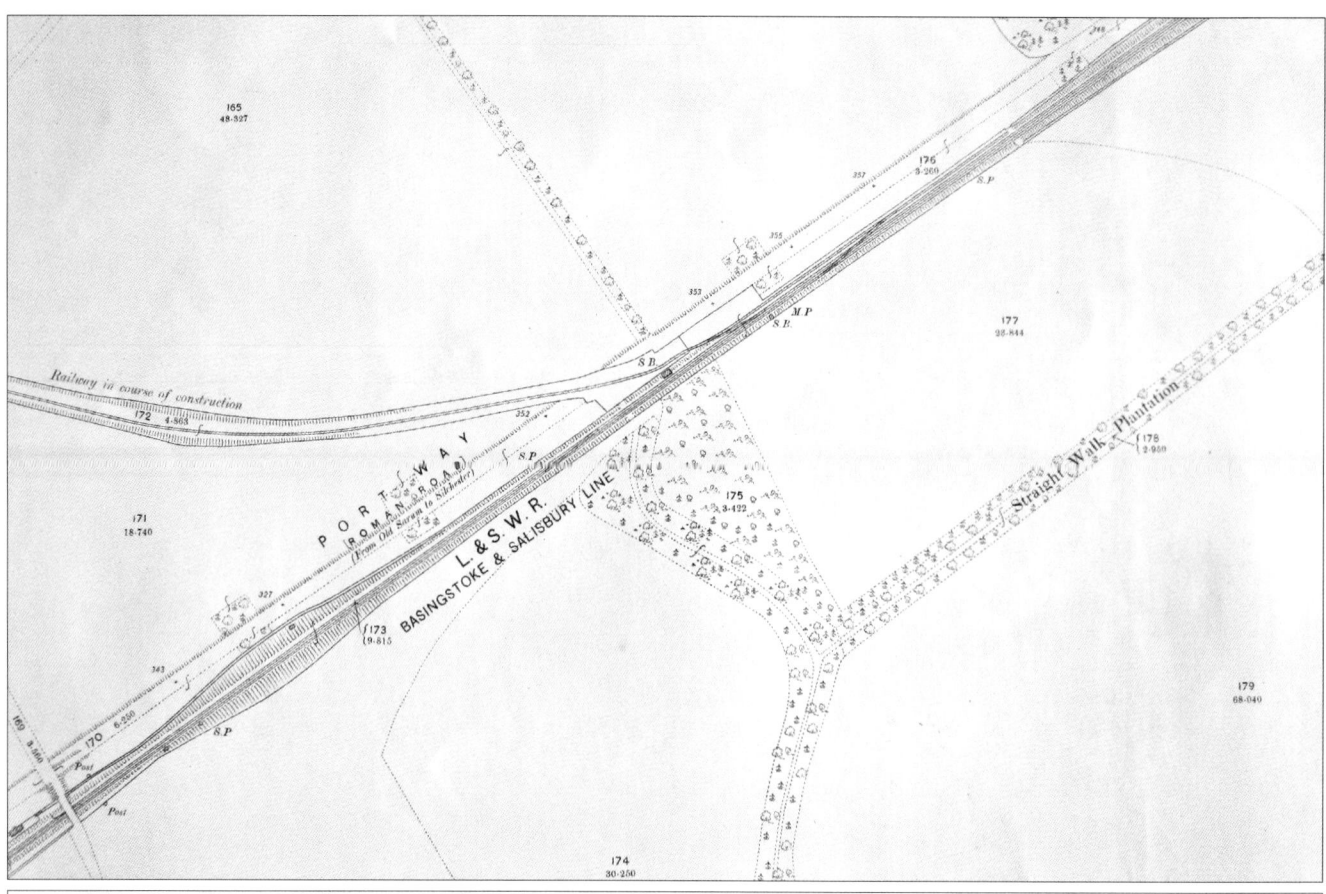

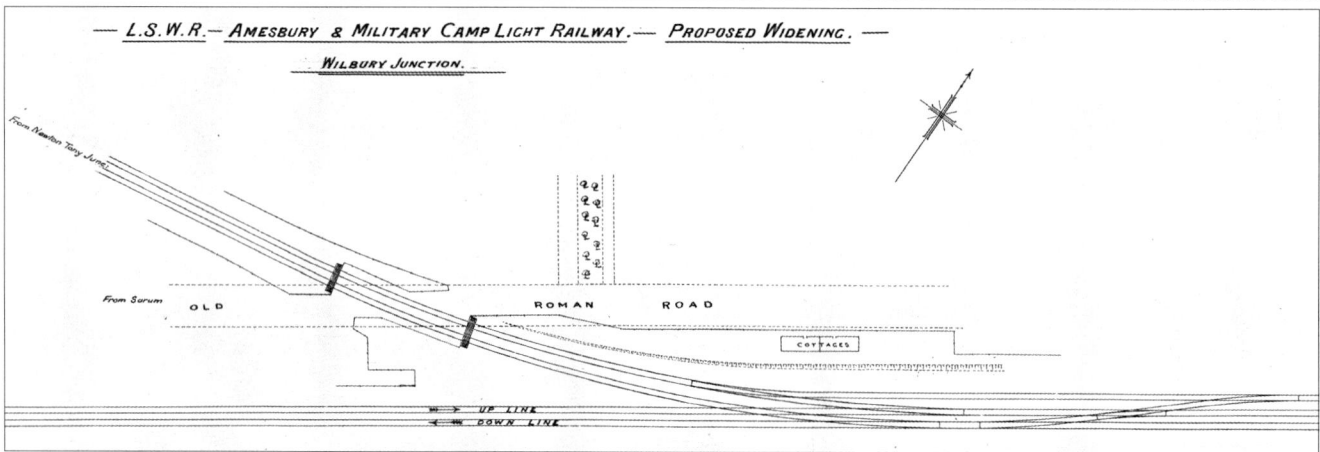

Top - *1901 Ordnance Survey map of Newton Tony Junction. (WSA)*

Centre - *An undated plan referring to the name 'Wilbury Junction'. An appended note stated, "Position of Signal Box to be determined on the ground in conjunction with Traffic Department."*

miles. This was to remain a fatal flaw even after services were diverted from the junction at Grateley to run through direct from Amesbury to the cathedral city. This disparity in distances and therefore in journey time ultimately affected the viability of the branch particularly when competing road services started to bite in later years. The initial timetable of six return daily passenger services, two of which started or terminated at Andover rather than Grateley, was supplemented by one return goods working from Andover.

To accommodate the new line the layout at Grateley, the junction station on the LSWR mainline from London to Exeter which had opened on May 1st. 1857 when the village population stood at some 150 souls, was altered. The former up platform was converted into an island to allow the Amesbury trains to use the outside platform face and the road overbridge adjacent to the station required widening to accommodate the revised trackwork, total costs amounting to some £7,000. In view of the impending opening of the Amesbury line and of the fact that the signalling in the area needed updating, LSWR engineers recommended in November 1900 that the Andover - Grateley section should be the site for a trial of automatic block signalling and that a

Top - *From the excellent 'Track Layout Diagram' volumes by Pryer and Paul (section S3), a chronology of the junction facilities at Newton Tony.*

Centre - *Amesbury with the engine pit siding adjacent to the turntable.*

Bottom - *Newton Tony. (Both 'Railway Magazine')*

pneumatic signalling system should be installed at Grateley. A special train from Waterloo to Grateley on 31st. July 1901 conveyed a large party of railwaymen from the UK, the Continent and the USA, invited by the British Pneumatic Signal Co., to inspect the new installation at Grateley. Following a period of trial working, the automatic signals were brought into use on 20th. April 1902 a few days before formal opening of the Amesbury line for goods traffic. Although the principle of automatic block signalling was proven in this experiment, the pneumatic system was found to be expensive to maintain and, with savings of £1,000 p.a. being anticipated, conversion to conventional signalling took place in 1919 prompted by the need to install a new junction and signalbox at Red Post Junction, where the MSWJR line branched off the mainline, to cater for increased wartime traffic.

Although some commentators have suggested that a third independent line from Grateley to Newton Tony Junction was provided at the outset, the 1901 OS map clearly shows that there was no such line in situ at this time, merely a short siding at Newton Tony Junction in the Grateley direction. Following an inspection by Major Pringle (HMRI) on 28th. February 1902, this third track opened for traffic on 24th May 1902, scope for it being contained within the Act of 9th. August 1899. Its provision was presumably a reflection of the desirability of segregating branch trains thereby minimising interference with mainline services. This independent third track appeared on the map accompanying the proposed revised junction arrangements produced in 1903. It also appears on an undated map when the junction seems to have been known as Wilbury Junction. The widening works involved not only the replacement of Grateley station bridge, with wrought iron girders but two further bridges before Newton Tony Junction was reached. Although only one set of rails was ever laid enough land was taken for doubling if required. Grateley is situated just over the county boundary in Hampshire, the line crossing into Wiltshire 1½ miles south west of the station. The junction of the branch with the main line was known as Newton Tony Junction.

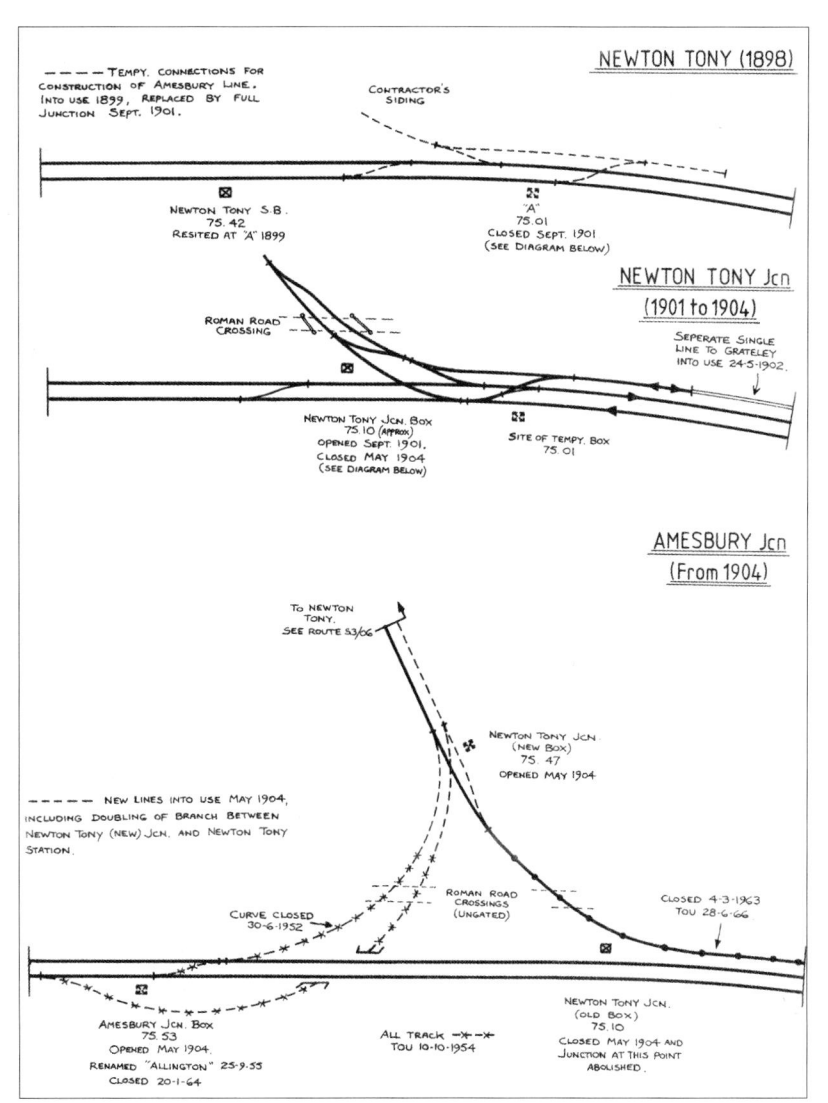

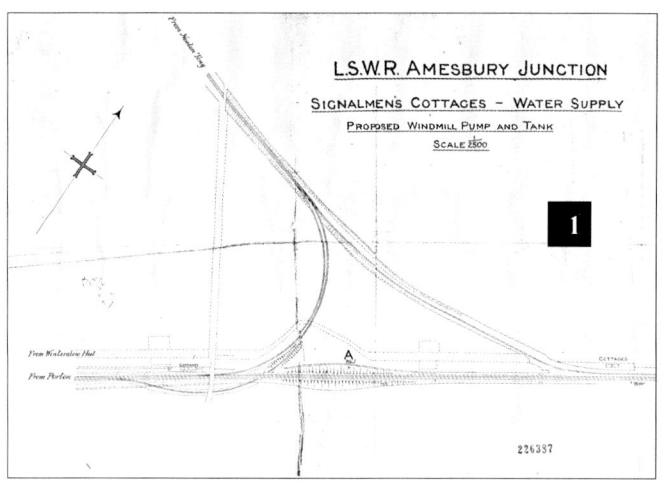

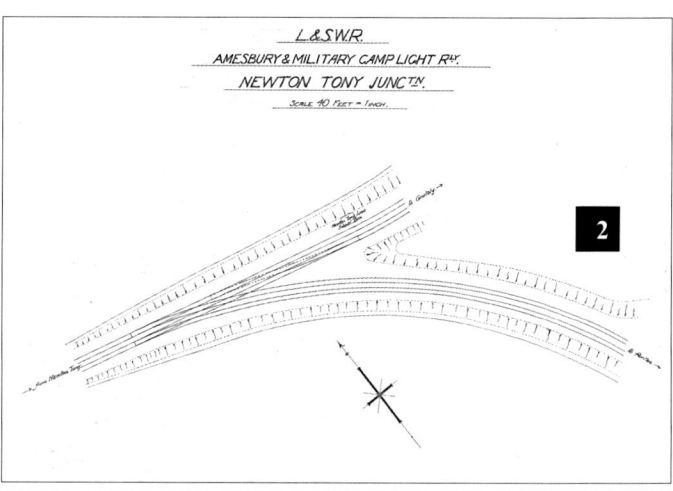

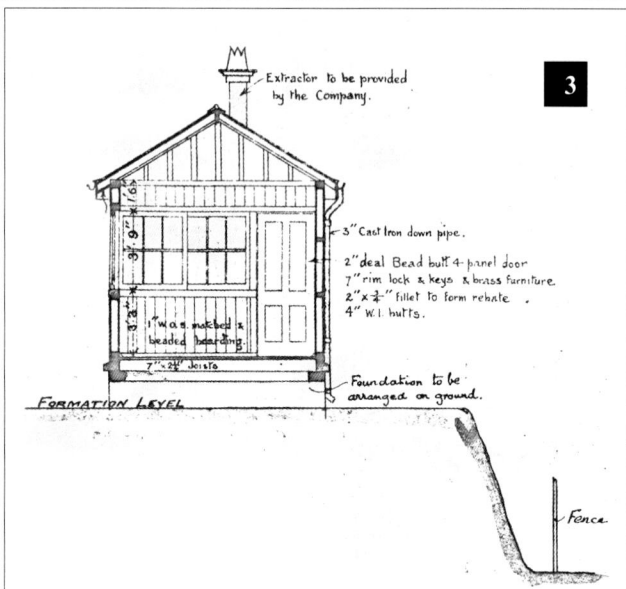

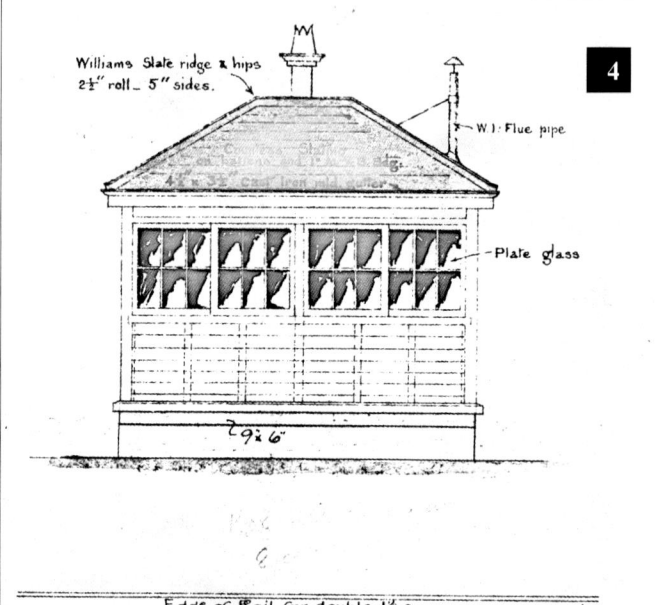

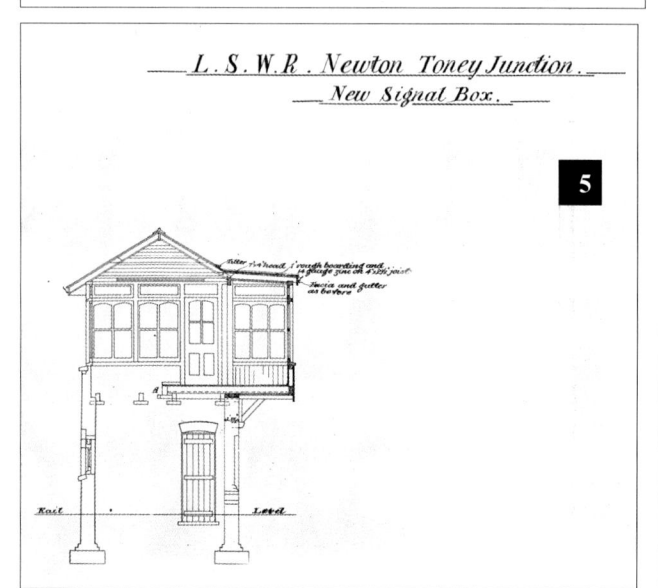

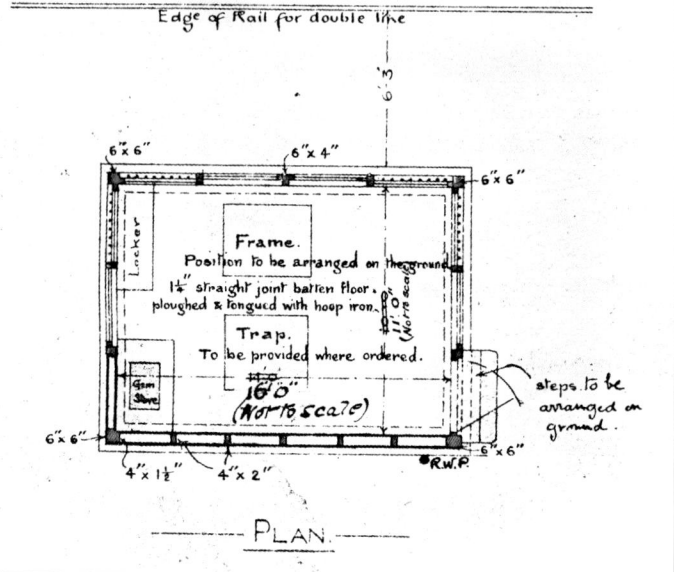

1 - Schematic diagram of the junctions with the main line, undated.
2 - Newton Tony Junction, undated, but adding to the confusion with a suggested double line of rails towards the east.
3 and *4* - Newton Tony Junction signal box as built. Its location would be as shown on plan No. 2: an undated sketch, circa 1904.
5 - End elevation of what would be Amesbury Junction signal box, see location plan on previous page. Clearly at this stage a final name had not be decided upon. The spelling 'Newton Toney' is referred to on pages, 18, 21 and 25.

The history of signalboxes at Newton Tony Junction is a little complex but in essence the original box was opened in August 1898, only to be closed the following year when a box with a 12 lever frame was opened slightly nearer to Grateley to provide access for the contractors working on the branchline then under construction. Main line trailing crossovers together with trailing connections from both lines were provided on to what was essentially just a contractor's siding at that stage. On 28th. April 1899 Major Addison (HMRI) inspected the new works at Grateley and the temporary junction arrangements at Newton Tony and found them to be generally satisfactory. This second box was replaced in 1901 in the V of the junction itself with a much more substantial box, with a 37 lever frame, to control the now full double track junction from the mainline which soon became single track on the branch. The box had levers to control a level crossing where the line crossed the old Roman road. This third box lasted until the junction modifications of 1904. A fourth box with this name opened in May 1904 half a mile further on towards Newton Tony village.

On parting with the mainline at the junction the branch curved away in a north-westerly direction passing under a road bridge and entering a cutting on a falling grade before climbing briefly to enter Newton Tony station which was situated 3¾ miles from Grateley. The station layout here consisted of a passing loop and two platforms with buildings located on the up platform only. Originally a signalbox was provided next to a small corrugated ironclad building on the platform but this was later moved nearer to the only gated level crossing on the line. Sidings were located to the rear of the up platform and until October 1903 the station nameboard read

Top - Grateley looking east at the time of the inauguration of the power signalling at the station. (Railway Magazine)

Centre - A WW1 era postcard of Grateley with a train of military traffic seen standing in the Amesbury branch platform.

Bottom - 1922 map showing location of Boscombe Down airfield siding.

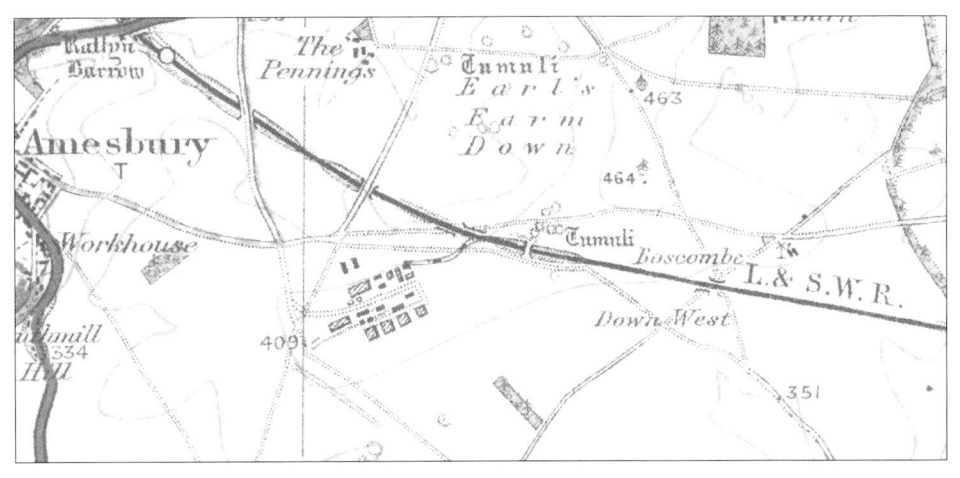

```
COPY.                HEADQUARTERS,
                       Southern Command,
C.R.S.C. 200531/5 (RT)   Salisbury.

                     11th March, 1919.
Dear Sir,

     With reference to your letter
A4/71584 dated 25th February, arrangements
have now been made to work the Boscombe Down
Branch with the Inland Waterways and Docks
engine, which was formerly working on this
Branch.  Will you kindly arrange to have it
passed over your system between kkx Ratfyn
Junction and Boscombe Down.

     Immediately these arrangements are
made, I shall be glad if you will recommence
placing traffic at Boscombe Down Jctn.

                Yours faithfully,

        (sd)    H. W. Perkins.

                Lieut.Colonel, A.D.R.T.
                Southern Command.


Geo. F. West Esq.,
    Supt: of the Line,
    London & South Western Railway Company,
        Waterloo Station,
            LONDON, S.E.1.
```

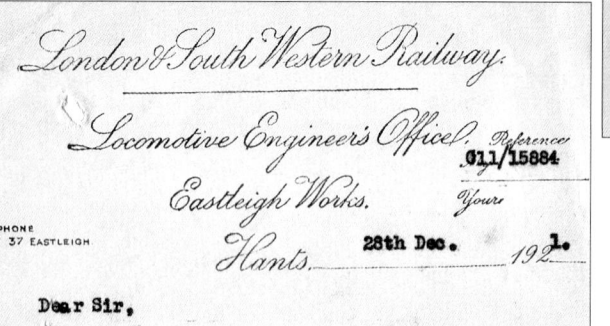

London & South Western Railway.
Locomotive Engineer's Office,
Eastleigh Works.
Reference 011/15884
Hants. 28th Dec. 1921.

Dear Sir,

Loco "Salisbury" at Boscombe Down.

In connection with the above, the Locomotive Foreman at Salisbury is arranging to take out the Steam Crane and Loco Van leaving Salisbury at 915a.m. to-morrow and stand on down line off Boscombe Down. After the 10.5 a.m. ex Bulford has passed Boscombe Down, he will pick up the three pairs of wheels and load them in a wagon on the spot. He will then proceed to Amesbury with wagon, steam crane and van and return to Salisbury, leaving Amesbury about 11.30 a.m. We will provide our own Loco Van and Guard for the service. The wheels will be sent to Eastleigh Shops the same day.

Will you please note and make what arrangements are necessary so far as your Department is concerned.

This is in confirmation of my 'phone message of this morning.

Yours faithfully,

For R. W. URIE.

S.W. Milford Esq.

London & South Western Railway.
Locomotive Engineer's Office,
Eastleigh Works.
Reference 011/15884
Hants. 24th January 1922.

Dear Sir,

Loading of Locomotive wheels at Boscombe Down Siding.

With reference to your letters of the 2nd and 23rd instant, in addition to the services you refer to, I would mention that we are undertaking repairs to the engine in question. When these repairs are completed, it is proposed to render an account embracing all our charges.

Yours faithfully,

For R. W. URIE.

S.W. Milford, Esq.,
SOUTHAMPTON WEST.

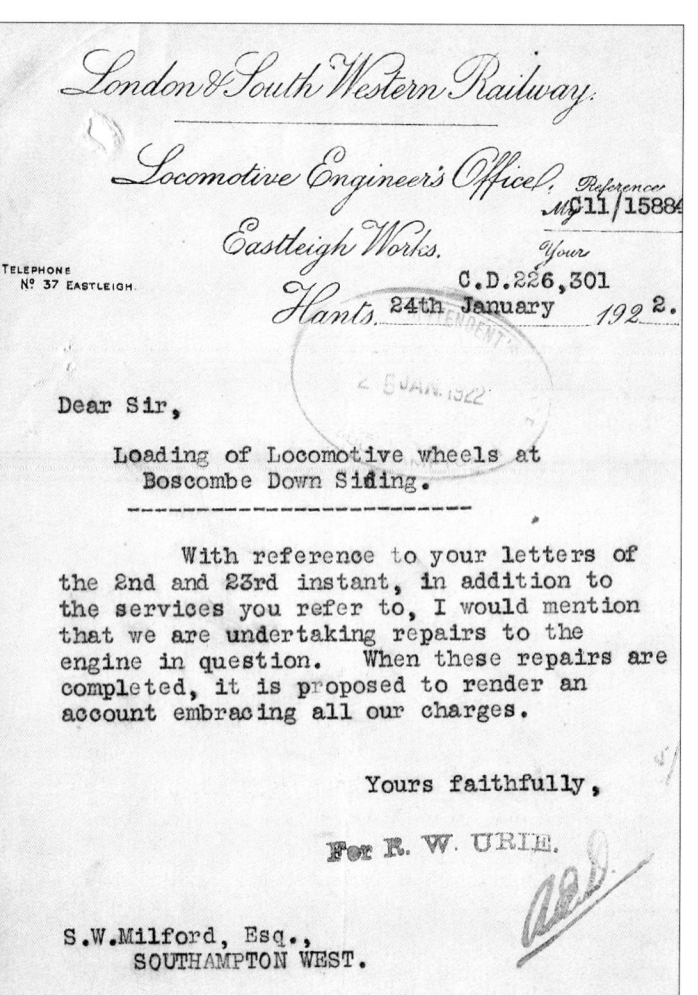

Correspondence re MOD locomotive at Boscombe Down.

"Newton Toney" after which the "e" was dropped to become "Newton Tony". Leaving the station the line climbed out of the valley of the River Bourne, initially at 1 in 51, and then a short level section led to a further climb at 1 in 93 to reach the summit on Boscombe Down. Eight bogies was the limit on this section for one locomotive. The "Railway Magazine" in describing the route waxed lyrical about the views from the train stating that *"on a clear day the spire of Salisbury Cathedral nearly 8 miles distant can plainly be seen as can the famous Beacon Hill where a splendid view of the new manoeuvring ground on Salisbury Plain and Bulford Camp is obtained."*

The line then crossed the Salisbury – Tidworth (A338) road and passed to the east of the Boscombe Down facility. Boscombe Down opened in 1917 as a flying training unit and after being home to various squadrons the base was taken over in 1939 by the Aeroplane and Armament Experimental Establishment that had been set up at Martlesham Heath after its initial work at Upavon Central Flying School. The A & AEE have remained at Boscombe Down ever since. The base acquired its own sidings into the camp in 1917, shortly after the original title of Red House Farm Airfield had been dropped, and work on the new aerodrome begun, the construction of which was rendered much easier by the provision of a direct railway connection. The cost

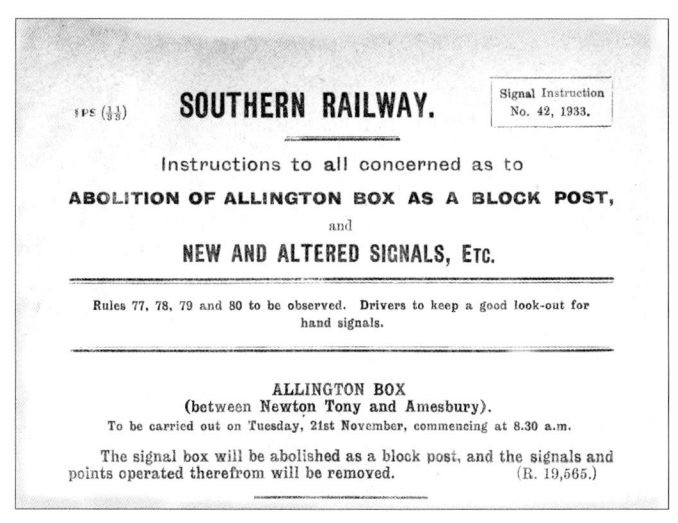

Southern Railway Signal instruction of 1933.

of this work to the LSWR was only £1,781 as the WD met the bill for sleepers, timbers, and earthworks. A new Boscombe Down signalbox was installed in late 1917 or early 1918. This was only intended to be short-lived during construction work at the airfield and it closed at the end of 1918. In January 1919 160 wagons and vans were dealt with at these sidings and on the 31st. of the month the sidings were handed over to the RAF and it was reported that all wagons and the locomotive used to shunt them had been removed as the men formerly operating the siding had been demobilised. A request was made in March 1919 to allow military motive power, described as the "Inland Waterways & Docks locomotive", passage over the LSWR line from the LMR sidings at Ratfyn Junction to Boscombe Down to enable traffic to be dealt with by the WD at Boscombe Down siding. In view of the small amount of traffic offering, approx. 4 trucks daily by that time, the SM at Amesbury had suggested that it could be more economically dealt with at Amesbury and moved by road to Boscombe Down thus allowing the siding there to be closed permanently. The military were reluctant to accept this proposal indicating that there were large amounts of machines to be despatched there by rail in addition to the conveyance of coal, petrol and stores, and they considered that handling of this traffic at Amesbury would result in congestion and delays. In May the Military advised that there was some delay in procuring a driver and fireman for Boscombe locomotive duties and that doubts existed as to the state of repair of the locomotive earmarked. Problems were resolved and a locomotive was transferred from Ratfyn to Boscombe Down at 10:30 on 14th. June 1919 although the WD did warn that it was not expected that workings would begin immediately. By August there had obviously been a change of heart and the Military advised that the locomotive currently at Boscombe Down was destined for Richborough MOD and that it could "run on its own wheels but not under steam". Having disconnected the coupling rods and provided a man to travel on the locomotive the LSWR District Superintendent informed the Military that the locomotive would be taken forward on 19th. August on the 6pm goods working. By May 1920 the Military advised that the siding was no longer required for military purposes.

Unfortunately there is a blank in the correspondence record until February 1921 when a further, or is it the delayed original (?), consignment of wheels from the former WD locomotive "Salisbury" was scheduled to be collected from Boscombe Down. In September further correspondence indicated that it was proposed to remove the military locomotive from Boscombe Down to Swindon. December saw a letter from Eastleigh sent out by Robert Urie stating that a steam crane and van would be proceeding to Boscombe Down on 29th. Inst. to pick up locomotive wheels and that as some repairs would be undertaken on the locomotive, it is not clear whether this would be at Eastleigh or on site at Boscombe Down, a combined charge would be raised for this work and for transporting the wheels. A Special Traffic Notice dated 13th. January 1922 referred to a special train with steam crane leaving Salisbury at 09:15 reaching Boscombe Down at 10:00 to collect locomotive wheels before proceeding on to Amesbury. The siding had gone and the airfield fallen out of use by the early 1920s, although the airfield was destined to rise phoenix-like in later years.

In January 1944 the War Dept wrote to the SR requesting the provision of sidings just to the east of the former Allington Signalbox, which had closed in November 1933, for the Air Ministry at Boscombe Down. On 28th. January a notice from Southampton Control indicated that the provision of a new siding with trailing points from the down

Title page of Newton Tony Curve Light Railway plans of 1902. (WSA)

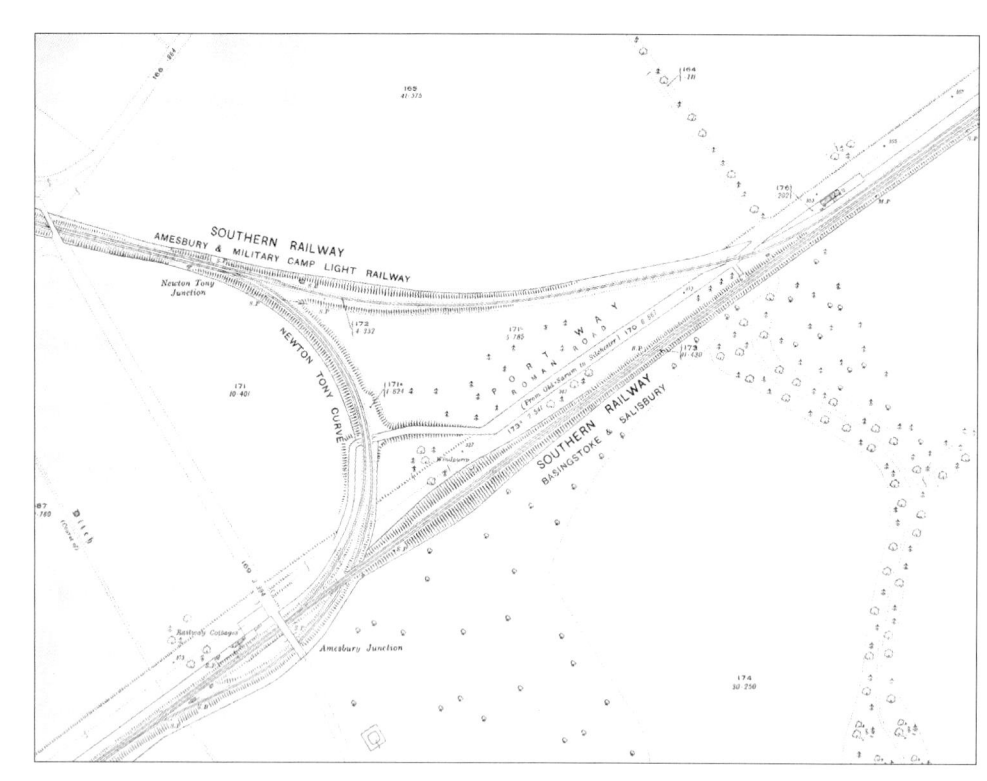

Left - OS map showing triangular junction near Newton Tony in 1925. (WSA)
Bottom - View looking towards Newton Tony with burrowing down line to Salisbury rising up in the foreground and up line from Salisbury above it. (Martin Dean Collection)
Opposite top - View looking from Newton Tony Junction with the main Andover - Salisbury line in the background. (Martin Dean Collection)
Opposite bottom - From the burrowing down line, a view looking back towards Newton Tony Junction. The main Salisbury line passes over the bridge. This was destined to be the most westerly burrowing junction of the LSWR. (Martin Dean Collection)

line would be provided on 1st. February with catch points in the siding at the clearance point of the connection with the down line. The cost of these works was a not inconsiderable £2,548 which reflected their extensive nature. On 10th October 1945 a Colonel Trench of the Board of Trade inspected the new connection next to an ungated level crossing to the south east of Allington to serve temporary sidings laid for the construction of a large runway at Boscombe Down. The sidings were laid with 95lb/yard rail and a two lever Ground Frame electrically released from Newton Tony was provided. At its peak up to 12 trains/day arrived at the sidings, which subsequently, on completion of the airfield, were dismantled, although a connection to the branch was maintained until 1948.

The line continued on passing the site of the former Boscombe Down signalbox and entered a shallow cutting on the level and then descended at 1 in 60 towards Amesbury station situated some 4¾ miles from Newton Tony Junction. Although built ostensibly as a light railway the station at Amesbury was far removed from the typical "Colonel Stephens" shack and boasted two through platforms with a footbridge, a 24 lever signalbox, a 45ft. turntable, several sidings including three dock roads served by a platform devoid of buildings, for ease of military access. Trains from these sidings could be hand signalled to allow access to and from the branchline. The two main platforms at Amesbury were both signalled for the departure of up trains. There was also a Station Master's house and a row of three pairs of railway cottages. At the north end of the site a ground frame hut containing three levers originally was provided, this being subsequently increased to 18 levers following the opening of the Bulford extension. The generous provision of facilities was a reflection of the substantial military traffic anticipated. A consistent water supply was most important here in view of the long distance nature of many of the workings and the need to turn round locomotives and empty stock generally within the hour. As mentioned previously, work had already commenced at Amesbury on the proposed extension to Shrewton and a cutting about 350 yards long had been excavated beyond the station. This area was used to provide four lengthy accommodation sidings. Initially, as the newspaper had reported, six services each way daily were provided with none on Sundays. The journey time for the 7¼ miles from Amesbury to Grateley was 20 minutes with one intermediate stop. Connection could be made at Grateley for services to Andover and to Salisbury. The "Railway Magazine" concluded that the *"railway opens up a district of much interest to the tourist and antiquarian,*

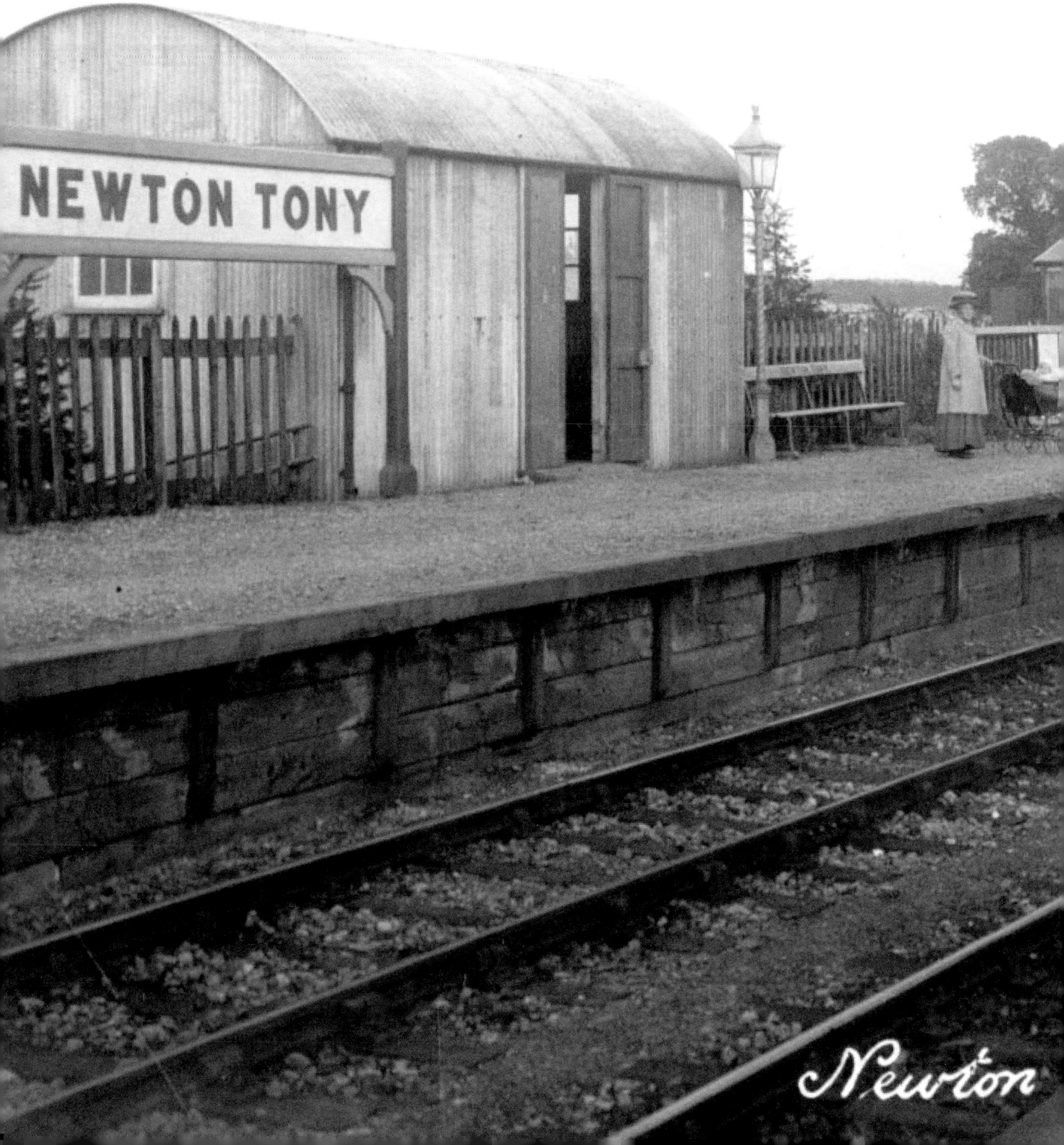
NEWTON TONY
Newton

Newton Tony Station looking towards the main line junction and Grateley. The steep gradient, descending at 1 in 100 immediately at the end of the platform will be noticed. This image is of the original station buildings and the only one so far located from the period. It dates from sometime between 1 June 1902 and 1 May 1914, at which latter date fire destroyed the facilities - see overleaf. (John Alsop)

FIRE AT NEWTON TONY STATION

From:

'The South Western Gazette' 1 June 1914.

"We regret to report that a disastrous fire broke out at Newton Tony Station on Friday 1 May, which resulted in the greater part of the station and contents being consumed.

"The fire, which broke out about 12.30 pm, was first observed in the roof of the booking office, the discovery being made by the porter on duty, who at once raised the alarm and, together with several helpers, strenuous efforts were made to subdue the flames, but a strong breeze was blowing at the time and the building burnt very rapidly, mainly due to the fact that it was composed of match-boarding inside and a layer of felt, which in its turn, was covered by galvanised iron.

"The station-hose was attached, but there was not a great pressure of water available. The station master (Mr O P Norwood) was on his annual leave, but happened at the moment to be at home, and he, together with the relief station-master (Mr Shepherd) was soon on the spot, and with the assistance of signalman Cleave, and other willing helpers, everything was done that was possible to stop the progress of the flames.

"The roof and sides of the building soon collapsed, some of the red-hot sheets of galvanised iron narrowly missing the workers. During the progress of the fire a light engine from Amesbury arrived on the scene with some of the staff, who brought fire buckets and obtained water from the tender of the engine. A message was telegraphed to Salisbury and Bulford, but as the signalbox was well alight and was full of smoke and crackling woodwork, its transmission was attended with considerable risk and inconvenience. Indeed the roof fell immediately after Mr Cleave had sent the message saying they were burnt out.

"The telegraph instrument was soon destroyed, and from that time until early Saturday morning communication with the other stations was cut off, but the service of trains was not interfered with. Soon after this the Company's manual (fire engine) from Salisbury arrived with their brigade by special train, and in a very brief space of time got to work, but unfortunately the ruin was then completed, although they succeeded in totally extinguishing the burning remains.

"The flames had done their work so rapidly that the till and contents and a few of the books and a clock, were all that could be rescued, it being impossible to get near the booking-office owing to the intense heat and dense smoke, the latter being seen at Bulford Camp, five miles distant. So great was the heat that the edge of the platform caught fire, but was immediately extinguished. At one period it was feared that the goods shed and lamp-room would share the same fate, but by breaking down a fence these were saved.

"Some idea may be formed of the way in which the staff worked when we add that within an hour at the utmost, temporary telegraph and telephone instruments had been fitted in the goods shed, which is now doing duty for booking, parcels and goods traffic. The levers in the signal box were all that remained, but these were soon got in working order, and are now encased with tarpaulins.

"The cause of the fire is unknown, but it is generally supposed that a spark from the signal-box chimney was blown under the edge of the roof of the booking-office, and being fanned by the high wind, set fire to the roofing felt.

"The whole of the books, ticket, invoices, insurance cards, accounts, returns, etc., having been destroyed, much inconvenience and labour have been thrown upon the staff. Traffic was only very slightly delayed, and by early on Saturday morning all the electrical instruments had been fixed in the temporary signal-box, and everything was so far in working order.

"We are indebted to Mr Percy Norwood, son of the station-master, for the photographs taken during the height of the fire. Mr Norwood, it will be remembered, was instrumental in saving the life of a man at Liss Station, and was decorated by the King, as reported in our issue of March last." (- for replacement station building plans see page 74.)

Newton Tony Station with the replacement buildings and new signal box looking down the line towards Amesbury and Bulford. (John Alsop)

and the Druidical remains of far-famed Stonehenge are only about 2 ½ miles from the station. It is a most enjoyable walk or drive from Amesbury to the historic stones. The opening of this railway will give the public exceptional facilities for visiting this district."

REVISED JUNCTION ARRANGEMENTS

It is convenient here to deal with subsequent changes to the junction of the Amesbury branch with the LSWR mainline. The prophetic words of the Salisbury & Wiltshire Journal were soon borne out in practice and the LSWR directors first discussed new junction arrangements in March 1903 less than a year after the official opening. The proposals were approved in June and the consequent Light Railway Order for the work issued. Whilst the existing east facing junction was adequate to serve the longer distance movement of troops and materiel from sites such as Aldershot and those members of the public wishing to travel towards London, considerable local pressure had built up since opening to provide a shorter direct passenger service to Salisbury removing the necessity to travel via Grateley thereby shortening journey times, distance covered and, of course, fares paid ! Originally the estimates for the new spur lines and junction arrangements were established as £14,975. This was later reduced to £9,900, through the simple expedient of not removing surplus excavation material from site, the actual final cost being £10,600.

Revision to the junction required the track between Newton Tony station and the new divergence to be doubled and a new 13 lever signal box named Newton Tony Junction opened at the divergence of the east and west facing spurs. A pair of cottages for the signalmen was erected here at a cost of £550. A single line then ran eastwards towards Grateley along its own independent track whilst a double line of rails curved to the south west, one line of 22 chains connecting to the LSWR up mainline whilst the other of 32 chains burrowed underneath the mainline to connect with the down mainline thus avoiding conflicting movements. In view of the limited number of scheduled passenger trains travelling to Salisbury at this time, the provision of such an expensive junction was questionable. Certainly Newton Tony Junction was a lot quieter than other locations on the LSWR mainline from London where burrowing had been resorted to and was far less busy than some spots, such as Woking, where the provision of such a junction arrangements would have been very beneficial. A new signalbox was installed at the junction on the mainline known as Amesbury Junction replacing the original Newton

Men from the Isle of Wight Rifles at Amesbury in 1910. (Peter Daniels Collection.)

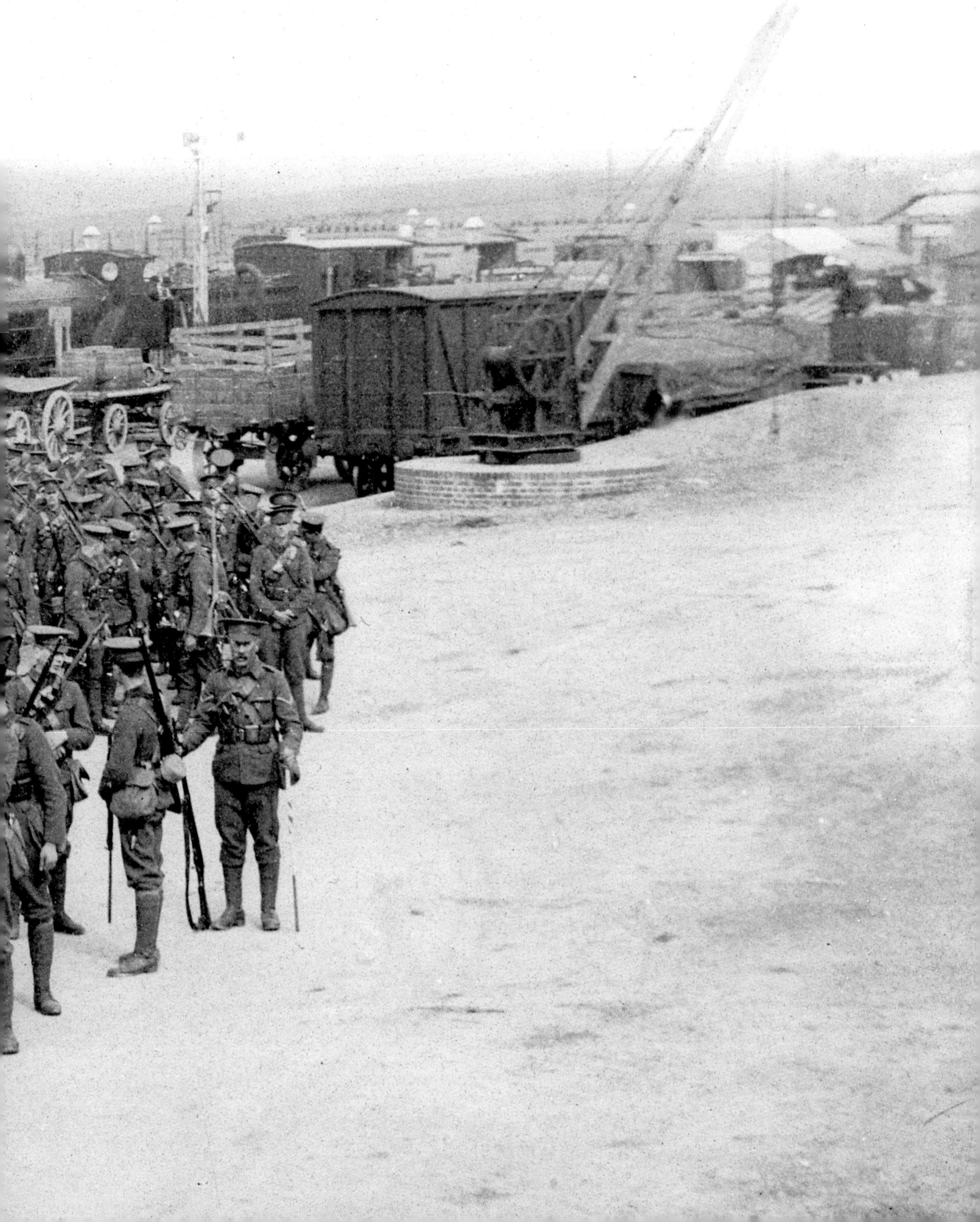

Amesbury Station looking towards Bulford and the abandoned Shrewton extension. (John Alsop)

Bulford Station looking north towards Bulford Camp and Sling. (John Alsop)

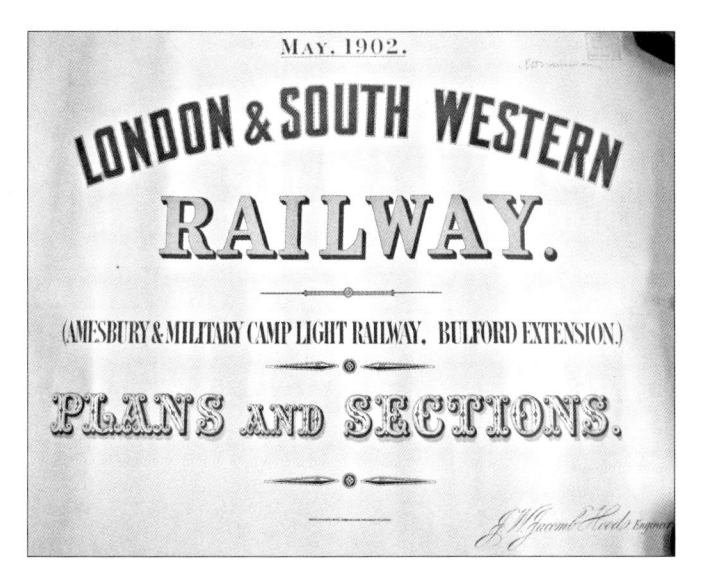

Title page of the Bulford Extension Railway 1902. (WSA)

Tony Junction box which closed and the original connection of the branch with the mainline was removed as were all the signals installed in 1901. By December 1903 the new curve at Newton Tony Junction was reported as being nearly complete. Passenger services between Amesbury and Salisbury over the new junction were inaugurated on 8th. August 1904 reducing the journey time, which was approximately 50 minutes but varied depending upon the connections at Grateley, to just 37 minutes and the distance from 17½ to 11 miles. However, only six services were diverted to run to Salisbury, three continuing to take the old route to Grateley or Andover Junction. By 1909 there was just one return passenger working remaining between Bulford and Andover Junction via Grateley, a 5pm from Waterloo to Bulford but no return and 1 return goods working from Andover Junction to Bulford. In 1919 Salisbury became the origin and destination of all scheduled passenger services, the last weekday train from Andover Junction via Grateley running on 1st. June, the Sunday night train for returning troops continuing on this route until 3rd. October 1920. When diversion of all trains to Salisbury occurred, passengers for Andover, London and stations to the east could either change at Porton station which was located some 2¾ miles west of Amesbury Junction or could continue to Salisbury and retrace their steps by express services which did not call at the smaller stations.

EXTENSION

An additional factor in persuading the LSWR of the desirability of altering the junction arrangements may well have been a request from a Colonel Scott of the Royal Engineers in March 1902, even before official opening of the Amesbury line, asking if the railway company would undertake an extension from Amesbury to Bulford where a large military camp had been constructed, although the majority of buildings here were wooden huts rather than permanent brick built structures. Some of these huts, put up in 1903, can still be seen on Headquarters Street. Only the riding schools, now occupied by the Command Study Centre, the NAAFI Stores, the Garrison Gymnasium, and the terraced homes nicknamed "Merthyr Tydfils", owing to their similarity to housing provided for Welsh miners which were not built until the 1930s, were constructed of brick. As for the officers and their wives, they made do with converted huts or found private accommodation in nearby villages. The military authorities at the time stated that "*it was wholly unsatisfactory*" that troops detraining at Amesbury station then had to march 3 or 4 miles to camps at Bulford and Sling. Large quantities of stores, equipment and ammunition likewise had to be taken by road. With the other large military presence on the Plain in the Warminster area naturally a west facing junction on the mainline made even more sense in allowing the easy transfer of men and materiel. It was further suggested by the military that this line should continue beyond a proposed Bulford Camp station crossing a road and terminating at a goods station at Sling Barracks.

This camp at Sling was initially created as an annexe to Bulford Camp in 1903 and soon after 1914 New Zealand troops started work on building wooden huts here. They were later joined by Canadian troops, joiners, bricklayers, and civilian workers. By 1918 there were 4,300 men based

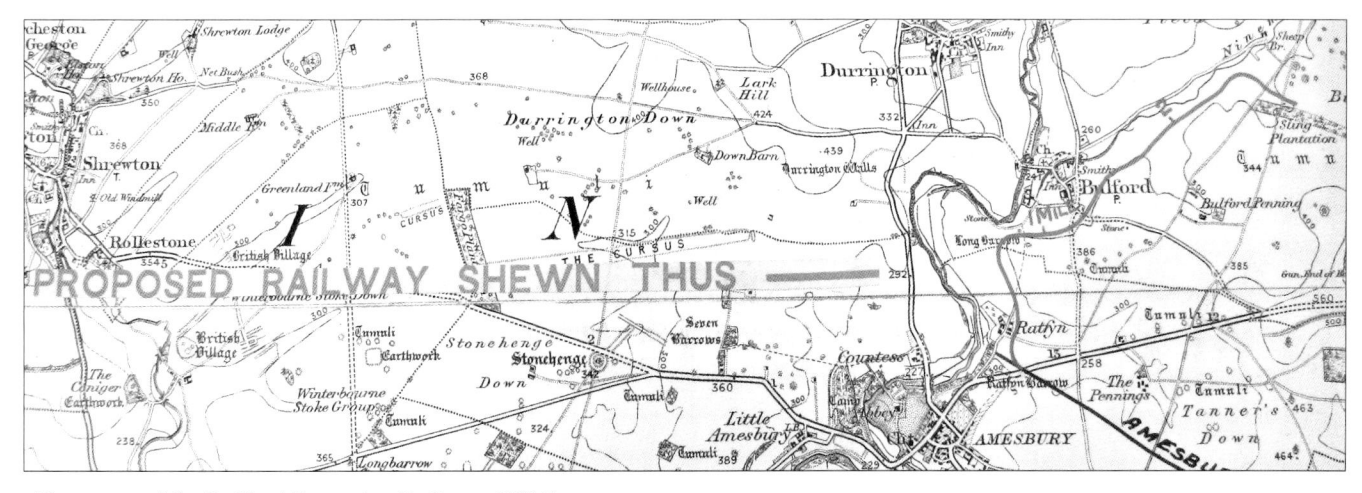

The route of the Bulford Extension Railway (WSA).

Left - *Amesbury Station before the foot bridge was built and showing the unusual double shelter on the up platform, looking towards Bulford Camp. At the end of the canopy two men are seen, perhaps painting, one using the conveniently parked coach as access. (John Alsop)*
Middle - *A train on the large embankment of the Bulford extension just south of Ratfyn Junction. The site of this today has been swallowed up by the dual carriageway A303. (Fuller of Amesbury)*
Bottom - *The Bulford Extension line as it gains the embankment just north of Amesbury station looking towards Bulford Station. (Derek Fear).*

An idyllic and very English scene looking from Telegraph Hill towards Bulford Station. (Peter Daniels Collection)

A very early view of Bulford Station taken before the large platform awning was built and with much activity taking place on the platform. (John Alsop)

Bulford Station showing the out of proportion 90 foot canopy that had been supplied by the LSWR after the War Department had complained about the meagre amount of roof covering provided. (John Alsop)

Bulford Station with an O2 tank engine and a couple of old pre-grouping coaches forming the branch set. Having run round it's carriages, the train is about to depart on the return journey back to Amesbury and Salisbury. (John Alsop)

at Sling including some New Zealand conscientious objectors such as Archibald Baxter and his brothers Alexander and John who had been forced to join the army and sent all the way from New Zealand to England to make an example of them. After the end of the war the camp became a repatriation centre and at the time there was unrest in other camps as a result of delays in demobilising troops. To try to restore order a harsh regime was enforced and route marches ordered. The men requested a relaxation of discipline as the war was over and they were far from home, however this was refused and the troops rioted, stealing food from the mess and emptying the Officers Mess of alcohol. To try and resolve the situation the officers and men were promised no repercussions, but this promise was not honoured and the ringleaders were arrested and shipped back to New Zealand. After the war a Kiwi was cut into the chalk on Beacon Hill, which can still be seen today, to commemorate the link with New Zealand.

Somewhat unusually however, the applicant for the Extension LRO was not the LSWR, as might have been expected given that they were constructing it, but the WD. This was similar to the process to be used in 1905 with the Bentley to Bordon branch in Hampshire. Application for a Light Railway Order was made on the 15th May. Also unusual was the fact that the WD concluded an agreement with the LSWR, dated December 31st. 1903, to pay interest at a rate of 3½ % p.a. on the estimated capital cost of the line. In effect they were subsidising the construction of the extension which would be undertaken by the LSWR's own staff. The first true military railway had been built during the Crimean War (1854-56) the main route running from the harbour at Balaclava to a supply point at the rear of British lines some 7 miles distant. From here a number of subsidiary lines were laid to the various batteries. A large number of navvies were shipped out to undertake construction and the line proved to be of the utmost value in moving stores and ammunition. Motive power was a combination of horse, stationary engine and rather underpowered locomotives. Although it was somewhat disparagingly dubbed the "Great Crimean Railway", it did play a key role in the fall of Sebastopol by providing a supply line that was far more efficient than the primitive roads of the area.

Work began on the Bulford extension early in 1904 under the direction of the LSWR Chief Engineer J W Jacomb Hood. One of the locomotives known to have been employed on this work was Manning Wardle 0-6-0 ST No. 407, formerly called *"Pioneer"* which the company had obtained from a contractor from Okehampton for £500 in 1881 and which had been used in Southampton Docks. It was agreed that the LSWR would work the single line as a normal passenger route to Bulford station, the section to Bulford Camp and onwards to the compound at Sling would be worked as required by the WD and not be open to the public. The final cost of the Bulford extension was reported in October 1907 as £28,809. Although enough land was taken for a double line the route from Amesbury remained single track until the end of services. Major Pringle (HMRI) visited the line on 3rd. April 1906 and passed it for passenger traffic. On 16th May the LSWR Directors were informed of the successful inspection and announced that the line would open for traffic on the 1st June. This extension increased the

Top - *Bulford Camp Platform, devoid of buildings, looking towards Sling Camp Platform. (Unknown)*

Bottom - *Sling Plantation Army Camp. (Fuller of Amesbury).*

length of the line from Amesbury by 1¼ miles to Bulford and a further 1 mile to Bulford Camp plus ½ mile on to Sling giving as total mileage from Newton Tony Junction of 7¼ miles.

Leaving Amesbury the new line passed under London Road (formerly A303) bridge and swung northeast passing a short siding on the left at the delightfully named spot of Ratfyn and rose on a grade of 1 in 113 easing to 1 in 597 before descending at 1 in 111 to cross in quick succession the Bulford – Amesbury road and the Bulford – Durrington (A3028) road before arriving at Bulford station. This, the terminus for the public passenger service, comprised a wooden, later replaced by concrete, edged platform on the down side together with a run-round loop. The aesthetics of the station building, built of brick and timber, would not be helped in 1915 by the provision of a particularly large canopy out of all proportion to the size of the building. Originally just two small awnings covering merely the entrances from the platform to the station offices had been provided but the WD had complained that the meagre roof covering provided insufficient protection for waiting troops and a canopy 90 feet in length was provided at an estimated cost of £235. A small signalbox was located on the platform and three sidings and a Goods Shed completed the facilities here. The line then curved to the east and with easy grades of 1 in 100 ran through a shallow cutting reaching Bulford Camp station. A long open concrete faced platform, ideal for troop assembly, and a small booking office were provided here. A run-round loop and a long siding of 645 yards parallel to the branch line in the direction of Bulford were also provided. Only goods were then conveyed on the final stretch to Sling, the line falling at 1 in 100 before climbing at 1 in 63 then at 1 in 260 crossing three roads by ungated crossings, the last of which was over the Marlborough road to reach the army compound of Sling on the north side of a plantation of the same name. A platform for unloading goods was provided here together with a passing loop and a siding. All public trains were now extended to Bulford with a journey time of seven minutes allowed from Amesbury. Although there have been some published reports that the single line was doubled to Bulford in May 1909 this is not borne out by OS maps which show single track throughout the life of the line.

3. OPERATION

IMPROVEMENTS......TIMETABLES......MILITARY TRAFFIC......
ACCIDENTS…...SIGNALLING…...MOTIVE POWER…...COACHING STOCK

IMPROVEMENTS

Between the opening of the Bulford extension and the First World War a number of improvements were made as might be expected in response to the increasing use being made of the line by the military. It was claimed that, for its size, Amesbury was one of the busiest stations in the country before and during the First World War. Principal amongst these improvements was the decision, in 1909, to continue the double track from Newton Tony to Amesbury. This was largely brought about by the extensive manoeuvres planned for that year by the Territorial Army. By late May 1909 work was complete and an intermediate signalbox named Allington was provided between these two points. Other works, of a lesser nature, included the extension of a siding at Newton Tony, at an estimated cost of £90. Following the fire here on 1st. May 1914, which destroyed the main station building, all that remained was the lever frame and part of the Gents urinal. The LSWR approved the reconstruction of the station building which in addition would include a new waiting shelter on the down platform at an estimated cost of £411, £300 of this being covered by the Company's fire insurance fund. Local residents were delighted to have the waiting shelter as they had been making representation to the LSWR to have such a facility for some time.

At Amesbury plans were submitted in 1906 for a proposed footbridge together with screening and roofing on the up platform and a cycle store which were costed at £350. In 1910 two pairs of cottages were built for an estimated cost of £556 and in 1914 a small stage for military baggage traffic to aid the despatch of troop trains was provided for £15. This was to overcome the situation whereby vans were prevented from being placed in position for the reception of baggage at the dock on the up line side at the same time that guns were being loaded. Also in 1914 the Goods Shed and Station Master's Office were extended for £220 and additional sidings provided. In 1916 five "high lamps" were installed, at an estimated cost of £38, thereby removing the need for a large number of portable flare lamps, and consequently saving the services of one man, illumination being required round the clock for dealing with troop movements.

At Bulford telephonic communication was provided in 1907 at an estimated cost of £41. An old carriage was to be placed in the siding to serve as a room for the telephonic instrument and as a shelter for the men employed at a further cost of about £18. In 1909 a goods store and an extension of the loading dock were estimated at £245, the WD paying interest on the outlay as they did on most of the work undertaken on the extension. In 1910 additional siding accommodation was provided for £377. In 1914 an extension to the station buildings and gents WC were made costing £125 the same year that Bulford saw the parcels office go up in flames as a result of a relief parcel porter pouring petrol, which he had obtained from one of the local cabmen, into a lighted paraffin lamp. Although the fire was quickly extinguished it caused damage to the office and the cloakroom, the unfortunate porter ending up in Salisbury Infirmary with serious burns. Additional sidings were provided at Bulford and at Sling in 1915.

The somewhat isolated nature of the stations at Amesbury and Bulford were fair game to those of criminal intent and on 12th January 1913 the goods shed and booking office at Bulford were forcibly entered and £6 4s 7d stolen. December 1913 saw burglaries at both stations, the booking office at Amesbury being entered on the 30th December, with the aid of a crowbar from the permanent way hut, and the princely sum of 12/4½d taken from the till and a desk drawer was also forced and a further 12/- stolen. On the same night better pickings were to be had at Bulford when the sweetmeat machine was relieved of £8 3/- . The police investigated both robberies and apparently used bloodhounds to try and trace the culprits. Although the animals picked up and followed a trail from Amesbury to Bulford and thence to the Camp, the scent was lost however and nobody was apprehended. The following year at Bulford Camp station an army picket spotted a blaze in the old carriage used as an office and store, thought have been started deliberately or by an unauthorised person entering for a crafty smoke in the structure. Although prime suspects in the vicinity were always likely to come from the ranks of servicemen, criminal intent was not confined to them as on 27th May 1913 a deficiency of £11 0s 5d in the goods account was laid at the door of the Goods Clerk who was summarily dismissed, it being subsequently found that he was responsible for further losses of £31 2s 8d. Whilst of interest in their own right, these events not only show that antisocial behaviour is nothing new but are a useful insight into the sort of receipts held on the branch at the time.

TIMETABLES

For the opening of the line to Bulford the revised train service consisted of nine trains daily in each direction, three for Grateley and six for Salisbury. The first train left at 7:03 am giving a Waterloo arrival at 9 minutes past 10 am, a considerable improvement on the timetable operative on the opening of the Amesbury branch. The last train back from Salisbury left at 9:12 pm. There was one train from Salisbury on Sundays at 8:40 in the evening which provided a connection at Porton from the 5:40 pm departure from London for returning servicemen together with an 11:59 pm departure from Andover Junction connecting with the 10 pm London departure, which ran fast to Amesbury omitting Grateley and Newton Tony arriving in Bulford at 35 minutes past midnight for those wishing to squeeze every last drop out of their weekend pass. One return goods working daily ran from Salisbury to Bulford and one from Basingstoke. From 1914 a milk van service was provided for the benefit of local dairy farmers between Bulford and Waterloo.

The branch was probably at its busiest in the lead up to, and for the duration of, both world wars when massive amounts of men and machines were moved about the country, mostly by rail during the first conflict and to a lesser extent during World War 2 when road transport played a much larger role. During World War 1 there was much disruption to non-military railway traffic on the branch and even soldiers stationed at camps served by the railway were often unable to use it as they wished when they were on leave. A frequent complaint from soldiers based at Sling camp was that despite being only a couple of miles from Bulford station it was often *"difficult to catch a train to anywhere !"* This did lead some enterprising local garage owners into the taxi and hire car markets from which they made a good living for a while. Such was the congestion at times that in 1918 for example goods for Netheravon Airfield were routed via Pewsey some 10 miles away by road, on the relatively uncongested GWR network, rather than via Bulford just 5 miles distant.

Every summer in the early years of the 20th.C saw a large number of train movements transporting not only regular Army units but Territorial and Volunteer units to and from manoeuvres on Salisbury Plain. In 1909 for example, the LSWR ran 170 special troop trains over the week prior to the August Bank Holiday, 90 of these being for territorial units with 29 trains leaving Waterloo and nine leaving Nine Elms during the weekend conveying 22,000 men, 1,700 horses and 32 guns bound for Amesbury. A graphic example of the volume of troop movements catered for by the railways occurred during the Christmas leave period in 1910 when the LSWR ran some 237 special troop trains involving over 180,000 men. Special timetables were issued to cover these train movements and the opposite page shows that covering the return of Territorial Forces from Amesbury over the period 14th - 17th August 1909. On Sunday 15th. for example there were no less than 20 troop trains due to leave Amesbury between 08:55 and 16:00, the timetables giving fascinating details of the Unit conveyed, the number of Officers and Men, the number of horses and vehicles, the number of guns, with the new machine guns receiving special mention, and the tonnage of baggage.

MILITARY TRAFFIC

Special Traffic Arrangements for the summer of 1914 reveal the volume of special trains run for the military in the run up to the outbreak of hostilities. On 25th. July, for example, a 12:25 departure from Exeter ran to Sherborne conveying the Wessex Divisional Signal Royal Engineers comprising three officers, 65 men, three horses in horseboxes, 31 horses in trucks and 6 four wheel wagons. Their return working was scheduled from Bulford on 8th. August. Other trains on that day conveyed the Army Service Corps of two officers and 75 men from Bridgwater, the 5th. Somerset Light Infantry of four officers and 115 men from Yeovil, 60 men from Crewkerne, three officers and 70 men from Chard all travelling to Bulford by a service at 9:15 am from Chard Junction with through coaches from Chard, Yeovil, and from Bridgwater, via the S&D, attached at Templecombe arriving at Bulford at 12:12 pm. A further arrival at Bulford, at 2:38 pm brought the 4th. Dorsets consisting of four officers and 100 men from Crewkerne, two officers and 80 men from Sherborne, and four officers with 110 men from Gillingham. The initial task at the outbreak of war in 1914 was the mobilisation of reservists and the return of TA units from their various summer camps to their bases. Embarkation of the first five Divisions of the British Expeditionary Force (BEF) commenced on 10 August, War Office sailing schedules from Southampton determining rail timings such that trains were booked into the docks at 12 minute intervals. Between 10th. - 31st. August 670 trains ran to Southampton Docks, the BEF being despatched punctually and with little disturbance other than some small reductions in normal passenger and steamer services for a few weeks. In October 1914 the landing of Canadian troops at Plymouth required 92 special trains to take them to the Plain.

Despite the best efforts of the War Office and the Railway Executive Committee, who had assumed its wartime role of exercising the government's power to take over control of the railways during wartime, on 4th. August 1914, troops remained eager to spend their weekend leave in the fleshpots of the capital. On Sunday evenings in 1916 for example the LSWR despatched four special trains to Bordon and Liphook, two each to Bordon, Dinton and Shawford and one each to Tidworth, Eastleigh, Farnborough and Aldershot.

In 1916 Australian training battalions were formed in England from which reinforcements could be posted to Australian Divisions fighting in France. Battalions such as the 42nd, which arrived from Queensland by way of Egypt and the Suez Canal, found themselves deposited at Amesbury Station. They undertook their acclimatization and final training on Salisbury Plain where camps had been established at a number of locations. That at Larkhill seems to have been particularly unpopular with the men as one soldier wrote home *'It has been raining like fun here and things about Larkhill are pretty sloppy. It's a rotten place when it rains and a jolly sight worse if it keeps fine for any length of time. The dust is that fine that it will get in anywhere; do what you will you can't get away from it.'*

Saturday, November 25th 1916 witnessed the departure of the 42nd. from Salisbury Plain the Battalion at last emerging as a smart, well equipped, highly trained fighting unit, with

LONDON & SOUTH WESTERN RAILWAY.

SPECIAL NOTICE No. 1,355, 1909.

TIME TABLES

FOR TRAINS CONVEYING THE

FIRST LONDON DIVISION

OF

HIS MAJESTY'S

TERRITORIAL FORCES

FROM

AMESBURY,

On SATURDAY, 14th, SUNDAY, 15th, MONDAY, 16th, and TUESDAY, 17th AUGUST, 1909.

As mentioned in the text, the rationale for the building of, and for many years the principal traffic on, the railway was that of military origin. There are numerous references to special trains running for this purpose, one example for 1909 is seen here. (Contemporary illustrations of soldiers at the stations follow.) On the occasion reported here 12 special trains operated on 14 August and 20 on the next day. What also makes this interesting is how, with typical military / railway planning, each train was scheduled to depart from a particular platform, numbered as such on the station plan accompanying the notice and reproduced above.

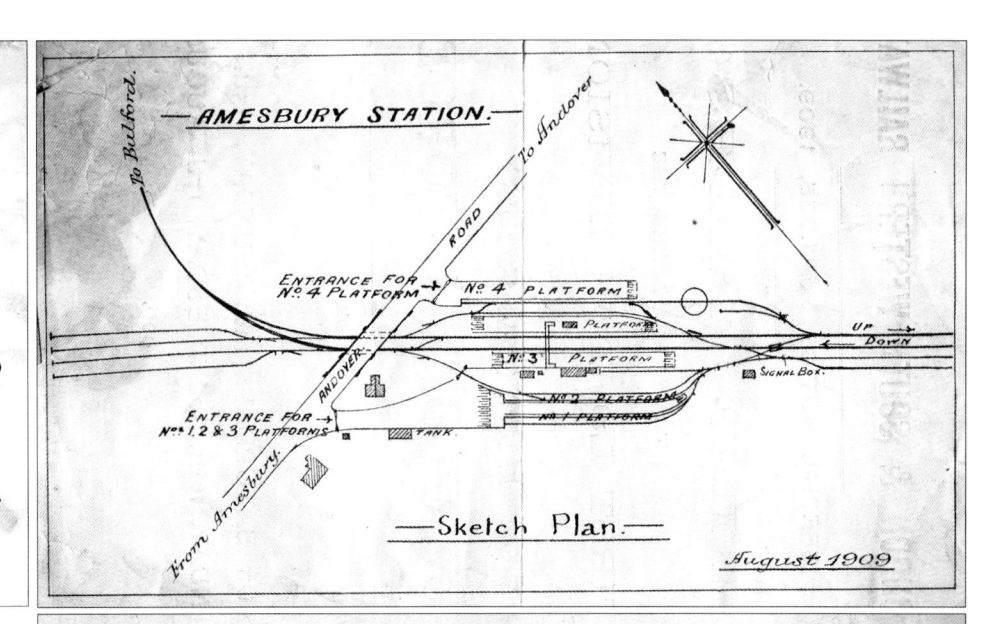

AMESBURY STATION.

— Sketch Plan. —

August 1909

TIME TABLE FOR RETURN OF TERRITORIAL FORCES FROM AMESBURY.

On SATURDAY, 14th August.

Train.	Number of Departure Platform at Amesbury.	To	Arrival Time.	Unit.	Officers.	Men.	Horses. In Boxes.	Horses. In Trucks.	Vehicles. 4-wheel.	Vehicles. 2-wheel.	Guns.	Limbers.	Tons of Baggage.
9 5 a.m.	4	Waterloo	11 45 a.m.	1st Field Ambulance	9	120	19	16	7	—	—	4	2
9 30 a.m.	1	Nine Elms	12 7 p.m.	1st Brigade R.F.A.	5	142	5	80	4	4	4	4	8¾
9 50 a.m.	2	Nine Elms	12 28 p.m.	1st Brigade R.F.A.	4	141	—	87	6	1	4	4	5
10 15 a.m.	4	Woolwich	3 0 p.m.	2nd Brigade R.F.A.	6	165	8	110	4	—	4	4	6
10 50 a.m.	4	Woolwich	3 30 p.m.	2nd Brigade R.F.A.	5	165	8	110	4	—	4	4	6
11 15 a.m.	2	Nine Elms	1 56 p.m.	3rd Brigade R.F.A.	4	110	8	91	1	—	4	4	7
12 0 noon	1	Nine Elms	2 54 p.m.	3rd Brigade R.F.A.	4	110	7	100	1	—	4	4	6
12 25 p.m.	2	Nine Elms	3 13 p.m.	3rd Brigade R.F.A.	4	110	7	100	6	—	—	—	—
12 50 p.m.	4	Waterloo	3 35 p.m.	4th Brigade R.F.A.	—	20	12	121	1	—	—	—	—
		Lewisham	4 28 p.m.	4th Brigade R.F.A.	10	130	(Change at Waterloo.)						1
1 30 p.m.	3	Waterloo	4 8 p.m.	5th Battn. City of London	26	600	5	1	—	—	2 M.	—	15
2 0 p.m.	2	Waterloo	4 38 p.m.	8th Battn. City of London	7	355	5	3	—	—	1 M.	—	—
2 35 p.m.	1	Waterloo	5 28 p.m.	8th Battn. City of London	13	600							

On SUNDAY, 15th August.

Train.	Number of Departure Platform at Amesbury.	To	Arrival Time.	Unit.	Officers.	Men.	Horses. In Boxes.	Horses. In Trucks.	Vehicles. 4-Wheel.	Vehicles. 2-Wheel.	Guns.	Limbers.	Tons of Baggage.
8 55 a.m.	4	Waterloo	11 30 a.m.	1st Battn. City of London	20	502	5	3	—	—	1 M.	—	14
9 20 a.m.	2	Waterloo	11 53 ,,	2nd Battn. City of London	18	373	4	3	—	—	1 M.	—	7
9 40 a.m.	1	Waterloo	12 13 p.m.	3rd Battn. City of London	23	475	4	1	—	—	1 M.	—	7
10 0 a.m.	4	Waterloo	12 35 ,,	4th Battn. City of London	21	371	6	7	1	—	4 M.	—	12
10 0 a.m.	4	Waterloo	12 35 ,,	T. & S. Column	8	130	(Change at Waterloo.)						
		Woolwich	1 48 ,,										
10 20 a.m.	2	Waterloo	1 1 ,,	T. & S. Column 3rd Bgde. Co. for Nine Elms (detrain at Waterloo)	2	40							
10 20 a.m.	2	Waterloo	1 1 ,,	2nd Field Ambulance	8	109	9	17	6	1	—	—	4
10 40 a.m.	4	Nine Elms	1 20 ,,	H.A.C.									
11 0 a.m.	2	Waterloo	1 35 ,,	3rd Field Ambulance	1	84	3	14	5	1	—	—	4
11 20 a.m.	4	Nine Elms	2 5 ,,	H.A.C.									
11 50 a.m.	1	Waterloo	2 37 ,,	R.G.A.	7	160	3	50	4	—	4	4	5
12 15 p.m.	2	Waterloo	2 51 ,,	6th Battn. City of London	4	100	6	2	—	—	2 M.	—	22
12 35 p.m.	3	Waterloo	3 9 ,,	6th Battn. City of London	18	600	—	—	—	—	—	—	10
12 55 p.m.	4	Waterloo	3 33 ,,	7th Battn. City of London	14	350	5	—	—	—	2 M.	—	10
1 30 p.m.	2	Waterloo	4 4 ,,	9th Battn. Co'ty of London	28	517	5	1	—	—	1 M.	—	21
1 50 p.m.	4	Addison Rd	4 48 ,,	10th Battn. City of London	25	212	1	1	—	—	2 M.	—	15
2 15 p.m.	2	Waterloo	4 40 ,,	11th Battn. Co'ty of London	20	334	5	3	—	—	—	—	12
2 35 p.m.	1	Waterloo	5 9 ,,	12th Battn. Co'ty of London	6	200	4	1	—	—	—	—	15
2 55 p.m.	3	Waterloo	5 29 ,,	12th Battn. Co'ty of London	17	455							
				Rear Parties.									
4 0 p.m.	4	Waterloo	6 40 ,,	8th Battn. City of London	1	30	—	3	1	1	—	—	—
				5th Battn. City of London	1	30	—	3	1	1	—	—	10
				4th Brigade R.F.A.	1	15	1	7	3	1	—	—	
				1st Field Ambulance	1	10	—	2	1	1	—	—	

M—Denotes Machine Gun.

47

Princess Beatrice's Own Isle of Wight Rifles at Amesbury Station for manoeuvres 1910. On the left two horseboxes are seen close to the turntable. (John Alsop)

PRINCESS BEATRICE'S OWN
I. of W. RIFLES.
SALISBURY PLAIN, 1910
MOORES MOTOR WORKS
ANDOVER.
CARS FOR HIRE. REPAIRS
ST MALO

A Territorial Regiment arrives on a double headed special train at Amesbury Station 1908. (John Alsop)

every man fit and eager to get to grips with the enemy. Their strength was 33 officers and 994 other ranks. One soldier's reminiscences, which give a flavour of the times, were recorded thus *"As Reveille sounded at 4.30am a cold bleak morning was revealed on which we partook of our last breakfast at Number 11 Camp, Larkhill. After the meal, a period of tremendous hustle and bustle ensued. There was strapping and unstrapping of equipment, the packing of packs, to say nothing of the unceasing struggles to get all personal possessions, gear, ammunition, rations, blankets and utensils securely buckled to our bodies. At length we fell in for final inspection, then off we went on the four-mile journey to Amesbury railway station, gaily marching to the strains of "Colonel Bogey" played by the Battalion Band. The Battalion left Amesbury on three trains, which arrived at Southampton at 11am, noon and 2pm' on its way to play its part in the mud of the Western Front."*

On 24th. September 1917 New Zealand troops, who had disembarked at Plymouth, were taken by special train from Millbay station to Bulford being told that a meal would be provided at their first stop. Unfortunately this proved to be at signals at Bere Ferrers and, being ignorant of the geography, many jumped out of the train here and 10 were killed by the oncoming 14:12 service from Exeter to Plymouth. An interesting snippet of film can be viewed on the New Zealand Film Archive website which shows the training of New Zealand recruits at Sling Camp featuring grenade practice, Lewis gun drill, trench fighting, and the final inspection and departure from Bulford station of a reinforcement draft for France in 1918. The train is hauled by a brace of Adams locomotives running bunker first. A letter home from a member of the ANZAC forces revealed what he thought of Sling Camp –

"A little after midnight we reached Bulford siding and from this point we marched in the dead of night through sleeping camps until we reached this damned joint. Upon our arrival we were given some supper and then we turned in to our new quarters ready to sleep the clock around, the time now being 2 am. Alas! At 6. am. a camp Sergeant stamped his way through the hut bawling in a raucous voice 'Rise and Shine - Rise and Shine'. Heavy-lidded we crawled from beneath our blankets and from that moment we have been on the go with a vengeance..."

King George V was a frequent visitor to the troops stationed on the Plain and on 4th. November 1914 he arrived by train at Amesbury whence he travelled by car accompanied by Lord Kitchener, Field Marshall Lord Roberts and the premier of British Columbia, to Bustard camp and on to West Down North and Pond Farm camps where inspections of Canadian troops were held. On September 27th 1916 he reviewed Australian and New Zealand troops at Bulford escorted by the Australian Major-General Monash who delivered the king back to his train just one minute before it was due to leave, the monarch commenting upon the *"splendid timing"* and stating that the Australian Division was *"very fine...I don't know that I've seen a finer one."* He also reviewed New Zealand troops at Bulford in 1917, Brigadier General Herbert Hart's diary recording the occasion as follows –

"1st May. Beautiful day. The troops commenced moving out of Sling Camp at 9 o'clock to the review ground at Bulford Field. 7,000 New Zealanders were present. At 11.30 the King arrived, accompanied by various Generals, and inspected the assembled troops then taking the march past. He then presented some medals, the senior officers & women present were presented to him and he left by a special train at 1 o'clock. The politicians addressed the troops briefly and then returned to Sling Camp for a late lunch."

Associated with this military traffic was additional business for the railways resulting from family and friends who came

Soldiers marching through the High Street at Amesbury in WW1. A wonderful contemporary film of troops entraining at Bulford station appears on Film No: F17937 which is referenced on the New Zealand film archive:

http://data.filmarchive.org.nz/search/catplus/catplus-nzef.php#

Multiview Postcard of the time showing troops arriving for Salisbury Plain Camps. (Fuller of Amesbury)

by train to visit service personnel. Prior to the Great War details of the nearest railway stations serving the numerous summer camps on the Plain were published in "The Times" for the guidance of visitors. When camps became permanent year round traffic resulted from this source not only for the railways skirting the plain but also for those short branches that had breached it.

When working military trains on the branch from Great Western originating stations the GWR locomotive would travel through to Amesbury with an LSWR pilotman provided by Salisbury shed. More often than not an assisting locomotive would be required from Newton Tony onwards for the heavy troop trains and this too would be provided by Salisbury depot. On one occasion an LBSCR locomotive and crew were reported running through from Havant with a Home Counties Brigade contingent to Grateley using an LSWR pilotman and guard. On 21st. June 1914 a troop train conveying 100 men of the Cambridge University OTC and their horses arrived at Grateley where a pilot was attached as far as Amesbury, the train locomotive continuing unaided over the lesser grades to Bulford. Even several months after the 1918 Armistice military traffic continued to be heavy requiring one locomotive duty at Basingstoke and six at Salisbury generally for the whole day, some eight goods workings requiring the use of a pilot over the Boscombe Down incline. Many of the military specials travelled over the M&SWJR line from the north to Andover Junction where an LSWR locomotive was coupled to the rear of train to take it on to Newton Tony where an assisting engine was generally required to take the train further to Amesbury. It would not be until well into 1920 that demobilisation was complete from Salisbury Plain camps much to the frustration of the many homesick servicemen.

During World War 11 the branch also played an important role and, in the run up to D-Day, local inhabitants can recall heavy guns being brought up by special trains to the Plain from the coast for test firing. In preparation for Operation Overlord, the invasion of Europe, the Plain was one of the most vital training areas, General Dwight Eisenhower describing it as *"the best training ground in the United Kingdom"*. At the end of the war locals also remember trainloads of captured German equipment being taken up the branch to Bulford Camp no doubt for salvage and/or destruction. During the Suez Crisis of 1956 with its rapid mobilisation of reservists a number of trains from Waterloo and elsewhere ran on the branch which stayed open 24 hours a day to receive them and to despatch the returning empty stock workings. Many of these trains were delayed by a log jam at Andover Junction one Sunday evening when trains were backed up on the mainline awaiting platform space and transfer of personnel to buses for onward journeys to a number of camps in the area.

ACCIDENTS

Accidents on the branch were few, one of the first, being more of a potentially dangerous incident than an accident, was recorded in 1914 when on the 25th January the 11.35pm empty stock working from Bulford to Salisbury suffered a broken coupling somewhere between Newton Tony and Amesbury Junction. It appears the engine crew were unaware of what had happened as, despite the rear portion of the train having been brought to a halt, they continued to

Troops marching near Stonehenge before WW1. (Fuller of Amesbury)

run until stopped near Laverstock Signal Box, a signalman either here or at Porton box having noticed the train running without a tail lamp. The enginemen, guard and signalman were subsequently admonished. Adams 4-4-0 locomotive No. 584, of Class X2, ran into some wagons which were parked on the up platform loop at Grateley on 28th. October 1914, whilst working the 11:50 special empty goods from Amesbury. Newton Tony was the scene of a derailment on 23rd June 1915 when at 7.54am the goods engine in the course of crossing from the down to the up line by the west crossover came off the road. The down Line was blocked until 11.15am, and with the consequent single line working until that time delays to both passenger and troop trains were inevitable. Damage to the track was put at £195 and both driver and signalman were deemed responsible.

A special empty troop train on the 22nd September 1916 passed signals at danger at Newton Tony Junction, continuing on to Newton Tony station on the Up (wrong) line which was unoccupied, at the time the signals being clear for a train from Salisbury towards Amesbury. The driver misread them but, realising his mistake, continued wrong line to Newton Tony. He was later suspended following an enquiry. On the 22nd January 1921 an engine became derailed at Amesbury having worked a special troop train from Kensington. On arrival at 2.30am, the train was run into the down military dock. The engine was detached from the train in order to turn for working back the empty stock. The points leading from the down siding to the down running line at the western end were the scene for the subsequent mishap. The lack of a ground signal here necessitated hand signalling and the porter on duty had overlooked the setting of the catch points as he beckoned the engine towards the trap he had inadvertently set. Damage was limited and the line was cleared by 6.50am.

Ratfyn Crossing on the Bulford extension was the scene of an incident on 21st December 1923 when, despite cattle guards, a cow wandered onto the line and was killed by the 9.05pm Salisbury to Bulford train. An incident similar to that of 1921 at Amesbury station occurred here again on 28th August 1929, the engine of the 5.25am goods train from Basingstoke to Bulford derailing at around 7.50am at the catch points to the down siding at the Bulford end of Amesbury station. The engine was re-railed by the Salisbury crane by 1.05pm. A local porter was held to be at fault forgetting to set the down siding points properly and for hand signalling the train to move forward. This incident along with the previous one in 1921 are unlikely to have occurred if a 1916 proposal had been enacted to install a ground signal to protect movements at this point thus avoiding the need for hand signalling and the consequent risk of human error. An estimated cost of just £17 for the work would surely with hindsight have been a cost effective solution. On the 1st January 1934 the 8.00am train from Bulford to Salisbury hit a car at Allington Level Crossing at about 8.14am and carried the vehicle for some 170 yards, smashing it quite extensively. The crossing was ungated

JUNCTION AND BRANCH SIGNAL BOXES

	Opened	Closed	Size	No. of Levers	Lever Centres	Notes
Grateley (1)	1870	20-7-1901		20 extended to 21 in 1899	4⅛"	
Grateley (2)	20-7-1901	2-5-1968	35'4" x 11'9" x 12'	72 (1) 66 (2) from 16-4-1921	3" (1) 4⅛" (2) Tappet locking	Pneumatic locking frame. New frame 1915. Mechanical locking from 1921.
Newton Tony Junction (1)	1899	September 1901		12		Box replaced another break-section box on main line with the same name previously located half mile nearer Porton. Relocated in 1899 to provide access to contractors building new railway.
Newton Tony Junction (2)	September 1901	7-8-1904		37		Tyer's No 6 Tablet to Newton Tony, replaced by 'Lock & Block' when line doubled.
Amesbury Junction * (reported box and [part of] frame second hand, ex Newton Tony Junction)	7-8-1904 (According to Pryer, opened in may 1904.)	20-1-1964	16' x 11' x 8' 6"	16 Sykes 'Lock & Block' on main line to Porton (west) and Grateley (east). Fitted with closing switch.	4⅝"	* Allington from 25-9-1955 According to the SRS Register, "Box operated by Railway Policeman".
Newton Tony Junction (on new site)	7-8-1904	17-10-1954	16' x 11' ground level	13	4⅝"	

and protected only by whistle boards 400 yards on either side. A report into the incident blamed prevailing dense fog as a key factor. A minor derailment occurred on the 24th January 1951 when a coach became derailed at 9.44am when the 9.40am Bulford to Salisbury train passed the stop signal at danger and passed over a set of points just as they were being operated. The driver was reprimanded for his carelessness and the signalman was told to be more observant. As far as is known no fatalities, other than the cow, were recorded during the life of the line.

SIGNALLING

The Electric Train Tablet Tyer's system No. 6 (ETT) was used to control movements on the branch when opened, the sections being Grateley to Newton Tony Junction, Newton Tony Junction to Newton Tony station, and Newton Tony station to Amesbury. When the line was extended to Bulford the second section was enlarged to cover the new line. In April 1935, when the signalbox at Bulford was downgraded to ground frame status, the "No Signalman Key Token" system was introduced between Amesbury and Bulford. Following singling of the route between Newton Tony and Amesbury in 1953 the Train Staff & Ticket (TST) system was introduced on 25 October. After the section onwards to Newton Tony Junction was singled on 17th. October 1954, the TST system was adopted for the whole branch until complete closure.

Council Rating (Appendix VIII) records give a good impression of the facilities at stations on the line and those for the 1930s are reproduced at Appendix x. During the inter-war years there was some retrenchment as witnessed by the request of the WD to take out of use the short section of the route from the west side of Marlborough Road crossing into the goods terminus at Sling. A plan of 1933 shows the proposed truncation at Sling with the provision of an additional siding and three loading docks to serve a proposed bakery, store and a meat store. Although the rails were removed those embedded in the road were left in situ to preserve the right of way. This was followed in 1939 by the section from Bulford Camp station to the west side of Marlborough Road being similarly treated although the rails were fortuitously not removed. As it transpired this proved to be a wise move as in 1940 the line was re-opened for WD traffic and in March 1942 the WD requested that the SR relay track and re-open the original Sling terminus on the eastern side of the road. The WD picked up the tab for this work amounting to £450. Other economies made by the SR included, in December 1932, dispensing with the Station

Newton Tony Station (1)	May 1904	3-8-1915	Open GF on station platform	10* extended to 13 from April 1909		* second hand frame of unknown origin dating from 1898. Instruments in station office
Newton Tony Station (2)	3-8-1915	17-10-1954	11' x 9'6" x 8'*	13	4⅛" Tappet locking	* constructed of 'Muriblocs'
Newton Tony Crossing GF	17-10-1954	4-3-1963				
Allington	25-5-1909	21-11-1933	Ground level	9	4⅝" Tappet locking 'Knee Frame'.	
Boscombe Down	20-01-18 (may have been 1917)	9-4-1923 (may have been 12.1918)	Ground level	8		
Amesbury	By April 1902	30-09-1964 GF wef 4-3-1963	Ground level	19 extended to 25 (or 24?) in 1904	4⅝" Stevens 'Knee Frame'.	Frame second hand ex-Grateley Tyers No. 6 Tablet to Bulford - Ratfyn 1914 to 1919. Thence 'No Signalman Key Token' to Bulford post 9-4-1935.
Amesbury GF NBP		1-6-1906		3		
	1-6-1906	4-3-1963	Hut	18 reduced to 10 from 19-12-1954		
Ratfyn aka Ratfyn Junction	22-10-1914	1929	Ground level replaced by GF in hut wef 6-11-1919	10		
Bulford	1-6-1906	4-3-1963	Ground level on station platform	7		GF wef 9-4-1935

Master's post at Bulford resulting in a saving of £250pa., the station thereafter coming under the supervision of the Amesbury SM. To appease WD concerns regarding their ability to contact the Station Master whenever the need arose, a telephone extension line was installed from the Booking Office to the SM's house. The intermediate signalbox box at Allington was abolished as a block post in November 1933 and all signals and points operated from the box were removed. Bulford signalbox was downgraded to a ground frame in April 1935.

MOTIVE POWER

Locomotives operating services on the branch initially were naturally of LSWR origin and Adams T1 and 02 class 0-4-4Ts and class A12 0-4-2Ts nicknamed "Jubilees", because they appeared in Victoria's jubilee year 1897, were well represented on passenger work whilst class 0395 0-6-0 tender engines were to be seen on goods workings. Initially locomotives were provided by Basingstoke shed but after the diversion of trains to Salisbury the shed here provided motive power for the branch. These types were within the weight limits imposed by the LRO. Due to the gradients on the line most troop trains and many of the heavier freights had to be double headed. The LSWR had considered using a steam rail motor from the outset for the Amesbury to Salisbury passenger service but in the event the decision was taken in January 1904 not to proceed with this limited accommodation option until the volume of traffic offering could be reviewed. In later years Drummond M7 tanks and 700 class tender locomotives took over workings with occasional appearances by Maunsell moguls, Standard types and Bulleid Q1s. With the relaxation of restrictions permitted by the BoT all types except 4-6-0s and heavy pacifics (Merchant Navy) were permitted and moguls and light pacifics (West Country/Battle of Britain) were occasionally seen although piloting was generally the rule using 4-4-0s of classes T9, L11 and L12. The line never possessed a locomotive shed and motive power was provided from Salisbury reverting latterly to Basingstoke shed during the freight only existence of the line. The standard LRO speed limit of 25 mph applied except approaching within 300 yards of the level crossing at Newton Tony where 10 mph was the limit. A notice board was erected upon the opening of the line instructing drivers of down trains to shut off steam at that point. The Bulford extension was additionally subject to a 10mph restriction on the more severe curves. All wagons for the LMR exchange sidings at Ratfyn had to be propelled from Amesbury and after completion of shunting any returning wagons had to be hauled back to Amesbury. An M7 diagram, operative on Sundays commencing in 1948, included provision for working troop specials originating from Waterloo between Grateley and Amesbury if required, the Drummond tank having previously worked an afternoon return trip from Salisbury to Wimborne via the Fordingbridge line.

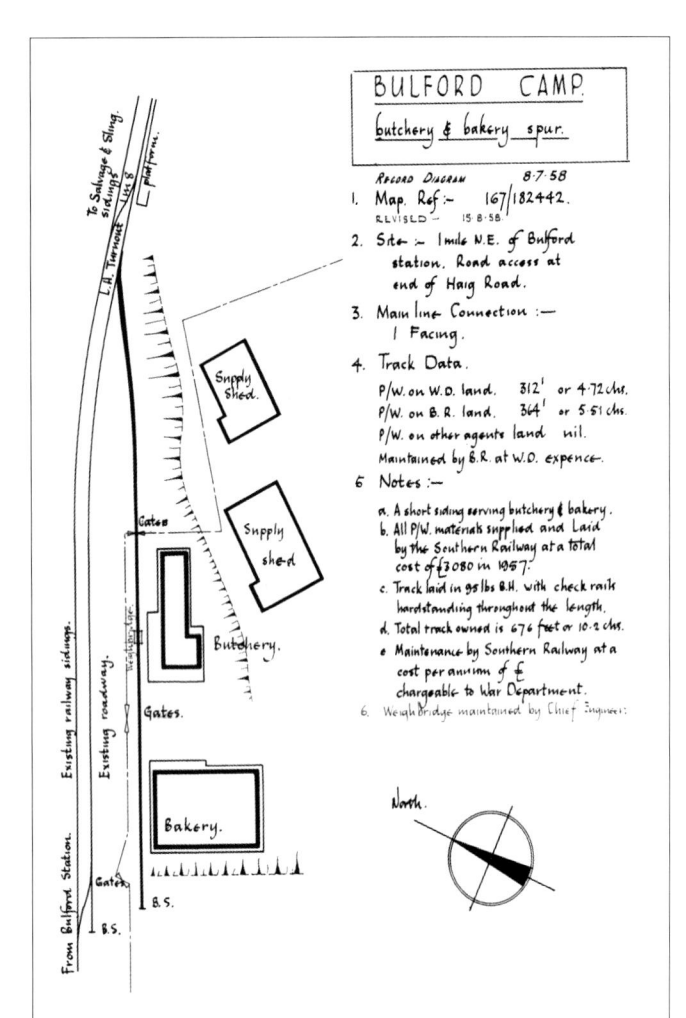

COACHING STOCK

The coaching stock was invariably of standard design with locomotives running round at each end although occasionally a push-pull two-coach set was used even though the locomotives were not motor fitted. One Salisbury carriage duty for the summer of 1919 saw a set leave Salisbury at 06:00, departing at 06:30 for Tisbury before returning to Salisbury taking on the 09:45 departure for Bulford. Returning to Salisbury it made a further two round trips to Bulford finishing at Salisbury at 18:24. Another duty, in 1944, involved three-car set No. 243 which was stabled overnight at Bulford and made seven return trips daily to Salisbury. However after the war, with rapidly declining patronage, a single ex LSWR composite brake coach would often suffice for the small amount of traffic offering towards the end, the coach being stabled at Amesbury overnight.

Left - *Track plan of Butchery and Bakery spur at Bulford Camp. (Mike Hitchen)*

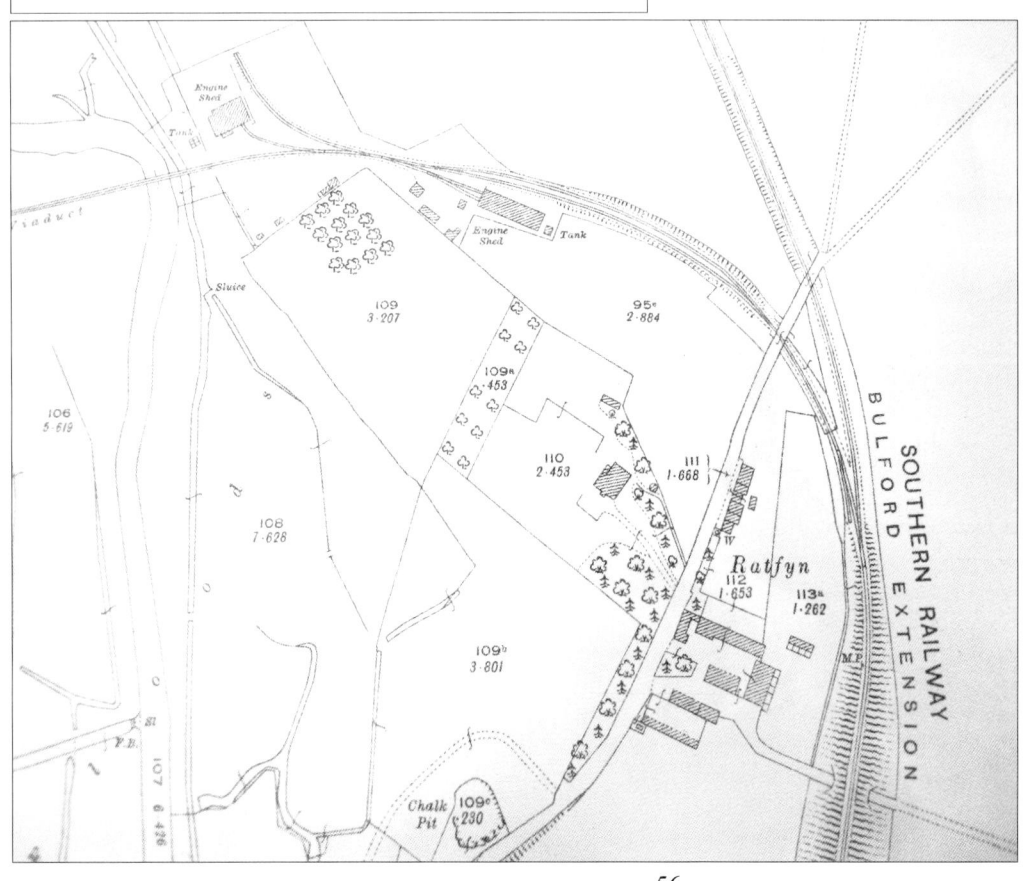

Left - *OS map of 1925 showing Ratfyn Junction with Larkhill Military Railway engine sheds located on both sides of the line. (Ordnance Survey)*

4. THE LARKHILL MILITARY RAILWAY
ORIGINS......CONSTRUCTION......THE ROUTE DESCRIBED......
CLOSURE.......TANK PRACTICE RAILWAY

ORIGINS

It is perhaps appropriate here to break off from description of the branch to relate the story of the associated Larkhill Military Railway (LMR) which branched off the Bulford line at Ratfyn Junction. The LMR was the longest railway to operate on Salisbury Plain being some 10¾ miles in length when all the many offshoots were taken into account. The plan to build this line followed from the decision to make a number of the camps being established on the Plain, which were initially merely tented, into more permanent constructions. Construction of these "Armstrong Huts", named after their designer a Major Armstrong, began in the autumn of 1914 being completed the following year. The First World War hutted camp remained in situ until 1966 when nearly all the old huts were knocked down and the present camp was built. The construction work was undertaken by the firm of Sir John Jackson a visionary civil engineer who saw that machinery was the key to success. Jackson always had the latest equipment and as a result was one of those who led the way from the navvy era into the modern machine age. In his foreword to the book "*Tower Bridge to Babylon*" dealing with the life and work of Jackson, Sir William McAlpine points out that the biographies of the large contractors have been largely neglected, although the ground-breaking projects of Brunel, Stephenson and others could not have been built without the great organisational skills of the contractors and their willingness to embrace new technologies. The Tower Bridge contract made his name and he put the innovative "steam navvy" to good use when he took over the major Manchester Ship Canal contract. Other projects included the Keyham extension to the Devonport dockyard and major works at Dover harbour. Overseas contracts included the Simon's Town dockyard in the Republic of South Africa, the Arica-LaPaz railway over the Andes, which most engineers said was impossible, and the barrage across the Euphrates in Mesopotamia. He thus brought a wealth of experience in railway construction both in the UK and abroad and in all probability found construction of the LMR somewhat less taxing than some of his more arduous contracts !

Peckett locomotive 'Queen Mary' and contractors stock. (Unknown)

Left - This splendid photograph shows Westminster in new condition on the Larkhill Military Railway sometime during WW1. (Fuller of Amesbury).

Bottom - A route guide showing the main line and the various branches of the Larkhill Military Railway. (Taken from 'Plain Soldiering' by N.D.G. James / Hobnob Press)

CONSTRUCTION

Jackson was the MP for Devonport and in the run up to the First World War he offered to do his patriotic bit by placing the services of his workers at Lord Kitchener's disposal at cost price. Before World War 1 there had been 3 tented camps at Durrington, Larkhill and Fargo. This offer was readily accepted and, in order to assist in the construction of more permanent accommodation to replace the tented camps, it was felt logical to bring in the raw materials by rail, a line of communication which would of course prove very useful subsequently for moving men and materials around the Plain. The GWR paid £574 for additional sidings at Sandford & Banwell on the Cheddar Valley line so that stone could be loaded for transport to the camps being built by Jackson on Salisbury Plain. In many ways the

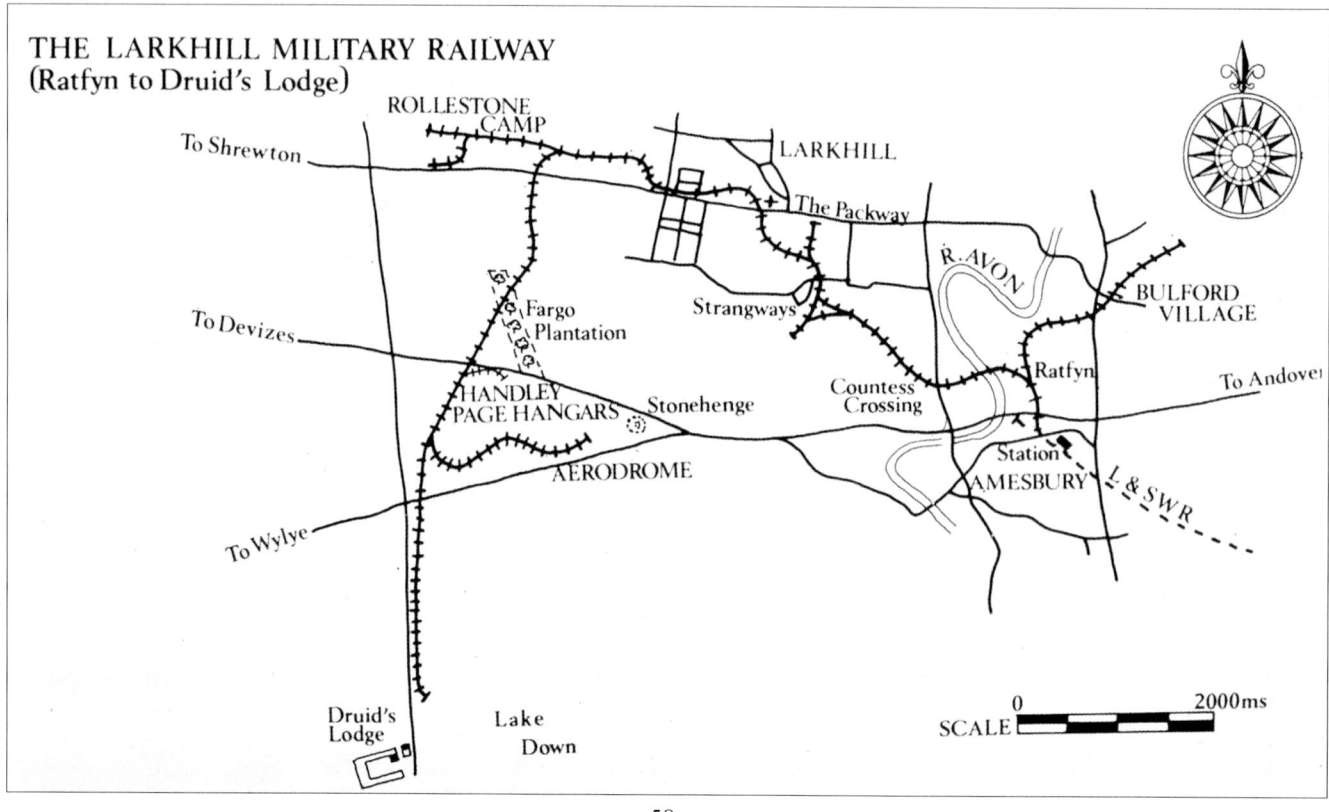

Photo by T.L. Fuller, Amesbury

Locomotive "Westminster" poses at the end of the River Avon girder bridge. (Fuller of Amesbury).

LMR was an echo of the original A&MLR extension to Shrewton, albeit taking a more roundabout route, which as we have seen was cancelled a few years earlier. A number of locomotives were used in the construction some of which stayed on to serve the line after completion. There were two Pecketts, an 0-4-0ST named "*Queen Mary*" and an 0-6-0ST named "*Westminster*", three Hudswell Clarks, an 0-4-0ST named "*Bulford*", a couple of 0-6-0Ts named "*Salisbury*" and "*Yorkshire*" were supplemented by a Sharp Stewart 0-6-0T named "*Sharpness*". There is also a report of an 0-6-0 Hawthorn Leslie tank delivered on 25 November 1914 to the contractors who named it "*Northumbria*". This locomotive had originally been one of a pair ordered from the manufacturers the previous year by the East Kent Railway. However shortage of money caused the order to be cancelled and the engines were subsequently sold elsewhere. After construction of the LMR was completed it passed to the War Department, probably in 1916, and was subsequently transferred to the Kinmel Park Military Camp Railway near Rhyl. At the end of the war it was sold to the Ebbw Vale Steel Iron & Coal Co as their No 36, passing to Richard Thomas & Co at Scunthorpe in 1936. There she lasted until 1965. After purchase by the WD, "*Queen Mary*" stayed on to work the line for a number of years, one report indicating that it was subsequently converted to an 0-6-0T.

"*Westminster*" was certainly there for a year or two and "*Salisbury*" stayed for a while.

"*Queen Mary*" features in a painting displayed in the Royal Artillery mess at Larkhill. However, remarkably one engine used on the line is still extant today. This is "*Westminster*", works no. 1378 built in 1914 to a War Office order and delivered to Sir John Jackson on 6th November 1914 for use on the LMR, and originally finished in holly green with polished brass and copper fittings. After working on the LMR, "*Westminster*" moved to the Fovant Military Railway in 1917 where it stayed until closure of that system in 1921. After its departure nothing is known of the loco until it came into the hands of Associated Portland Cement Manufactures at Dunstable in about 1950. In 1952 it was transferred to the APCM limestone quarries near Oxford where it worked until August 1969. The engine was purchased for just £50 and moved by Ameys of Oxford to the Kent and East Sussex Railway in September 1970. For a time it found a home on a private site at East Tisted Station on the old Meon Valley line where some basic restoration took place and it was steamed to a private audience on a few occasions. Since moving in October 1998 it can now be found on the Northampton & Lamport Railway.

THE ROUTE DESCRIBED

The line branched off the Bulford line some 700 yards north of Amesbury station at Ratfyn, known locally to railway workers as Wheelbarrow Junction, where a signalbox was located between October 1914 and November 1919. From 6th. November 1919 the box here was downgraded to a ground frame. The 1921 Working Timetable states that the line commences at Ratfyn Junction *"by points off the single line between Amesbury and Bulford, 610 yards on the Bulford side of Amesbury Starting Signal. The points face down trains. The military line is operated from a ground frame (known as Ratfyn Junction Ground Frame) controlled by the train tablet"*.

In 1918 six goods trains daily were scheduled from Amesbury to the exchange sidings at Ratfyn. Due to the somewhat isolated position of these sidings reports of pilfering of stores were not uncommon at this location. In 1915 after two or three months of losses a Sergeant Major from the RASC kept watch and apprehended nine labourers helping themselves to stores. The boundary of LSWR/LMR territory was marked by a gate as seen on the sketch map dating from 1917 on page 70. Curving away to the west the line passed over a minor road, to which the WD were to fix cattle grids, then opened out into a short loop before becoming single track again to pass a two road engine shed on the south side and a one road shed on the north side of the line. Details of the permanent way of the LMR are contained on a sketch map which shows that rails of 87lb/yard were laid abutting the LSWR track as far as the level crossing after which the loops consisted of a mixture of 82lbs/yard and 87lbs/yard material for a short distance then 60lb/yard with 33 foot rail lengths with 13 sleepers to a length secured by two dogs at each support.

Passing over the Wiltshire River Avon by way of a substantial girder bridge, some 180 m in length, the line then briefly diverged into four tracks before becoming single again to cross the Amesbury – Upavon road via an ungated

Aerial view clearly showing Ratfyn junction, lower right, with the LMR exchange sidings, engine sheds, and the line curving away to cross the River Avon on the girder bridge. (English Heritage)

A montage of photographs showing the River Avon girder bridge crossing (Fuller of Amesbury)

level crossing at Countess Crossing. A short siding was provided on the north side of the line after the crossing and the mainline then curved to the northwest for ¾ mile to reach a reversing triangle at Strangways which allowed the turning of locomotives without recourse to a turntable. I have always considered the provision of such a facility surprising on a line populated by tank locomotives, although it may have been justified to even out tyre wear, and have felt that this was a somewhat strange location for such a triangle, in the middle of the line. Perhaps it only became a turning facility after its original purpose was superseded. In fact a plan dated 28 November 1916 entitled "Extension of Fargo Branch, Proposed line to Lake Down" and countersigned by a Major in the RE who was the Officer in Charge, Military Camp Railways, Longmoor shows fascinatingly this triangle to be in fact part of a larger layout giving access to the west by a loop which turned northwards to rejoin the main line on the double track section north of the spur to the Flying Shed branch. An aerial photograph taken in 1930 shows what appears to be the original

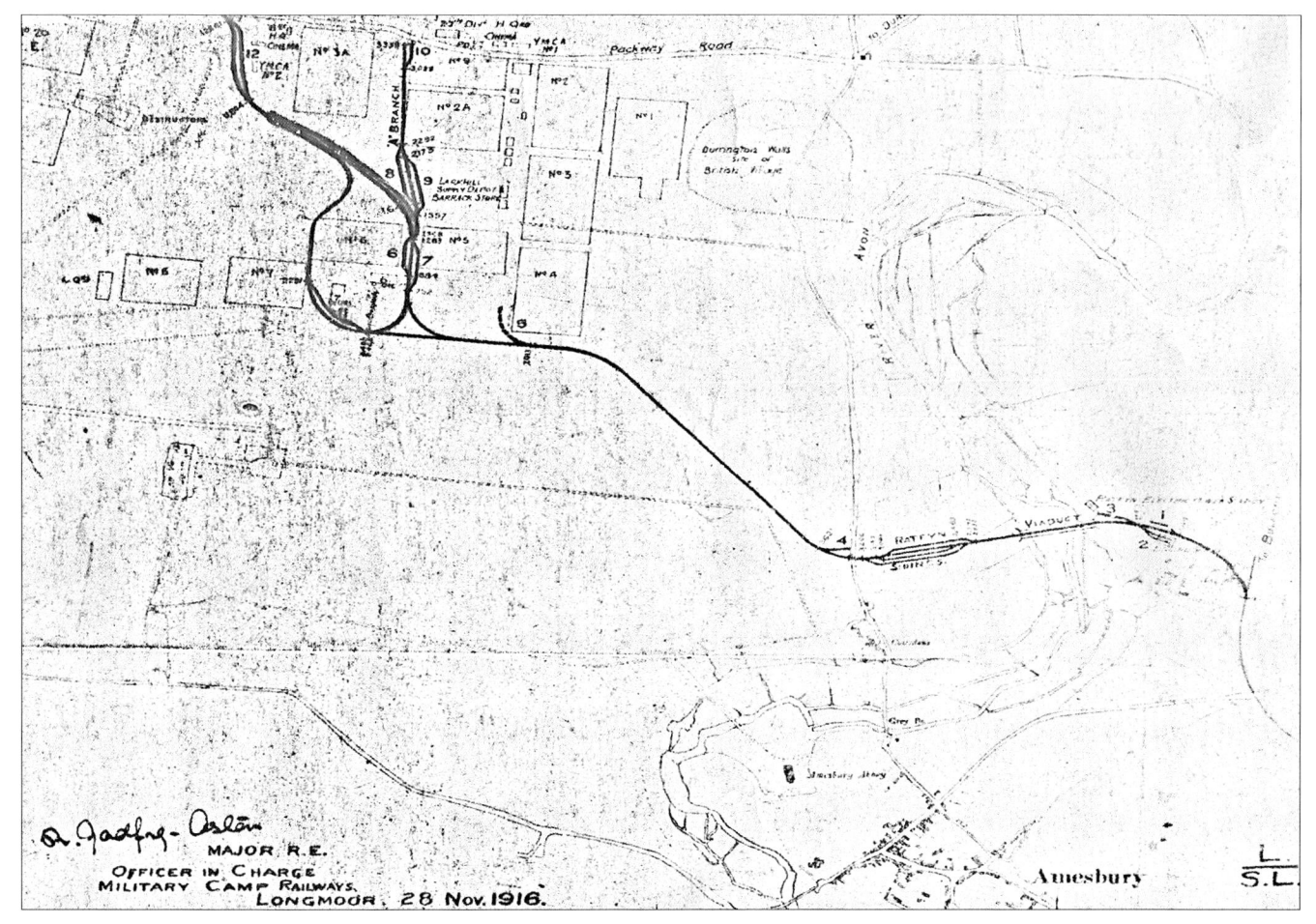

South east section from Ratfyn junction to Larkhill Camp showing evidence of a previously unrecorded layout to the west of the Strangways triangle, from the Military Camp Railways Larkhill Map of 1916.

61

An aerial photograph shows the Strangways turning triangle and the 'Flying Shed' branch heading northwards with the LMR main line making a reverse curve in a north westerly direction before crossing The Packway, top left.

trackbed curving northwards as described in the plan of 1916. It appears this aspect of the LMR layout has never before been identified and certainly does not feature on the standard reference map provided by N D G James in his book "*Gunners at Larkhill*" (See page 58). When this loop line closed, possibly when the new line further to the east to serve the Flying Shed was constructed, it may have been decided to retain a triangle for the purpose previously alluded to. There were an additional four sidings at the southwest extremity of the triangle, the main route turning sharply to the north over Fargo Road to the west of Lawson Road. At the north end of Lawson Road, close to its junction with Colquhoun Road were further sidings and a platform and station building for Larkhill Garrison. From 1920 Larkhill Camp became the headquarters of the School of Artillery.

At this point a branch, 47 chains in length, continued northwards known as the "Flying Shed" branch. This branch dates from the earliest days of the railway, before extensions to Stonehenge and Lake Down were undertaken, and served the huts built on the former flying field and passing close to the hangars of the British & Colonial Aeroplane Co. (BCAC), a forerunner of today's British Aerospace, situated in what is now Wood Road. These hangars were built to accommodate the newly established Bristol Flying School. As there were no flying facilities at Filton, BCAC set up a flight test base at Larkhill on land leased from the Army. The first flight of the famous Bristol Boxkite was made at Larkhill on July 30th 1910, the aircraft being nicknamed the Boxkite because of its appearance in flight. For several years factory fresh aeroplanes were sent from Filton to Larkhill and tested from there. In 1910 the War Office had little interest in flying but agreed to lease the site at Larkhill to BCAC and three sheds were erected. As each aircraft was built and flown new pilots were required to fly them so a flying school was set up on the Larkhill site with another school being established at the company's site at Brooklands. The former flying school is now commemorated by a stone plinth and plaque in Wood Road.

The mainline of the LMR continued west for ¼ mile and curved to the north. Before crossing The Packway close to Lawrence Road, a loop was provided for the adjacent Royal Engineers depot to ensure that wagons being loaded or

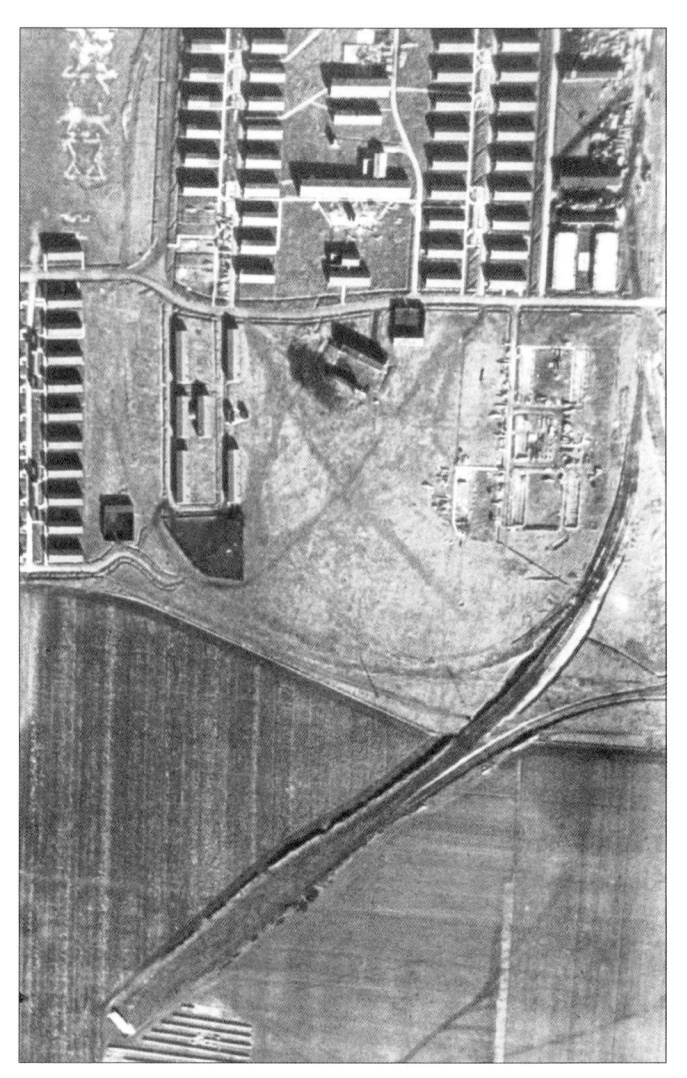

This 1930's aerial view of the Strangways triangle shows what might appear to be the earth work remains of the unrecorded track bed layout curving back round to the north.

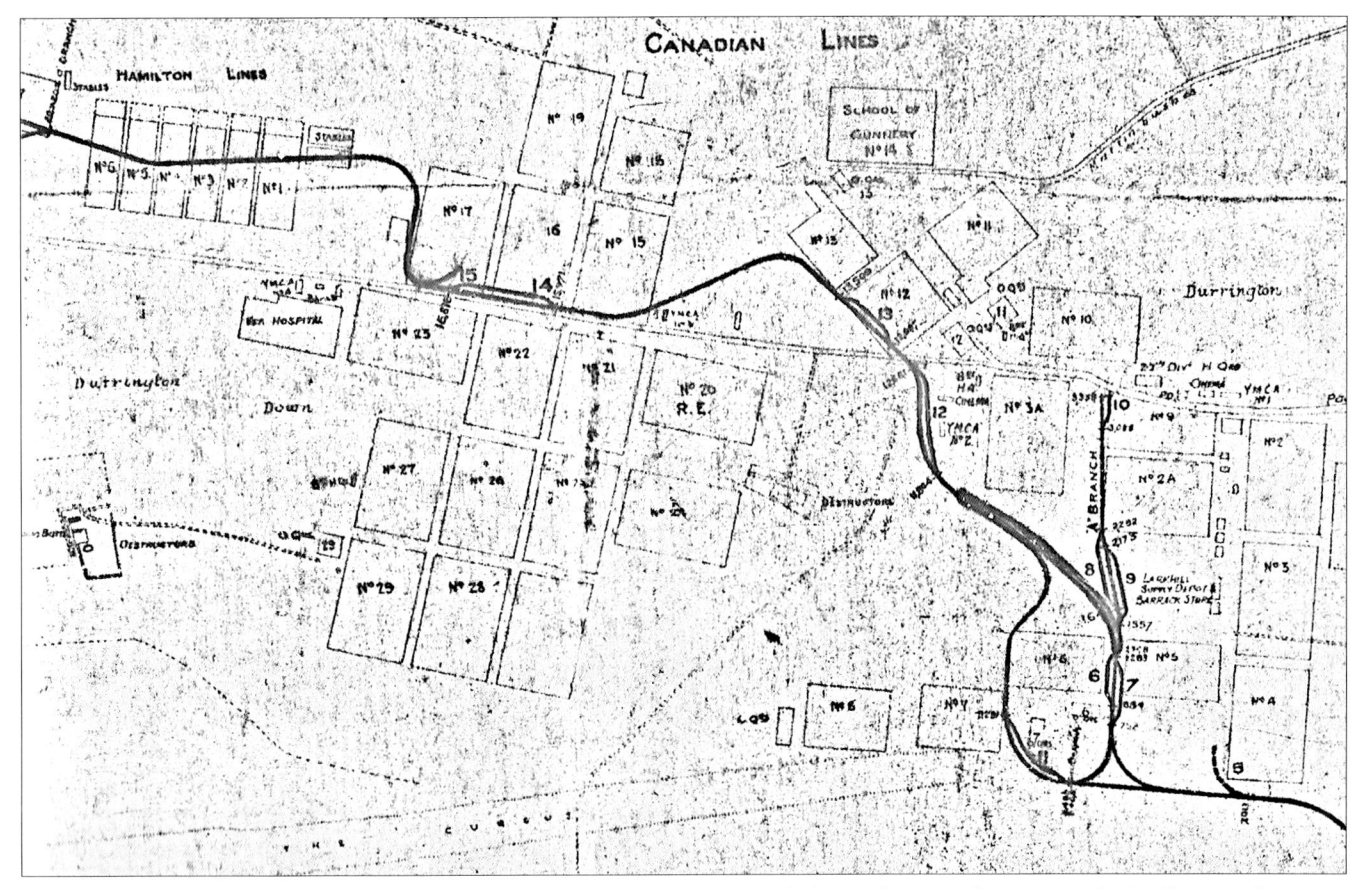

Showing again the unrecorded layout of Strangways, the section north of The Packway to the junction for Rollestone Camp and Fargo Branch, taken from the Military Camp Railways Larkhill Map of 1916.

unloaded did not obstruct the mainline. After completing a left hand 180 degree turn the mainline rejoined The Packway near the Roberts Barracks entrance. The Packway was, and still is, the main thoroughfare through Larkhill Camp and a number of services were provided on a site near to the Garrison Church. Formerly there was a Military Cinema, YMCA, Salvation Army, Vallers & Co. newsagents, Bollen's fruit store, and Sargent's Empire Stores and Refreshment Rooms. Running beside the Packway as far as Ross Road it branched away to the north and then west to Hamilton Battery. A short spur was provided here to allow the transhipment of ammunition onto the light tramway which served the battery guns. 700 yards beyond the Battery the mainline turned south whilst a branch continued west to Rollestone Camp where a balloon school was located. Shortly before reaching Rollestone a subsidiary branch turned south towards the original Fargo Ammunition Depot which at that time was north of the Packway. The mainline, on crossing the Packway continued as double track south in a straight line towards the 600 bed Fargo Military Hospital. Some 150 yards north of the hospital single track resumed and a siding was provided. A

Larkhill camp and LMR looking north towards The Packway in 1914. The aeroplane hangers built for Barber & Cockburn are visible on the centre skyline. (Fuller of Amesbury)

subsequent extension line headed on south and after cutting through Fargo Plantation crossed the Amesbury – Tilshead (A344) road 900 yards to the east of Airman's Cross. A spur to the south of the road and parallel to it provided a link some 450 yards in length to the Handley-Page aircraft hangars of the Royal Naval Air Service (RNAS). The mainline continued southwesterly towards a group of tumuli to the north of Winterbourne Stoke Clump, a small area of woodland adjoining the Amesbury – Wylye (A303) road. Some ½ mile before this road a further branch diverged to Stonehenge airfield which lay on either side of the main road.

It is perhaps hard today to envisage an airfield in such close proximity to this World Heritage site but this was the case for a few years last century. A postcard of the time even made great play of the fact by including an aeroplane in the view of the stones. It was laid down in 1917 and used as a training aerodrome for bomber squadrons. A variety of units were based there but it was also the location for the descriptively named No.1 School of Aerial Navigation and Bomb Dropping (SoANBD). This unit operated sixteen different aircraft types, and the fledgling RFC were joined by Handley Page aircraft from the RNAS in January 1918. The SoANBD moved to Andover in 1919, and the airfield was empty until the School of Army Cooperation occupied it in March 1920. It was scheduled to have become one of the RAF's permanent post-war stations but the plan changed, the School moving to Old Sarum in January 1921. The airfield infrastructure was gradually dismantled over the remainder of the 1920s. There is a headstone at the side of the road to the north west of Stonehenge at Airman's Cross commemorating the aircrew who crashed in the vicinity in July 1912. This, the first fatal air crash of the RFC, involved a Captain Eustace Loraine and his observer, Staff-Sergeant R H V Wilson who were killed when they crashed west of the stones after flying out of the nearby Larkhill aerodrome. The origins of Larkhill aerodrome go back to 1909 when a flying enthusiast called Horatio Barber rented a small piece of land in Larkhill. He built a shed to house his new aeroplane, and was soon joined by more enthusiasts. One of these was Captain John Fulton who served with an artillery brigade, and it was partly as a result of his interest that the War Office quickly realised the importance of aircraft and founded the first army aerodrome in Larkhill in 1910. A three bay hangar was constructed by the BCAC and in 1911 No 2 Company of the Air Battalion Royal Engineers was established here as the first flying unit of the armed forces to use aeroplanes rather than balloons. This evolved into No.3 Squadron RFC in May 1912, the first squadron to use aeroplanes. The aerodrome was closed in 1914 when hutted garrisons were built over the airstrip. The original BCAC hangar can still be found on the corner of Wood Road and Fargo Road and is the oldest surviving military aerodrome building in the UK. It was given listed building status in 2005.

Construction of camps at Larkhill with LMR train visible in the background. (Fuller of Amesbury).

A view of the LMR tracks running through Larkhill Camp, north of The Packway. (David Foster-Smith)

Having crossed the A303 the mainline then ran along the east side of the Salisbury road (A360) to terminate some 600 yards north of Druid's Lodge serving a hutted camp which was located on the west of the road and provided a link with Lake Down Aerodrome which lay to the east of the railway terminus. The mainline of this circuitous route from Ratfyn, which had thrown off numerous spurs, was 7.3 miles in length.

The LMR was operated by a small company of Royal Engineers of the Railway Operating Division (ROD), who were housed in a small camp to the east of Countess Crossing, in a similar manner to other military railways of the time. The LMR was not alone in serving camps on the Plain for the WD constructed railways to installations at Fovant, Porton, Sutton Veny and Codford. The gradients on the route were severe and, as far as is known, the line was never used to carry regular passenger traffic, although some reports speak of a regular Saturday service in 1924 when a carriage would be provided at a small platform near the church at The Packway Crossing at 1 pm. The carriage would then be taken to Amesbury for attachment to a Salisbury train, this provision proving very popular with service personnel who had a weekend pass. LMR motive power ran through to Ratfyn where LSWR locomotives took over for the trip to Amesbury and beyond. A notable trio of passengers known to have been carried on February 4th, 1915 were King George V and Queen Mary who, in the company of Lord Kitchener, inspected Canadian troops at Larkhill shortly before they left for France, a commemorative postcard being produced of the visit featuring the departing train. A special train steamed to a temporary station near the Bustard Inn where 25,000 troops were drawn up. The royal visitor conveyed the following message –

"Officers, non-commissioned officers and men : at the beginning of November I had the pleasure of welcoming to the mother country this fine contingent from the Dominion of Canada, and now after three months training, I bid you God's speed on your way to assist my army in the field."

The line did, however, carry a considerable amount of goods in the form of supplies and munitions. One of the more spectacular items of military hardware associated with the line was His Majesty's Gun 'Boche Buster'. This name is more properly applied to the carriage of this huge beast rather than to the gun itself. Serving throughout the last year of the First World War as a 14" rail mounted gun in France, using a gun originally intended for the Japanese Navy, it was reincarnated during the crisis years of the Second World War and on it was mounted a massive 18" Breech Loaded howitzer. Manned by 11th Battery, 2nd Super Heavy Regiment, the weapon was based at the Bourne Park railway tunnel, part of the Elham Valley railway line that had been taken over by the military, and it was intended to act as one of the final defences of the coastal area under threat of German invasion. The 18" Howitzer barrel No.1 Mk 4 had been constructed in 1918 and completed in 1919 and was designed as a partner piece

Believed to be the view from Durrington camp looking towards Larkhill camp and the Royal Artillery School of Gunnery on the north side of The Packway. This was rail served by the LMR as can be observed by the wagons stationed on the far right of the photograph. (Fuller of Amesbury)

Sargent's Empire Stores and Refreshment Rooms, located on The Packway, with a New Zealander seen in military uniform at the side door. Note that cars could be hired including Sunbeam, Renault and Overland, the latter being a little recognised marque today. In 1908, John Willys bought the Overland Automotive Division of Standard Wheel Co. and in 1912 renamed it Willys-Overland Motor Company. From 1912 to 1918, Willys was the second largest producer of automobiles in the United States after Ford.

The Packway looking east to Durrington village. A number of services were provided on this site near to the Garrison Church. There was a Military Cinema, YMCA, Salvation Army, Newsagent, Fruit Store, General Store and Refreshment Rooms. (Fuller of Amesbury)

A view of Rollestone camp possibly looking west. The LMR railway tracks at the very forefront of the photograph diverged from a junction located just west of Hamilton camp (Fuller of Amesbury)

This page, centre and bottom and opposite page - The four illustrations depicted come from the collection of David Foster-Smith. David's Grandfather - David Smith, was a navvy who became a Missionary in the final years of the nineteenth century. In his new guise David Smith was sent to live amongst the navvies and their families on various civil engineering contracts from that time through to the period around 1914. In the south these included the building of the Meon Valley Railway* and various military camps on Salisbury Plain. Whilst no paper record of his activities has survived, a vast archive of photographic material has remained in the family, including the illustrations seen on these pages - as well as others already included in this work. David Smith's role was to minister to the spiritual needs of the men, in practice this meant their moral welfare, achieved by keeping them occupied outside working hours and away, where possible, from alcohol: hence the choir, harvest festival, also lectures on first aid etc. We know that when navvies brought their families, similar activities were provided for the women and children in what were in effect, communal gathering places. Whether the hut(s) seen here were provided by the military / contractor or through the mission is uncertain. What we do know from his earlier work in the Meon Valley is that David Smith could be very persuasive! The flags within one of the buildings will be noted and understandable, those from the empire will be obvious, but not so some of the others, the Italian / French example and more especially that from Japan. David Smith was not alone in his work, indeed it would have been impossible for him to attend to the needs of what were several hundred workers, no doubt those seen *illustrated were others of like persuasion, although it is interesting also to note that whereas in the Meon Valley series of illustrations he features several times, in these David Smith is not seen.* **Opposite page** - *Sling Camp Mission Room & Institute.* **This page** - *Inside of the Larkhill Camp Mission Room & Institute on the Packway.* * *"The Meon Valley Railway Part 1: Building the Line", Noodle Books 2011.*

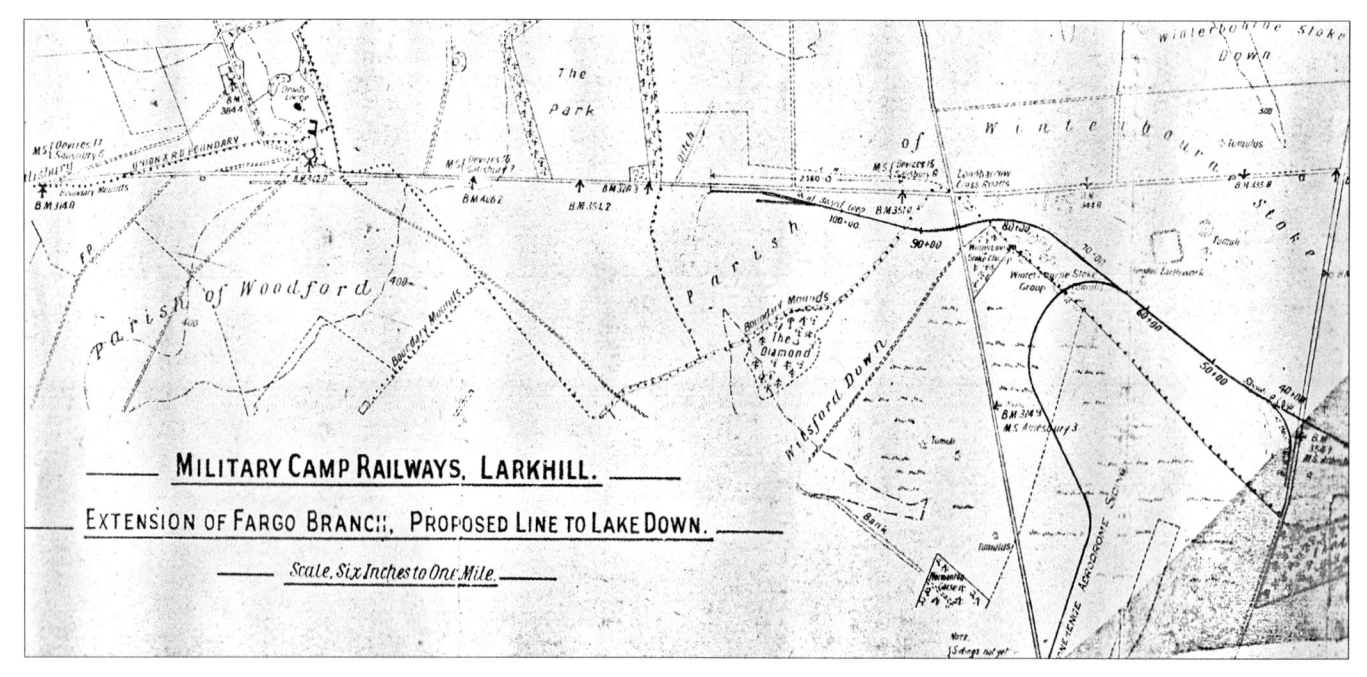

Top - *The Fargo Branch just south of the 600 bed Fargo Hospital, showing the Stonehenge Aerodrome and the proposed Lake Down Extension Line, taken from the Military Camp Railways Larkhill Map of 1916.*

Right - *Track plan of Ratfyn Siding. (Mike Hitchen)*

to the 14inch guns and was interchangeable with them on the same mountings. Four of these barrels were built, mounted in turn on one of the carriages for test firing and then put into store. In the 1920s the 14" barrels were declared obsolete and two 18" barrels were mounted. Periodically one of these was brought out to be deployed on Salisbury Plain either on a siding near Bulford or at the terminus of the LMR at Druid's Lodge.

CLOSURE

The Camp Railway Organisation was run from Longmoor which, during the First World War, operated more than a dozen camp lines having a total mileage of well over 100 miles. Following the reduction in military operations after the end of the war there were just two active Camp Railways remaining by 1921, Catterick and Larkhill with approximately 140 men on detachment working on them. Negotiations for handing over the Catterick line to the LNER were in hand in 1924, and Larkhill closed down soon after. The first part of the LMR to close was the newest section south from Fargo to Druid's Lodge, Lake Down and Stonehenge airfield the track for which OS maps shown to have been removed by 1923. The remainder of the route had probably ceased to operate by 1928 and an instruction dated 17 December 1929 confirmed that the LMR had been closed. Certainly most of the track had been removed by 1932, any remaining sections having gone by 1937. However, the SR recorded that despite the closure of the LMR the WD wished to retain a short branch from Ratfyn Junction for dealing with tank wagons of fuel oil for their electrical power station. Following removal of the Camp Line track, a short siding was retained as requested on the following basis –

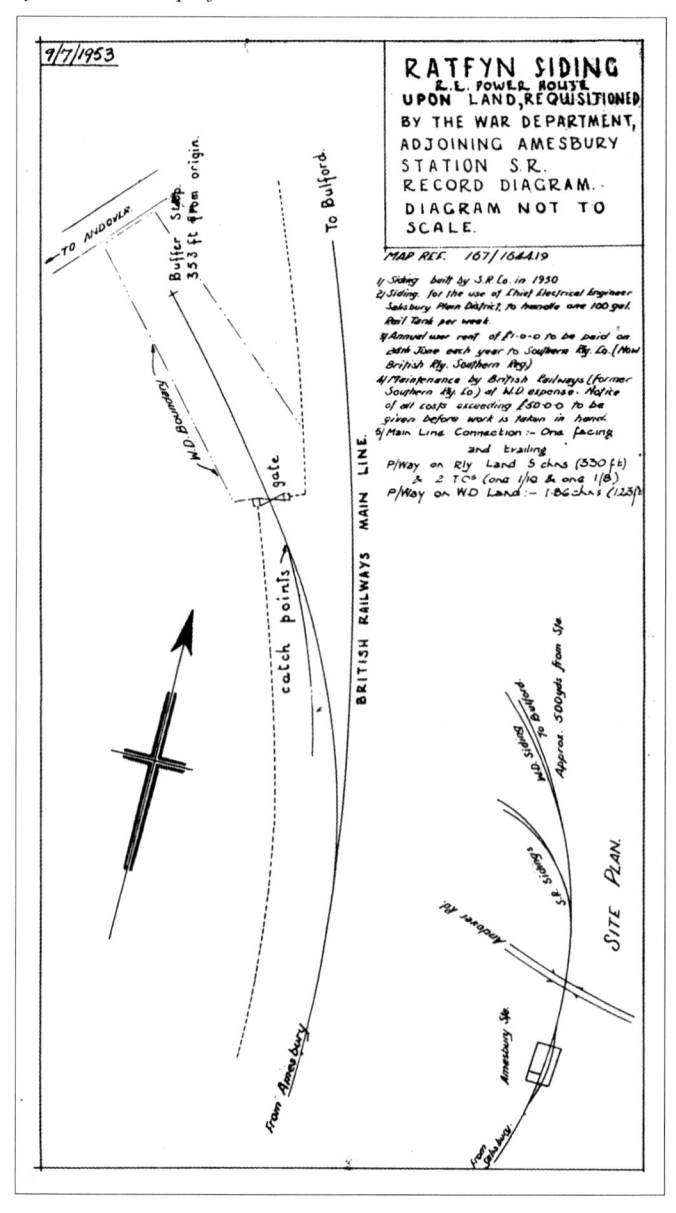

His Majesty King George V and Queen Mary accompanied by Lord Kitchener leaving Larkhill Camp after inspecting the Canadian Troops in 1915. (David Foster-Smith)

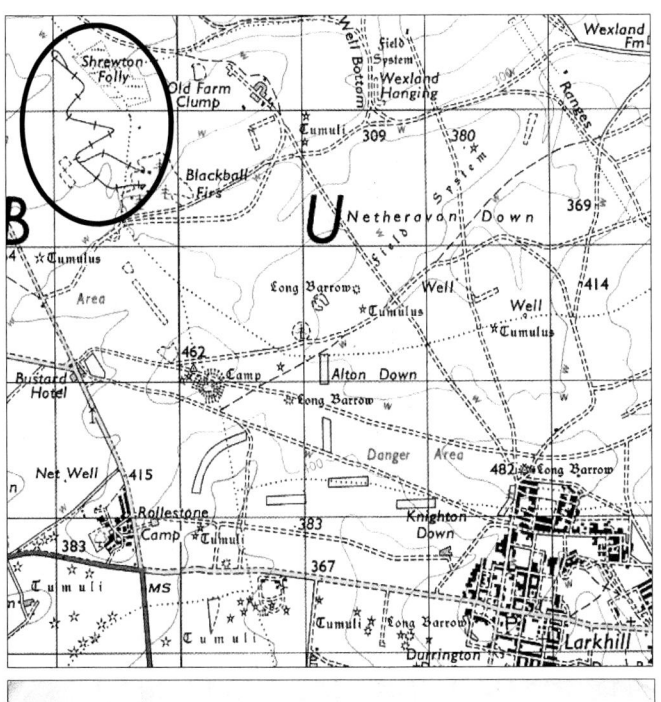

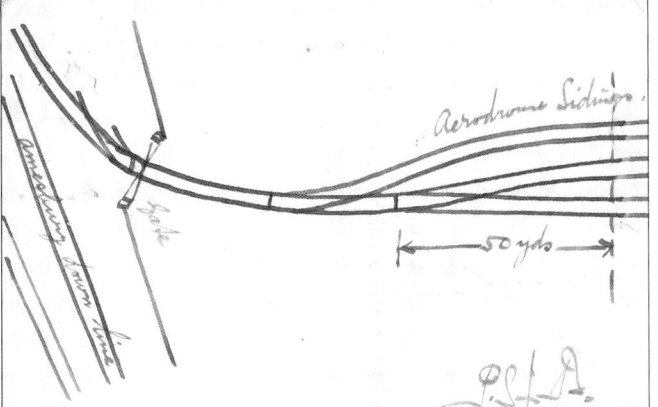

1. A rental of £1 per annum be paid by the WD for the SR Company's land.
2. Maintenance of the siding to be borne by the WD.
3. Amesbury station rates to be applied for conveyance of traffic to/from the siding, plus a haulage charge of 1/7d per loaded wagon.
4. The arrangement to be terminable on one month's notice.

TANK PRACTICE RAILWAY

Before leaving the military railway mention should be made of an isolated narrow gauge line known as the Tank Practice Railway. This was located 1½ miles north of Rollestone Camp and was built to a gauge of 2ft. 6 ins. in 1916 for tank firing practice. The track was sunk in narrow cuttings about 8 feet deep and 18 feet wide and the target, a hessian or canvas screen shaped like a tank, being placed on a trolley and towed by a small, naturally unmanned (!), diesel or petrol engine on a chassis. Trips were placed at various points along the line to operate the throttle thus causing the target to accelerate or slow automatically. Tanks would then blast away at this moving target. Track consisted of mineral quarry steel rails of usual section bolted to pressed-steel square ended sleepers. It was manufactured by Hudson of Gildersome Foundry in Leeds, the same firm that made much of the track for the Purbeck clay mine tracks near Corfe Castle. There were semi-circular turnround lengths at either end allowing continuous working from one control. An engine shed with associated turntable was provided, the total track length being some two miles. Being situated within the military firing range this was not normally accessible however a report of a visit made in 1971 mentions that the Army had recently lifted some track and filled in some of the cuttings to make vehicle crossings.

Map - Tank Practice Railway (circled) seen in the top left hand corner of this 1960 map. (With the kind permission of Ordnance Survey) Bottom map - A pen sketch of the original Boscombe Down sidings taken from a page of LSWR correspondence.

Much track was seen recovered lying in piles but some had been used as fencing at the entrance to the Danger Area on Black Heath. The site of the engine shed had been infilled with rubbish and a target frame was noted on its side and broken wheels and axles lay scattered around. The visitor managed to persuade the MoD to allow him to recover a four foot length of track affixed to two sleepers for preservation.

THE GENERAL INSTRUCTIONS SHOWN ON PAGES 47 AND 48 OF THE WESTERN APPENDIX IN REGARD TO LOADS OF TRAINS ON THE AMESBURY AND BULFORD BRANCH ARE SUPERSEDED BY THE FOLLOWING:

PASSENGER TRAIN TRAFFIC - The maximum loads for passenger and troop trains on the Amesbury and Bulford Camp line must be based on tonnage. When a vehicle does not bear a tare plate, the under mentioned method to be used for calculating tonnage:

Bogie coach or van when loaded to count equal to	28 tons
Six-wheeled coach or van when loaded to count equal to	16 tons
Cattle wagon when loaded to count equal to	15 tons
Horse box when loaded to count equal to	9 tons
Van U or P.L. van (4 wheeled) when loaded to count equal to	16 tons
Box wagon or Carriage or Road Vehicle truck when loaded to count equal to	10 tons

The total weight to be conveyed by ordinary and special trains will be as under

1. West Country or Q1 Class — Load = 300 tons
2. B Class — Load = 260 tons
3. C Class — Load = 200 tons
4. D, E, F or G classes and M7 tank Engines — Load = 170 tons

When an assisting engine is provided, the train can be made up to the combined maximum load for each class of engine used.

Vehicles for the Bulford Branch which are attached to down passenger, horse-box and milk trains, to travel via Porton, must be marshalled to arrive at Porton in the following order: Newton Tony, Amesbury, Bulford.

FREIGHT TRAIN TRAFFIC - The following loads are authorised:

When an assisting engine is attached at the rear of a train, the load may be made up to the maximum limit laid down for each class of engine, except that the vehicle limit shown must not be exceeded.

Section of line			Maximum Load inclusive of Van Class of Engine				
From	To	Vehicle Limit	Q1 West Country	B	C	D.E.F.H.I.J	K
			Equivalent to Loaded Goods				
Porton Grateley	Amesbury * Amesbury	50	34	29	25	22	20
Amesbury Amesbury	Porton Grateley	50	37	32	27	24	20
Amesbury Bulford	Bulford Amesbury	50	40	34	30	26	20

* When the load between Newton Tony and Amesbury, or vice versa, exceeds equal to 40 general goods wagons, an assisting engine must be attached at the rear and must in every instance run through from Newton Tony or vice versa, attached to the train and must not be uncoupled between these points.

When an assisting engine is provided at the rear, and also when from the nature of the load of a train worked by one engine only, or the weather conditions, the man in charge considers it desirable, the train must, before descending the decline to Amesbury in the case of Down trains, or to Newton Tony in the case of Up Trains, be brought to a stand before passing on to the falling gradient, and three-fourths of the total number of wagon brakes must be pinned down to ensure safe working of the train down the gradient.

The guard will be responsible for seeing the wagon brakes are pinned down as before indicated, and also for seeing the brakes are released on arrival of the train at Amesbury or Newton Tony, as the case may be.

One twenty-five ton goods brake van must be attached at the rear of every freight train running over the line.

A Earle-Edwards.
Divisional Superintendent   16 September 1947.

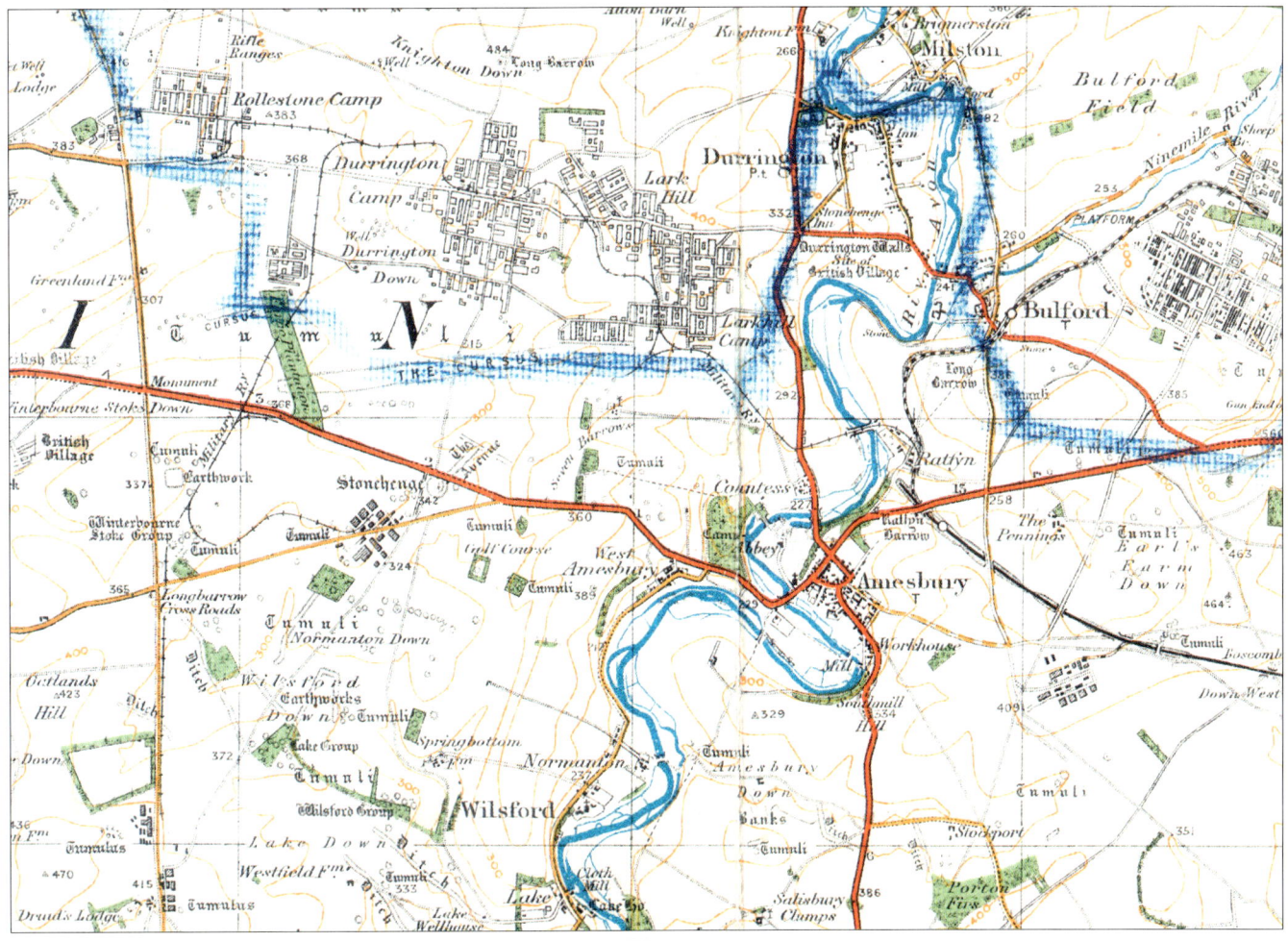

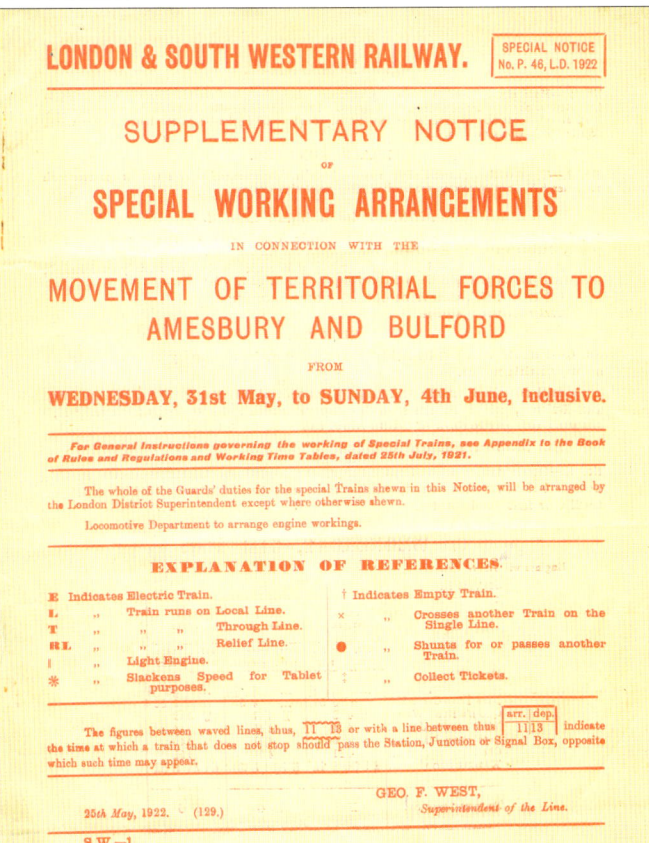

Above - The route of the Larkhill Military Railway is shown on this section of map reproduced from a 1920 Ordnance Survey map. The Blue edging shows, approximately, the WD area. Note also the siding to Boscombe Down seen lower right. (With the kind permission of Ordnance Survey)

Left - Special Traffic Notice for 1922. (A further, similar, notice has been found for Saturday 17 to Wednesday 21 June covering the return workings.) On the occasion illustrated four special trains were run to the branch using locomotives provided by Nine Elms, Basingstoke and Salisbury. In addition one train, running via the GWR to Basingstoke, continued with the GWR engine and an LSWR pilot driver. Another service originated from the LNWR arriving at Kensington where nine minutes were allowed for an LSWR engine to take over. In both the cases mentioned, 'foreign' stock would therefore have been seen on the branch. For weight purposes, certain services were also shown as double-headed either from Grateley or Newton Tony. In the reverse direction details of some of the stock formations are given, with as an example, : 'half a four coach set - three 80-seat thirds - 2 vacuum fitted cattle trucks - 2 P.L. vans - half a four coach set', a total of 11 vehicles. Other similar mixed formations are mentioned including even open trucks sandwiched between passenger vehicles, the latter being marshalled at either end of the train. (See example illustration on page 50.)

L.S.W.R. NEWTON TONY.

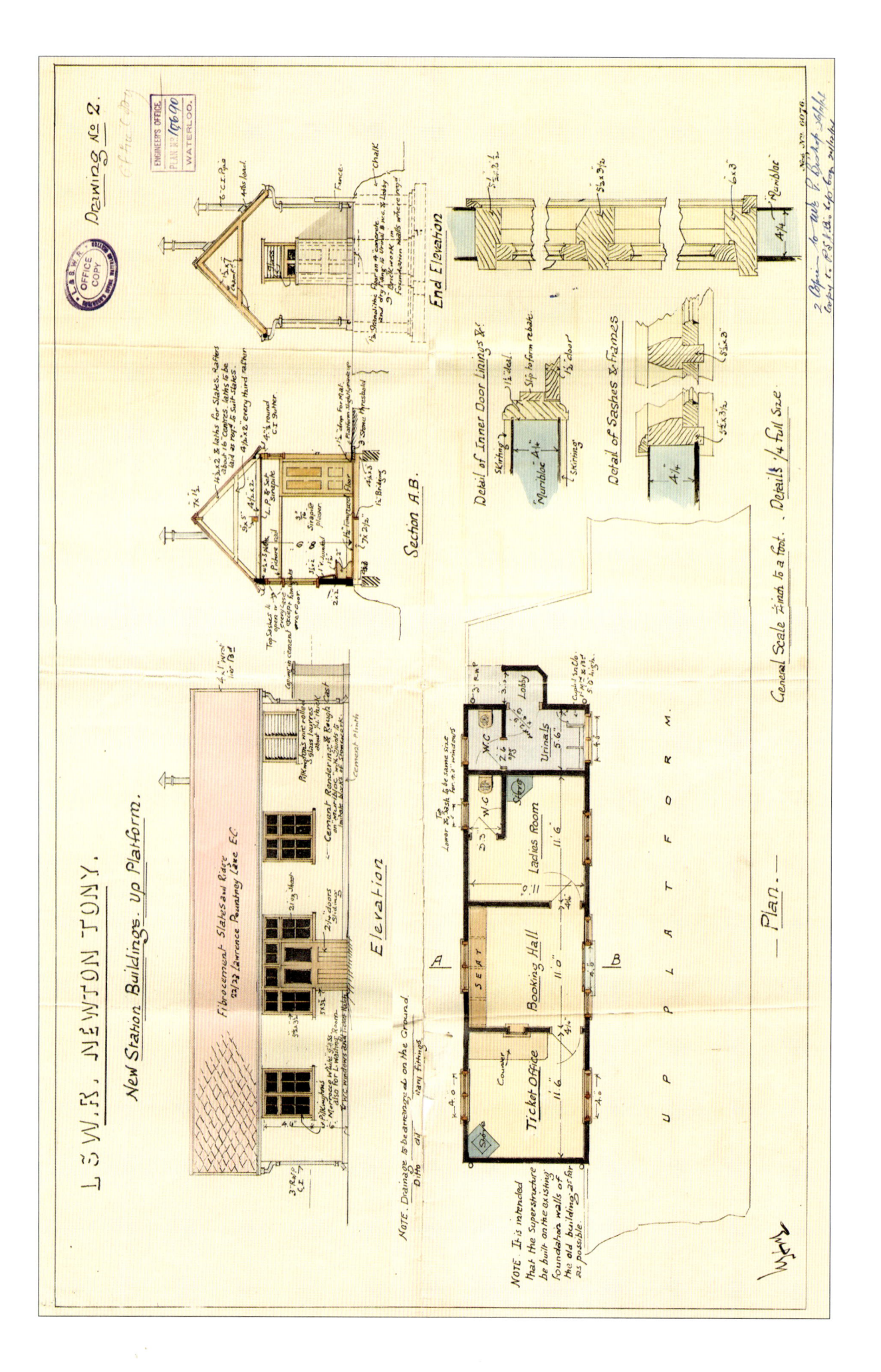

New Station Buildings. Up Platform.

Drawing No 2.

General Scale ½ inch to a foot. Details ¼ Full Size.

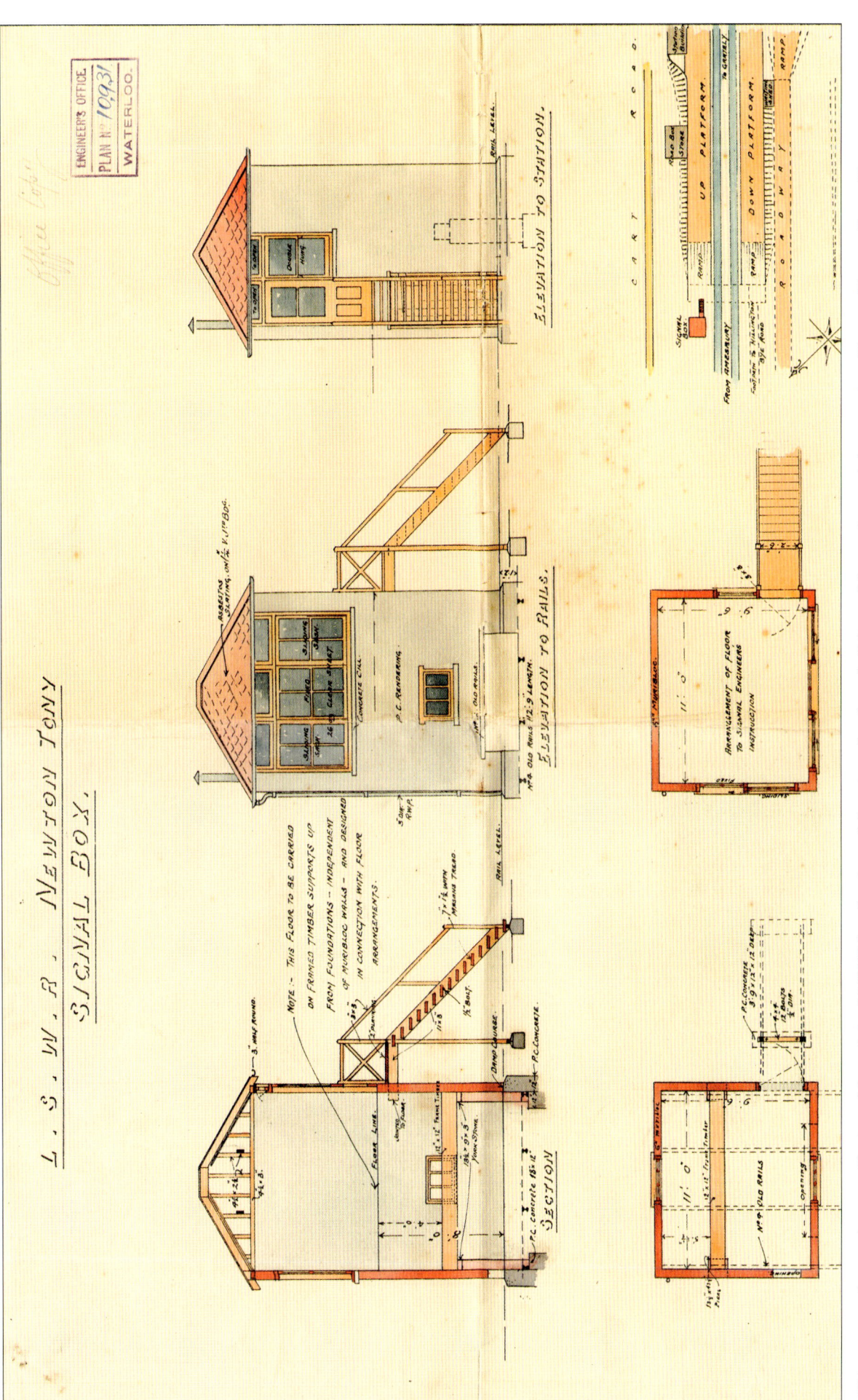

This page and opposite top - Copies of the original LSWR hand-coloured drawings for the rebuilding of the station and the new signal box at Newton Tony. These were replacements following the fire of 1 May 1914, referred to on page 34. (Kevin Robertson collection)

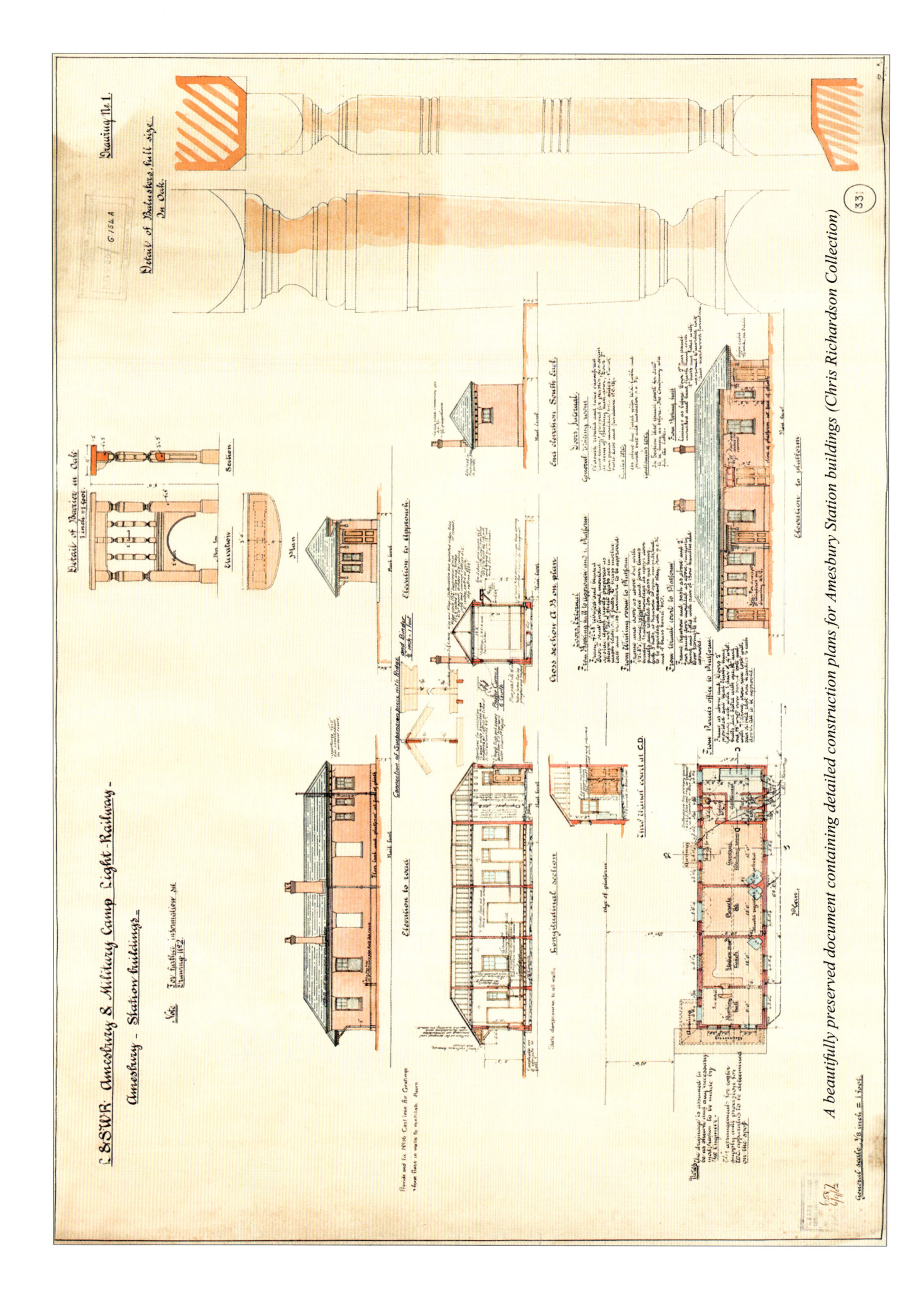

A beautifully preserved document containing detailed construction plans for Amesbury Station buildings (Chris Richardson Collection)

Contemporary coloured postcards showing the exterior and interior of Miss Perks Soldiers Home in Bulford Camp. From very early days a tent was erected on Bulford Down among the thousands of soldiers encamped there to provide refreshments, reading and writing materials, and evangelical teaching. This facility was operated by the Misses Perks, Louisa and Emma. After some years working under canvas and in the light of the decision by the War Office to establish a permanent camp at Bulford, it was decided that the "Miss Perks Soldiers Home", as it had become known, should similarly become of a more permanent nature. The building was estimated to cost £6,000 and was officially opened on 4th June 1903. The War Office had been quite willing to grant a site but the local military authorities wanted to relegate the Home to a position at the extreme end of the camp, right away from the men. Miss Perks appealed to Lord Roberts, Commander-in-Chief of the British Army, who is reported to have said "Give Miss Perks whatever site she wants!" and thus it was built on the main route through the camp. (Unknown)

A hand coloured photographic postcard depicting early days at Bulford Railway Station. (John Alsop)

Centre and bottom - Two further views of the Railway Enthusiasts Club "Rambling Rose" tour with M7 No. 30108 of 23 March 1963 - the same special features on the cover. Here the train is seen at a desolate looking Bulford Camp Platform prior to returning to Amesbury. The service had started at Farnborough venturing first to Basingstoke and the stub end of the line to Alton, the latter by this time curtailed at Thorneycroft Siding. After this it was back to the main line for Grateley and on to the branch to Amesbury and Bulford. Leaving the branch the train continued west to Salisbury before reversal and thence down to Southampton before taking the main line as far as Shawford Junction and then the DN&S route through Winchester Chesil as far as Newbury. The tour concluded with a trip along the Berks and Hants main line eastwards to Reading, via Reading Central goods and finally the SECR line to Farnborough. As might be said, "A Grand Day-Out". (Amyas Crump collection.)

Q1 No. 33017 hauls an eastbound freight through Grateley. The former Amesbury bay lies to the right of the nameboard, the loop being fully signalled at this time. (Alan Sainty Collection)

The down milk empties are passing Amesbury Junction behind H15 No 30489 in September 1959. The chalk face of the former fly-under connection may be seen immediately ahead of the locomotive. (K.R.Collection)

700 class No. 30368, a long time Bulford branch goods locomotive, is seen at Basingstoke shed on 11 February 1962 suitably adorned for the recent Christmas season being withdrawn in December that year. On the 18 May 1963 the last Schools class in BR service, 30934 "St Lawrence", steamed from Basingstoke shed, where it had been stored since withdrawal in December 1962, to Eastleigh towing 30368 which had also been stored at 70D following snowplough duty the previous winter. No. 30368 had led something of a charmed life for having been partially dismantled in 1960 at Eastleigh it was subsequently fitted with parts from classmate 30687 to enable it to work until withdrawal at the end of 1962. (Jeffery Grayer)

A Bullied Q1 33039 runs round at Bulford Camp platform on the Hampshire Venturer railtour of the 10 March 1963. (C H Gooch / Southern-Images.Co.Uk)

5. DECLINE

RETRENCHMENT......PASSENGER CLOSURE......GOODS SERVICES...... TOTAL CLOSURE…....DEMOLITION AND REMAINS

RETRENCHMENT

After the heyday of the war years the branch rapidly succumbed to the rundown of military traffic and the haemorrhaging of local passenger traffic resulting from the improved bus services, from the late 1940s on, which ran far more frequently than the trains and deposited passengers in the centre of Salisbury. Even as early as 1937 the travel writer S P B Mais in his book *"Let's get Out Here"*, which was an account of 26 walks from stations served by the Atlantic Coast Express, when describing a walk from Salisbury to Amesbury mentions that *"...from Amesbury I went back to Salisbury by bus"* and this in a publication for the Southern Railway ! One of the many local bus enterprises which started up was that of John Armstead who was the local carrier in Newton Tony before the Great War, his family being the village blacksmiths. As early as 1918 J W Armstead & Son started a motor service, later run by his son Harold, using Guy and Albion buses. The service continued to be locally owned until August 1986 when it passed to Bells of nearby Winterslow subsequently being taken over by Wilts & Dorset in May 1999. In June 1949, for example, Armstead's were operating two return journeys daily from Newton Tony into Salisbury on Tuesdays, one on Thursdays and Sundays and no less than six on Saturdays.

Review of railway timetables since the opening show a fairly consistent pattern of services, nine daily each way in 1906, which had increased to 10 down nine up daily in 1914, reducing to seven daily each way in both 1924 and 1944, services running solely to Salisbury after 1918. Unlike many branchlines a Sunday service remained important in returning service personnel from weekend leave there being two down services in 1906, four in 1914 falling to just one in both 1924 and 1944. The formerly well patronised Sunday trains were withdrawn just a year after the cessation of hostilities on 6th. May 1946 ostensibly due to fuel shortages. In 1951 a further national coal shortage caused

Armstead bus service at Salisbury Canal coach park in July 1964 displaying Newton Tony on the destination blind. REV 90 was one of the classic Bedford OB types so beloved of rural bus operators. (David Gillard Courtesy Ian Trotter)

A few days before the end of passenger services, 2 June 1952, and T9 30179 is seen with the branch train at Bulford. (S C Nash)

BR nationally to cancel many services, trains being progressively suspended during January and February as coal supplies dwindled. Cuts were made to a number of the less well patronised express services, secondary mainline, branch and off peak suburban services and special excursions other than to fixed events. This state of affairs lasted until after Easter when the majority of services were reintroduced with the exception of poorly patronised trains already under consideration for withdrawal when the cuts were implemented. In the case of the Bulford branch the full service was temporarily suspended from February to May and when it was resumed passengers found it had been drastically pruned to just one train/day each way which left Bulford at 9:40 am arriving in Salisbury at 10:13 and allowing just under 3 hours in the city before returning at 1pm. Whilst the coal shortage was no doubt the catalyst for this drastic reduction it was doubtless already in the minds of management to abandon the passenger service on the branch completely. Obviously such meagre provision was very unattractive to would-be passengers and such a situation could not long continue. Indeed this was to be the case, the end coming when, following revisions to the summer 1952 timetables from 30th. June, it was decided that the solitary train service to Amesbury and Bulford would be withdrawn in its entirety. Gross passenger receipts in 1950 had been £19,603 but a report concluded that closure would yield savings of £15,697 per annum.

PASSENGER CLOSURE

The final day of operation, June 28th. 1952, was little publicised and few of the 5,000 local inhabitants or indeed many enthusiasts turned out to witness the last rites. Drummond 700 Class 30317 and the usual single coach performed the melancholy duty leaving Bulford at 9:40 am. It returned with the 1pm train departing from the usual platform 6 at Salisbury, Bulford trains sharing this platform with Bournemouth trains, and ran some 10 minutes late. It was augmented with a Bulleid corridor coach to cope with any last journey travellers. By 2pm it was all over and 50 years of public passenger service had come to an end, the train returning empty to Salisbury. Drummond locomotives of Class 700 and T9 had been prevalent during the last years of operation, Class 700s 30690 and 30317 and Class T9 30719 all being noted at work during the final month. Newton Tony station closed completely at this time and in October 1954 the track was slewed between the two platforms to provide one running line. At the same time the section to Amesbury Junction was taken out of use and all traffic had to proceed via Grateley as originally planned. Although the Newton Tony Junction to Amesbury section had been singled a year earlier in October 1953, a loop was retained at Amesbury and the former double track formation was safeguarded *"so it can be replaced in a national emergency"*. Fortunately, or perhaps unfortunately for the railway enthusiast, this emergency never came.

Rear end of M7 No. 30023 at Bulford, 9 September 1950.

Quiet times at Bulford, an unidentified Adams 4-4-0 awaiting return to Amesbury.

The end of the public railway at Bulford, beyond this point the line continued to Bulford Camp and Sling.

Looking north at Amesbury with the extensive military loading platforms visible on the left. (Estate of the late Austin Underwood)

GOODS SERVICES

Amesbury and Bulford both remained opened for goods traffic. Three goods services were initially provided, one running daily from Salisbury via Grateley of course now that the direct connection had been removed, one daily from Basingstoke and a NAAFI train which ran on Monday and Tuesday and additionally as required between Amesbury and Salisbury. A large NAAFI stores depot was situated at Amesbury. The ground frame at Bulford was reduced to 10 levers after 1954. A correspondent of the Railway Observer reported in 1959 that *"This branch is liable to close completely in the near future as the only traffic is supplies for Bulford Camp and coal for Amesbury. The NAAFI supplies which formerly came by rail are now delivered by road and BR are endeavouring to send all goods traffic by road from Salisbury Milford Depot. On 22/4/59 I travelled on 07.25 from Grateley to Bulford freight train with 75078. Traffic proved to be very light, no wagons in yard at Newton Tony but at Amesbury and Bulford yards were fairly full."*

TOTAL CLOSURE

This view proved to be unduly pessimistic as the line soldiered on for a further 4 years. Class 700 30368, the only example to be based at Basingstoke shed latterly, was especially retained for working the Bulford Goods which also served most of the intermediate stations between Basingstoke and Salisbury. Basingstoke MPD duty No. 242, in 1953 for example, saw a Class 700 off shed at 5 a.m. for a 5:30 start to Bulford returning at 16:30 from Amesbury and due back at Basingstoke at 19:00. The revenue miles attributable to this trip were 67 miles. Troop trains continued to run on the branch on an ad hoc basis and a few enthusiast specials penetrated the line as far as Bulford Camp station. These included one hauled most unusually by some very exotic motive power in the shape of a Beattie well tank, 30587, which was more at home in Cornwall handling the china clay traffic from Wenford Bridge to Wadebridge. On May 14th 1955 this Class 0298 locomotive powered the Railway Enthusiasts Club (REC) tour from Andover Junction to Bulford Camp and return with

Seven years after public closure, the level crossing, signal box and protecting signals are seen at Newton Tony. The track had also now been reduced to a single line and the platform edge demolished. The signal box acted as a ground frame only. 23 October 1959. (James Harrold / The Transport Treasury H1145)

Amesbury still with the signs of wartime painting. The view is of the former military platforms. Notice the island canopy has been removed.

Branch line freight, 23 October 1959.

Seen at Bulford (top and centre) is U class No. 31611, and bottom on the Amesbury turntable.

(James Harrold / The Transport Treasury H1153/52/49)

A snowy and deserted Bulford station photographed in March 1965. (Derek Fear)

Site of the recently lifted Shrewton sidings with the Bulford extension curving away right. (Derek Fear)

Newton Tony station after the track was reduced to a single line. (Derek Fear)

coaching set No.124. Towards the end in 1963 the Southern Counties Touring Society (SCTS) "Hampshire Venturer" tour, which had begun from London Victoria behind preserved T9 No. 120, traversed the line starting from Salisbury and travelling via Grateley hauled by Q1 33039. The final excursion on March 23rd. was the REC "Rambling Rose" tour with M7 30108, in charge of push-pull coaching set No. 608, running from Farnborough to Basingstoke and visiting Thorneycroft's siding on the old Basingstoke – Alton line en route before proceeding to Andover Junction then up to Bulford before going on to Salisbury. It was reported that the M7 had small rose motifs inserted into the "0"s of the locomotive number which remained in situ until scrapping. The Goods Yard at the former junction station of Grateley closed on 10th. June 1963 although the Booking Office remained staffed until 5th. October 1969. Plans were mooted to close all the intermediate stations between Andover and Salisbury but Grateley was reprieved and today draws customers from a wide area and enjoys an excellent service of 22 departures to Basingstoke and/or London on weekdays with a similar number to Salisbury and beyond. The nearby stations at Porton and Idmiston were not so fortunate closing from 9th. September 1968. Amesbury Junction signalbox, which had not been renamed Allington until September 1955, some 3¼ years after closure of the Amesbury line to passengers, closed on 20th. January 1964.

Although passenger services continued a little longer on the nearby Tidworth branch, they succumbed on 17th. September 1955 when the branch passed into the hands of the WD who operated freight services to Tidworth until 31st. July 1963. Track remains in situ from Andover (Red Post Junction) to Ludgershall where there are numerous MOD sidings serving a medical equipment depot and a vehicle depot. The system has its own diesel powered shunter which, in 2000, was a Ruston & Hornsby diesel No. 423 "*Cromwell*". Traffic increased following the completion of the Channel Tunnel, allowing direct rail access to Germany, and again in 1999 during the Balkans conflict.

THE REMAINS

Track on the Amesbury branch was lifted in the summer of 1965 and many of the road bridges demolished, that at Bulford Camp being blown up by the military as a training exercise. Walking the course of the line in 2010 several features could still be seen even after the passage of the last train more than 47 years ago. At Grateley the site of the former bay platform used by the Amesbury trains has been surfaced and incorporated into the car park for the ever

This view looking east on the SR mainline shows the now disused Allington Signal Box, and behind, the former track bed of the burrowing spur line of the Amesbury and Bulford branch. (Derek Fear)

The disused Allington Signal Box seen in 1965. (Derek Fear)

Amesbury Station seen from the road bridge, the ground frame is evident on the right. (Derek Fear)

increasing number of commuters who use this station. Grateley is but a shadow of its former self though it did win the dubious distinction of being "*Best Unstaffed Station*" back in 1994. The site of the third track to Newton Tony Junction is still evident in the wider than normal formation of the mainline. At the junction the triangular layout can still be discerned although very overgrown, the burrowing junction to Salisbury having been infilled. There remain no signs of the former signalboxes at the junction although the divergence of the routes from Newton Tony to Grateley and towards Salisbury are still evident as a splitting of two grassy tracks. An overbridge is still in situ en route to Newton Tony spanning a cutting to the south of the village. Interestingly enough the overbridge is still maintained by Network Rail as evidenced by the stencil marking "ABY" carried on one of the brick supporting pillars. There are now no remains of the station or level crossing at Newton Tony apart from a flat grassed area where the platforms used to be and the much extended Station Master's house and adjacent railway workers cottages. The course of the old railway line is visible after crossing the road where a car park for a local nature trail crossing the RSPB Winterbourne Downs Nature Reserve has been provided with explanatory signboard although there is no mention of the area being a former railway line. The abutments of the former road bridge, where the line crossed the Tidworth – Salisbury road (A338), can be seen whilst the trackbed near Boscombe Down airfield has similarly been given over to a trail which extends to the northern limits of the airfield site and to the outskirts of Amesbury passing an old underline bridge and an overbridge no longer used by regular traffic.

Although Amesbury station site was redeveloped after closure it is at the time of writing a building site being the location of a new Tesco supermarket due to open in November 2010. There are some tangible reminders of the former railway presence since the solid edifice of the former Station Master's house still stands on the old London Road although a row of railwaymens' cottages opposite has recently been demolished. The new A303 has swallowed up much of the formation north of the town though Ratfyn the site of the former junction with the LMR is still traceable. In Bulford village a local landmark is the home signal, the arm of which is now somewhat battered, standing sentinel at the beginning of the original railway approach road. Bulford station was demolished and the site redeveloped in the 1960s by the erstwhile Property Services Agency. Since 1998 the Special Investigations Branch (UK), who have the mission " *to provide an efficient and effective investigative service throughout the United Kingdom and in overseas theatres, except Germany, in order to contribute to the Moral Component of Fighting Power*" have been based on the site. There are some remains located near the entrance of

The REC special of May 1955 was headed by Beattie well tank 30587 and is seen taking water at Amesbury. (Unknown)

Top - *No. 30587 rounds the curve from the mainline, the former spur to the burrowing junction led off to the right to the rear of the platelayers hut. (Unknown)*

Centre - *The REC tour and Beattie well tank No. 30587 ran to Bulford station, seen here, and on to Bulford Camp platform. (Unknown)*

Bottom - *No.30587 runs round coach set 124 at Bulford Camp platform to return to Amesbury. (Unknown)*

A view of Amesbury station from the road bridge looking south towards Newton Tony (Unknown)

Amesbury Signal Box located at the throat of the goods yards and platforms. (Unknown)

32 Section SIB. From here some embankments remain giving an idea of the route to Bulford Camp and Sling, the platform at the Camp being still visible in 1990 but this has since been demolished. Much of the concrete platform at Sling, situated behind an old pumping station, is still evident although heavily camouflaged in trees and undergrowth – a sad epitaph for what once must have been a hive of military activity.

There are a few commercial DVDs available which feature brief glimpses of trains on the Amesbury branch including the B&R Production Volume 85 Steam Routes West Part 2 (The Southern Way) featuring 33039 on a special in 1963, the Ivo Peters Collection Volume 11 featuring M7 30108 on the final special also in March 1963 and Steam World Archive Vol. 11.

The Larkhill Military Railway also displays some remains though, having closed a lot earlier than the LSWR branch, there are fewer as might be expected after the passage of some 80 years. A road now leads off from the former Ratfyn Junction towards the River Avon where naturally all trace of the former bridge has gone. Over the river the course of the line can be picked up to both the east and west of Countess Crossing where the former route is now a footpath leading to Larkhill and several cuttings and embankments are still visible including the remains of the turning triangle. It is said locally, though this may well be apocryphal as so many of such stories are, that the route of the LMR can be traced by a line of apple trees that have sprung up from the seeds of apples thrown out by troops on passing trains. Locally this route is known as the "Apple Track".

A good appreciation of the line can still be had from Google Earth with several stretches still clearly visible and on close inspection even some faint lines through fields can be readily identified as the former trackbed. The old "Flying Shed" branch can no longer be traced for, once the camps in the vicinity were completed, the track was removed shortly after, no trace of it even appearing on an OS map of 1926. The flying field itself closed in 1914 and a large part was used for hutted and tented camps. The remains of a platform near Strangways stables at the junction of Lawson Road and Colquhoun Road are hidden underneath vegetation. Larkhill Camp itself reveals little remains of the route but it can still be seen between Larkhill and Rollestone Camp. The spur towards Stonehenge and Lake Down is still evident where it crosses Fargo plantation but elsewhere all traces seem to have been lost. A water tower near the site of Druid's Lodge was at one time thought to be the source of water supply for LMR locomotives but this was in fact the water supply for the camp, the railway line terminating some 550 m. short of the tower.

The sizeable water tank provided at Amesbury Station by the LSWR, recorded on 19 September 1962. (South Western Circle)

Platform view of Amesbury station (S C Nash)

An excellent view of the Amesbury station turntable showing the REC's special rail tour Beattie tank locomotive being turned for its return journey to Andover Junction. (Unknown)

Cutting near Newton Tony, 23 October 1959. This is the bridge featuring on the frontispiece. (James Harrold / The Transport Treasury H1144)

The former burrowing junction with the main west of England line above. 23 October 1959. See also lower view page 79. (James Harrold / The Transport Treasury H1143)

The military railway towards Sling beyond Bulford (public) station, 14 May 1955. (R F Roberts)

Stations Masters: 1912-1922

	Newton Tony	Amesbury	Bulford
1912	O J Norwood		
1915	O J Norwood	E W Coome	E Harris
1916	O J Norwood		E Harris
1917	O J Norwood	F U Sansom	E Harris
1918	O J Norwood	F U Sansom	E Harris
1919	O J Norwood	F U Sansom	E Harris
1920	O J Norwood	F U Sansom	E Harris
1921	O J Norwood	F U Sansom	E Harris
1922	O J Norwood	F U Sansom	E Harris

'SOUTHERN RAILWAY MAGAZINE', 1923

"AMESBURY - Mr Voller (left) who has just been appointed Stationmaster at Amesbury, joined the Company's service at Midford in 1895, and after a few years at Frimley and Rogate, was transferred to Plymouth District goods Supt.'s Office. Later he went to Andover Town, and after a brief stay was appointed to a post in the Central District Supt.'s Office. After 11 years he was promoted to the Supt. of the Line's Office, and in 1917 became Stationmaster at Porton.

From the **'SOUTHERN REGION MAGAZINE'**, September 1953.

"At an informal gathering recently, staff and friends bade farewell to Mr Towler, the Amesbury Station Master, upon the completion of 47 years service.

"Shunter T Packer spoke of Mr Towler's popularity, which was reflected in the happy relations at the station. He called upon Mr Hambridge, Mr Towler's successor , to present a chiming clock (with a bouquet for Mrs Towler).

"Mr Hambridge wishes Mr and Mrs Towler long life and happiness, and everyone present expressed a wish that Mr Towler would soon be restored to full health and strength after a long period of illness which persisted up to his retirement.

"Mr Towler joined the service in 1906."

DEMOLITION

A selection of views taken at Bulford station during demolition of the line.

1. A group of fascinated onlookers observe the caterpillar tractor removing rails from the permanent way adjacent to Bulford station platform.
2. Contractors loosen the chair bolts in preparation for lifting a further section of track.
3. Sleepers pile up as track lifting proceeds
4. The tractor negotiates the platform at Bulford station
5. A group of guilty looking children retreat with their spoils. (The oak keys used to hold the rails against the supporting chairs were often prized for firewood.)

(All Peter Daniels)

3

4

5

No more trains to Bulford. (Peter Daniels)

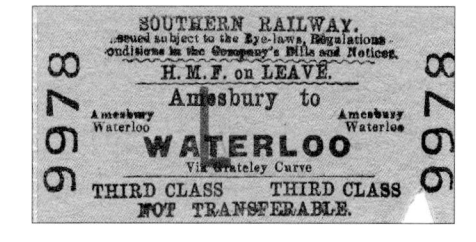

An aerial view of Amesbury with a head of steam visible indicating the presence of a train in the station. The sinuous course of the River Avon is also apparent in this view. Although the track of the LMR is no longer in-situ, the remains of the curve taking the LMR line away from Ratfyn Junction towards the crossing point on the river can still be seen. (English Heritage).

6. ICON OF THE PLAIN

One enduring feature of Salisbury Plain over at least the last four millennia is of course its most iconic landmark – Stonehenge. As seen in Chapter 1 the stones were threatened with some half dozen proposed railways passing close to the monument, only one of which, serving the short lived Stonehenge Airfield was actually built. A newspaper article from 1971 entitled "*All Change Please – for Stonehenge?*" reminded readers of the failed Pewsey - Salisbury proposal which would have seen a station near the monument opening up the possibility of through trains from London with consequent hordes of railborne visitors.

Today's tourist wishing to visit the stones by public transport more often than not arrives at Salisbury, the nearest railhead to the monument, by train before catching the bus connection that runs from the station forecourt every 30 minutes in the peak season. Had things turned out otherwise, as we have seen, there might have been a railway option from Salisbury available to 21st. Century travellers which would have seen them deposited at a station not far from the stones themselves. The problem with all the recent proposals to enhance the environment around Stonehenge is that they are all road based and following the scrapping of the £65m road tunnel scheme for the A303 in 2007, the present day still sees this site scarred by the proximity of roads and public car parking. In an attempt to remove cars from the immediate vicinity and, following public consultation on proposals to improve the setting and visitor experience at Stonehenge, the unanimous recommendation of the Project Implementation Group (led by English Heritage) was to locate the new visitor centre at Airman's Corner and this has been agreed by the Department for Culture and Media and Sport (DCMS). Public consultation, which took place from July to October 2008, indicated that the two preferred locations for the visitor centre were the Fargo Plantation, once crossed of course by the route of the LMR, or Airman's Corner, where the memorial to the fallen flyers is located.

The Project Implementation Group considered the feasibility of both these options and, taking into account the impact on the landscape, local environment and archaeology, determined that Airman's Corner represented the best possible solution. A much improved setting for the stones,

The ancient monument of Stonehenge, forever the enduring icon of Salisbury Plain. (Jeffery Grayer)

by removing intrusive buildings and car parking from the immediate vicinity of the site and by returning the section of road (the A344) immediately adjacent to the stones to grass, will result. A low-key transit system will run from the visitor centre to a drop-off point close to the stones, offering visitors opportunities to appreciate the landscape of the World Heritage Site and to view the surrounding monuments. A 4-trailer visitor transit system similar to that currently running at the Eden Project in Cornwall will be used. The distance between the visitor centre and the drop-off point is 2 km, giving a round trip journey time of 20 minutes. Each set of four trailers will have 72 seats and will have provision for the disabled. Of course the £20m visitor centre has had its detractors not least the Commission for Architecture and the Built Environment, who have criticised the design of the proposed centre, claiming the futuristic building does little to enhance the 5,000-year-old standing stones which attract more than 800,000 visitors each year. Recent government budget cuts have placed the whole scheme in jeopardy and it remains to be seen if and when the scheme goes ahead.

Although the courses of the old railway lines in the area have been affected by post closure developments large sections of them are still relatively clear. Reopening as a full rail link is almost certainly out of the question due to the high cost involved but local commentators have seen some potential with a light rail option which has been discussed from time to time in recent years. Modern trams with their light axle widths and ability to go round sharp curves could reduce the costs of rebuilding a route to the stones appreciably. Obstacles can be circumvented by incorporating stretches of street running which also means they can better serve local communities. Whilst the circuitous route via Larkhill to Stonehenge is unlikely to find favour either with the travelling public or with environmentalists, something along the lines of the erstwhile proposal of the GWR for a station serving Amesbury and Stonehenge located near enough to the monument to allow pedestrian access might be acceptable. The vision sees stations re-opening on the main line into Salisbury at Idmiston and Porton with new halts provided for Gomeldon, the Winterbournes and Bishopdown. In Salisbury, by reversing in the railway station and using the remains of the old Market House branch, a service could even perhaps terminate in the central car park giving an important boost to the city centre. It remains to be seen whether this is just a pipedream or whether such proposals might gain serious consideration, in view of their low carbon footprint, at some time in the future.

Were Wordsworth to cross Salisbury Plain today he would of course see many changes in the intervening 217 years not least in the army camps and firing ranges, but ironically the presence of the military over such large swathes of the land has had the effect of freezing time leaving much of the land comparatively undeveloped by man. The fact that all of the railway proposals to cross the Plain foundered and that only two small relatively short lived branchlines nibbled away at its south eastern fringes have no doubt also contributed to this lack of development. On the less accessible reaches of the Plain the poet would certainly find conditions much the same as he did at the end of the 18th. C. The feeling of remoteness, wide expanses of unspoilt landscape, and big skies can still be experienced today – long may it remain so.

More recent history - just over half a century ago. Q1s Nos 33006 and 33011 double head a westbound troop train bound for the Amesbury line, seen at Pirbright Junction in 1953/54. (Arthur Tayler)

A repositioned stop signal stands sentinel adjacent to the embankment leading to the former Bulford station. (Jeffery Grayer)

A sad epitaph for the former hive of activity that must have been the concrete platform at Sling buried in vegetation and still visible today to the north of Bulford Camp. (Jeffery Grayer)

Better days have been seen by this Larkhill Military Railway brick built platform adjacent to Strangways stables. A remarkable survivor more than 80 years after closure. (Jeffery Grayer)

The oldest aerodrome hangers in the country are now listed buildings. They were for many years used as a storage depot by the British Army. (Jeffery Grayer)

> ON THIS SITE THE FIRST AERODROME
> FOR THE ARMY WAS FOUNDED IN 1910 BY
> CAPT J.D.B. FULTON RFA AND MR G.B. COCKBURN
>
> THIS LATER BECAME 2' COY AIR BN RE
>
> THE BRITISH AND COLONIAL AEROPLANE COMPANY
> FORERUNNERS OF THE BRISTOL AEROPLANE COMPANY
> ESTABLISHED THEIR FLYING SCHOOL HERE IN 1910
>
> THE FIRST MILITARY AIR TRIALS
> WERE HELD HERE IN 1912

As the plaque indicates these are the listed former hangars of the British & Colonial Aeroplane Company at Larkhill Camp. (Jeffery Grayer)

Amesbury station during its death throes with a recent chalk infill in the distance in front of the road bridge. (Jeffery Grayer)

The former Amesbury Stationmaster's house is seen on the right with three sets of semi-detached railwaymen's cottages seen on the left, now demolished. (Peter Goodhugh)

A rusting overbridge remains on the outskirts of Amesbury adjacent to the Boscombe Down facility. (Jeffery Grayer)

The overgrown remains of a railway underbridge at Boscombe Down. (Jeffery Grayer)

Top - The present day site of the triangular junction near Newton Tony, the right hand fork to the former Salisbury burrowing junction, the left hand towards Grateley. *(Jeffery Grayer)*

Left - An overbridge near Newton Tony still has a code stencilled on, and remains the responsibility of Network Rail. *(Jeffery Grayer)*

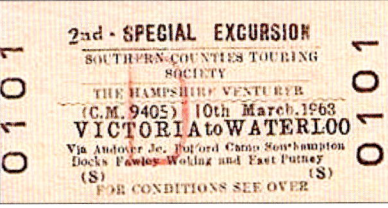

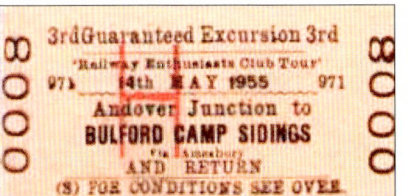

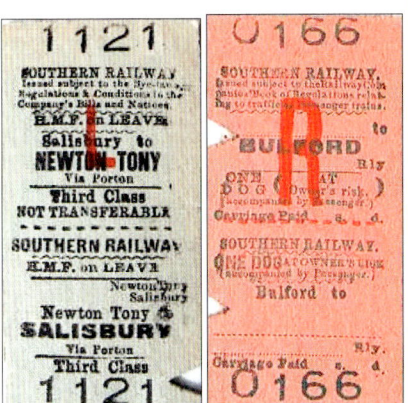

A collection of railway tickets and luggage labels that reflect a period stretching from the London & South Western Railway Company ownership, to the Southern Railway Company, and finally to the specials and rail tours run by the nationalised British Railways Southern Region in connection with the closure of the Amesbury-Bulford Branch.

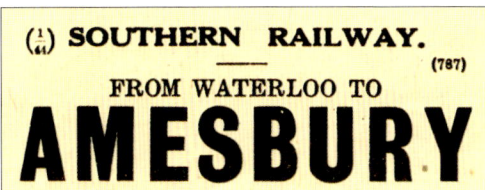

109

Airman's Cross memorial, by the roadside north west of Stonehenge. This was erected in memory of the very first flying duty fatalities ever incurred by the British armed forces on 6 July 1912. (Jeffery Grayer)

The old order in the shape of 3H Hampshire DMU No. 1124 approaches Grateley station with a Salisbury service in the 1970s. The former branch platform for the Amesbury line lies to the right of the unit where the large bush is growing from the former trackbed. Today the station area has been transformed with the provision of much car parking for the healthy commuter traffic. (Jeffery Grayer)

Modern day Grateley sees Class 158 units operating on the Waterloo – Salisbury – Exeter line. This view of a unit departing for Salisbury reveals the site, at the right hand side of the track, of the former third track serving the Amesbury branch. (Jeffery Grayer)

APPENDIX 1. CHRONOLOGY

Year	Event	Company
1846	Manchester & Poole Railway proposed	
1851	Westbury - Warminster opened	GWR
1856	Warminster - Salisbury opened	GWR
1857	Andover - Salisbury opened	LSWR
1862	Savernake - Pewsey - Devizes opened	GWR
1864	Wiltshire & Gloucestershire Rly. proposed	MR
1864	North & South Wiltshire Junction Rly. proposed	
1864	Wiltshire Rly. proposed	
1865	Upavon & Andover proposed	
1882	Andover – Ludgershall – Savernake opened	MSWJR
1882	Grateley – Amesbury – Shrewton – Westbury – Radstock - Bristol proposed (Bristol & London & South Western Junction Railway)	LSWR
1882	Pewsey – Salisbury - Southampton Rly. proposed	GWR
1887	Collingbourne & Avon Valley proposed	
1896	Light Railways Act	
1897	MOD begin to acquire areas of Salisbury Plain	
1898	Pewsey & Salisbury LRO granted	GWR
1898	Amesbury & Military Camp LRO granted	LSWR
1898	Ludgershall – Amesbury / Bulford Rly. proposed	MSWJR
1900	Patney & Chirton – Westbury opened	GWR
1901	Ludgershall – Tidworth – Shrewton Rly. proposed	WD / MSWJR
1901	Ludgershall – Tidworth opened	WD / MSWJR
1901	Amesbury – Shrewton Abandonment Order	LSWR
1902	Grateley – Amesbury opened	LSWR
1903	Amesbury & Military Camp Light railway (Bulford Extension) LRO granted	LSWR
1903	Bristol, London & Southern Counties Rly. proposed	
1904	Revised Newton Tony Junction opened	LSWR
1906	Amesbury – Bulford extension opened	LSWR
1914	Larkhill Military Railway (LMR) opened	WD
1923	LMR Fargo – Stonehenge/Lake Down closed	WD
1928	LMR closed completely	WD
1952	Bulford branch closed to passengers	BR
1955	Tidworth branch closed to passengers	BR
1961	MSWJR closed (Andover - Ludgershall remains open for freight)	BR
1963	Bulford Branch closed completely	BR

APPENDIX II.
TRACK DIAGRAMS

Newton Tony Station 1925

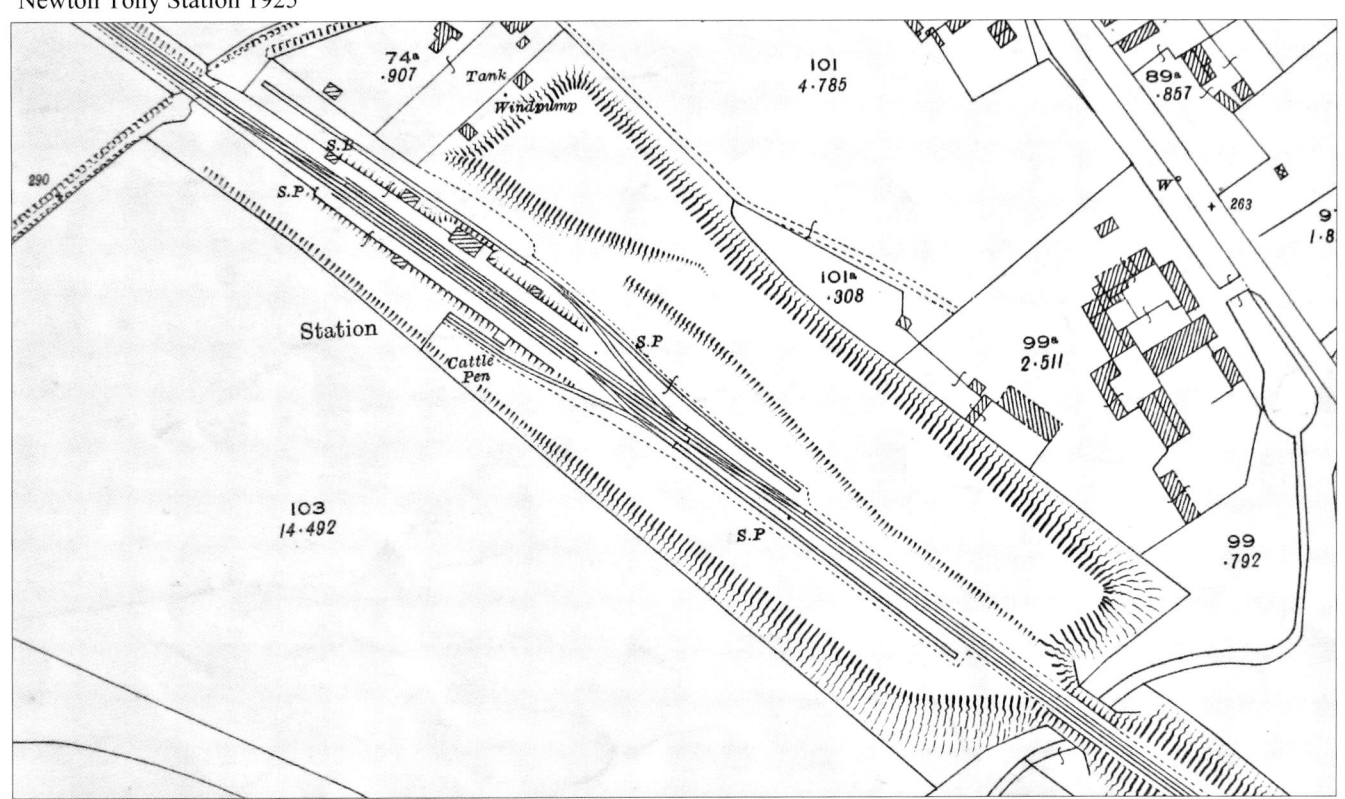

Amesbury Station 1924

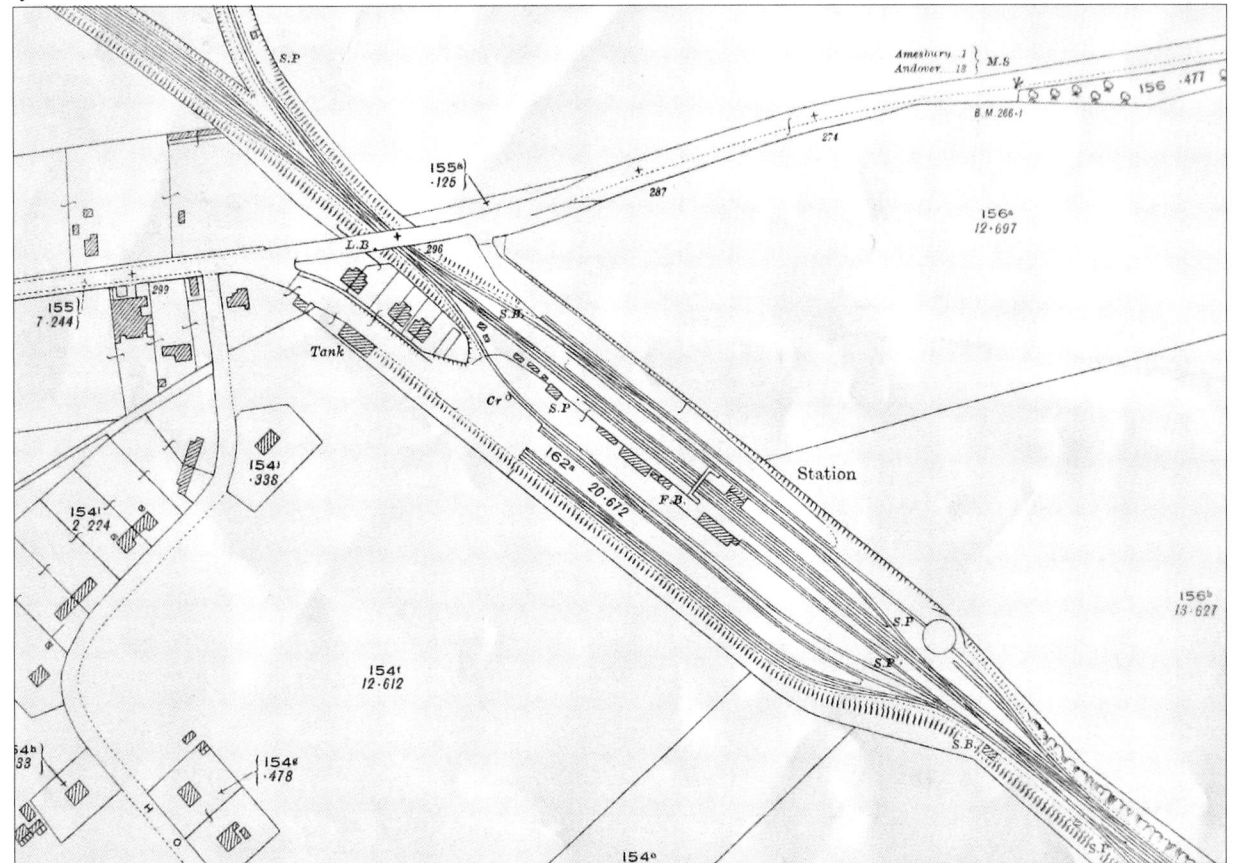

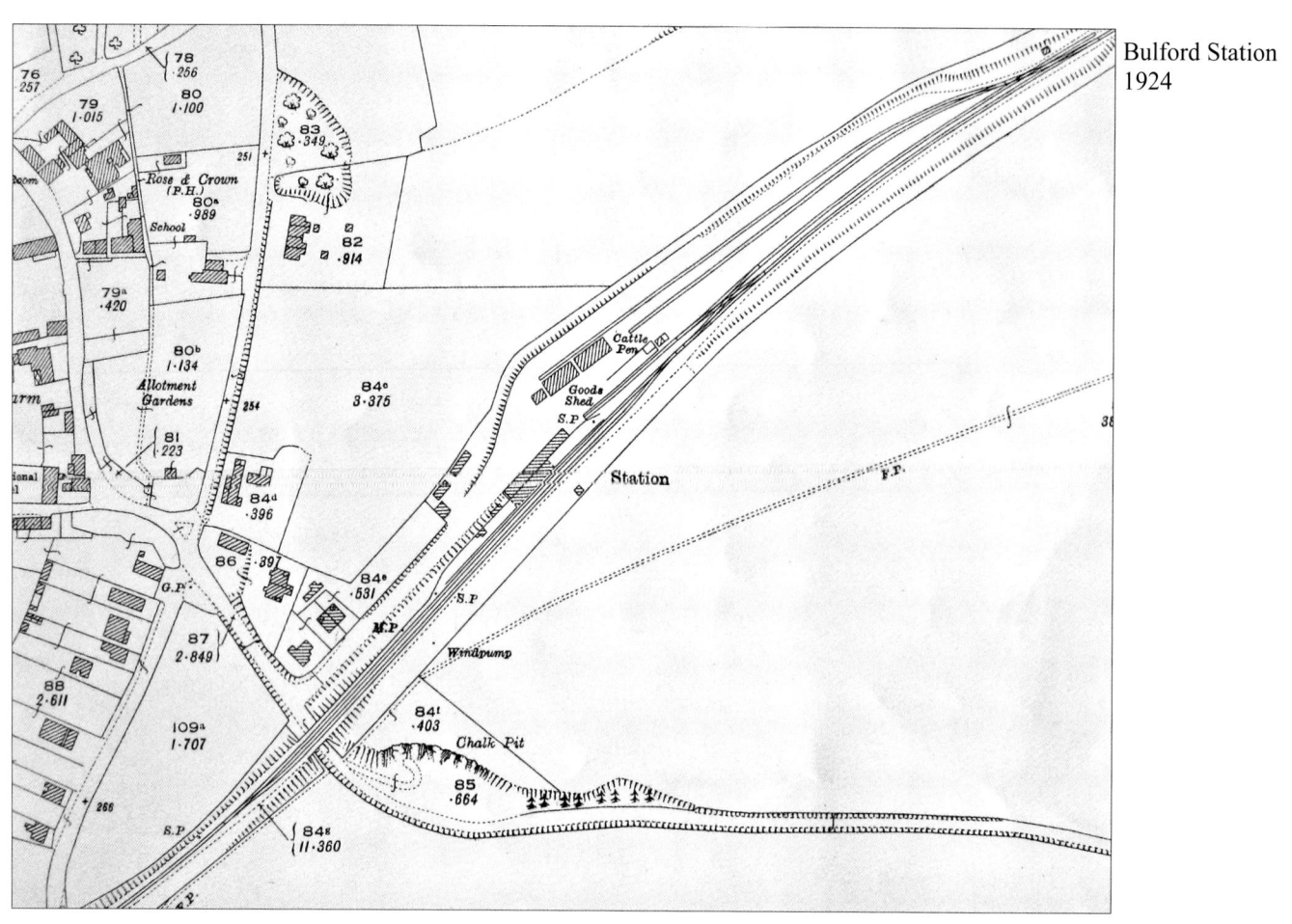

Bulford Station 1924

Bulford Camp Platform 1924

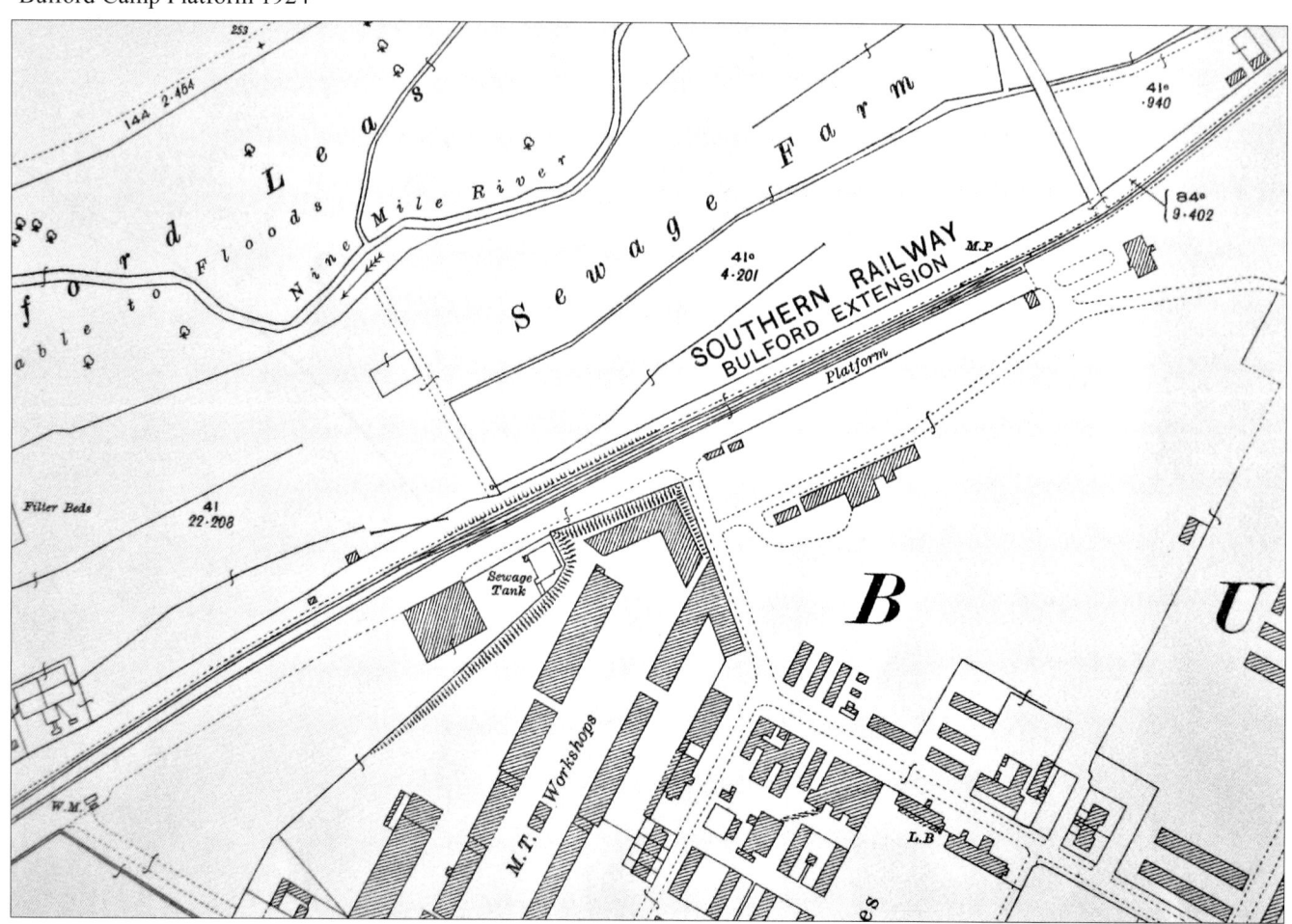

Sling Platform 1924

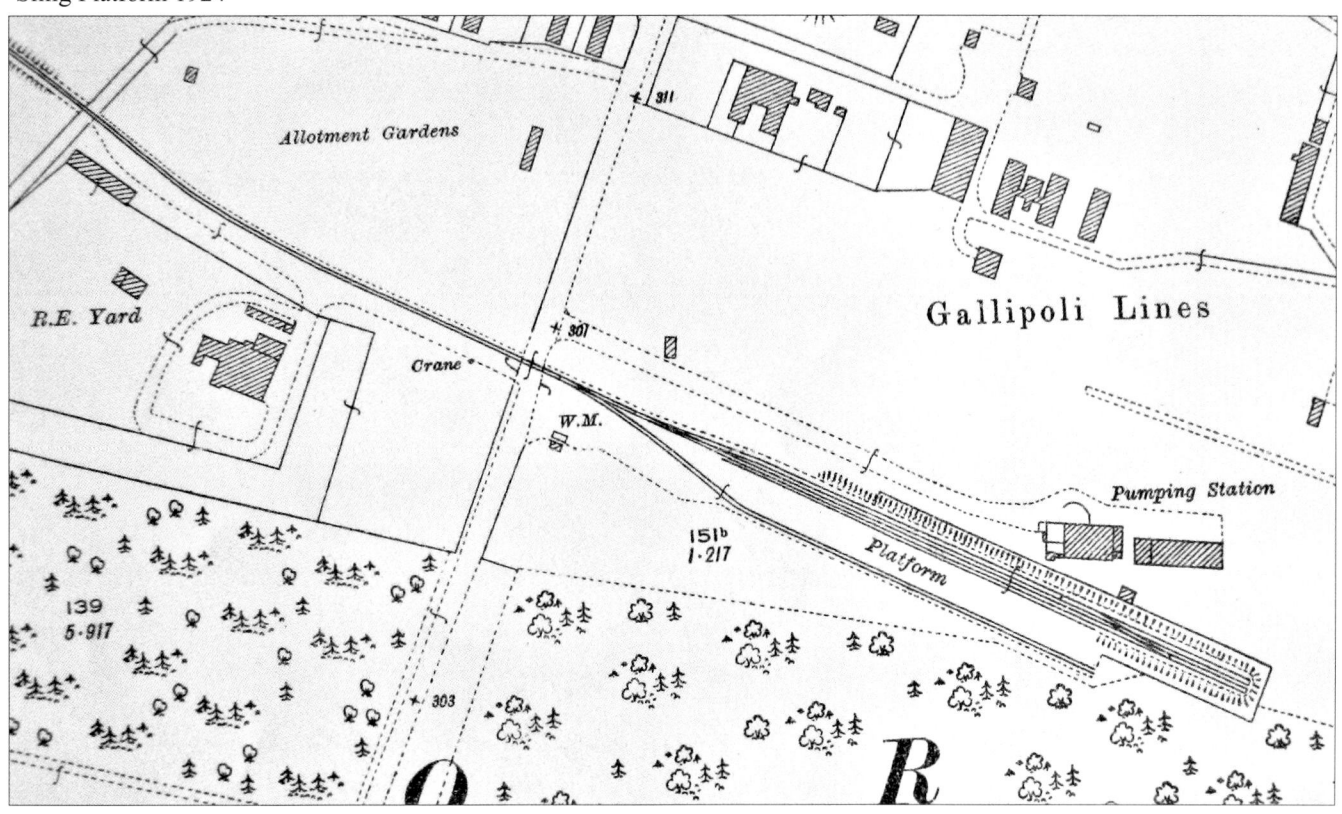

LMR route showing Flying Shed Branch 1924.

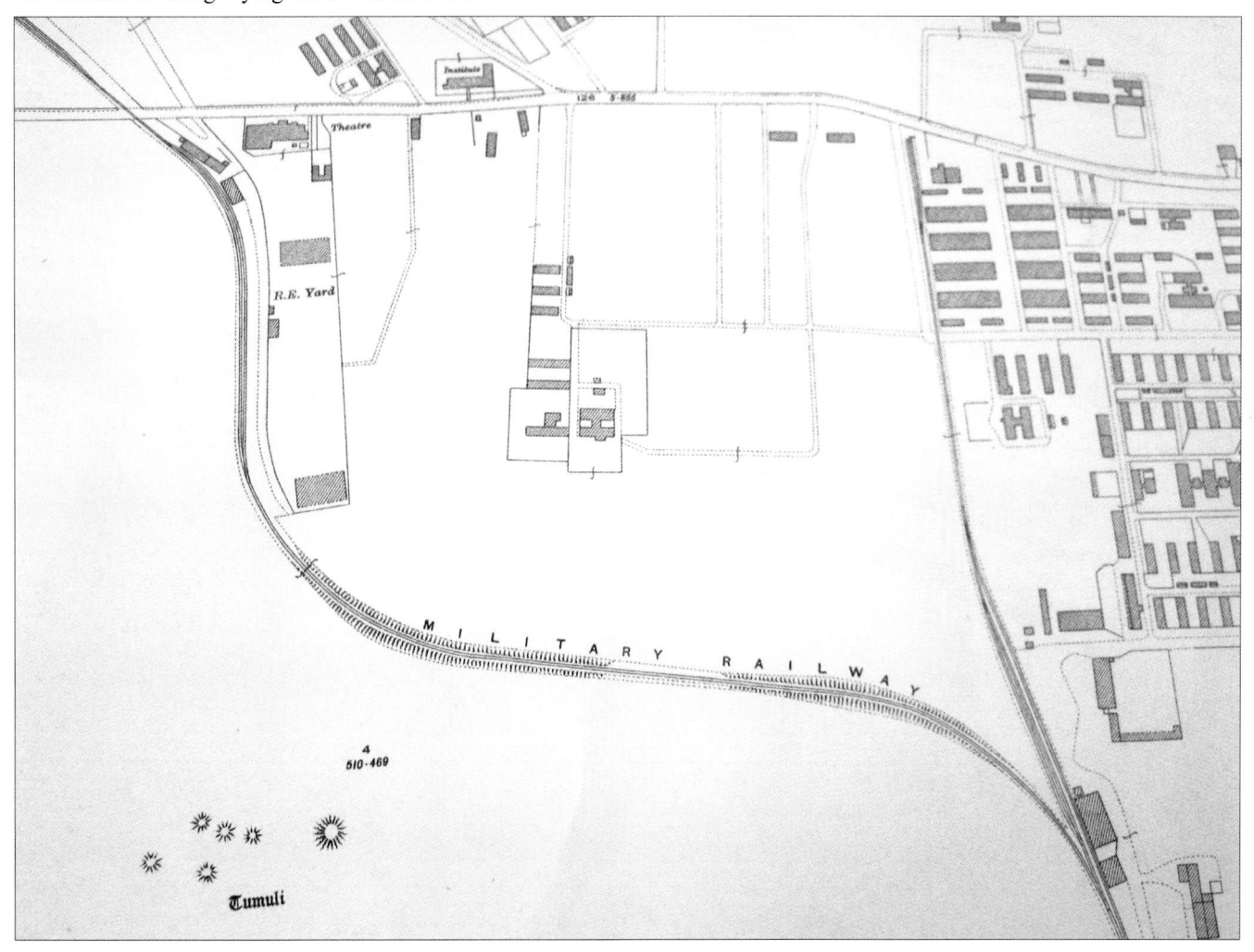

APPENDIX III. PLANS AND DRAWINGS

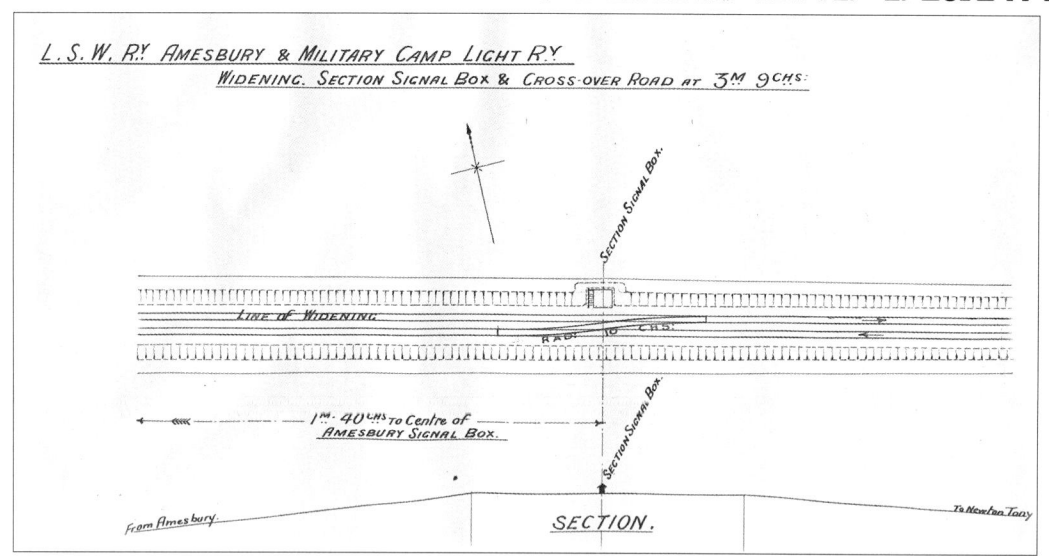

Allington break-section Signal Box, at 78m 15 chs from Waterloo.

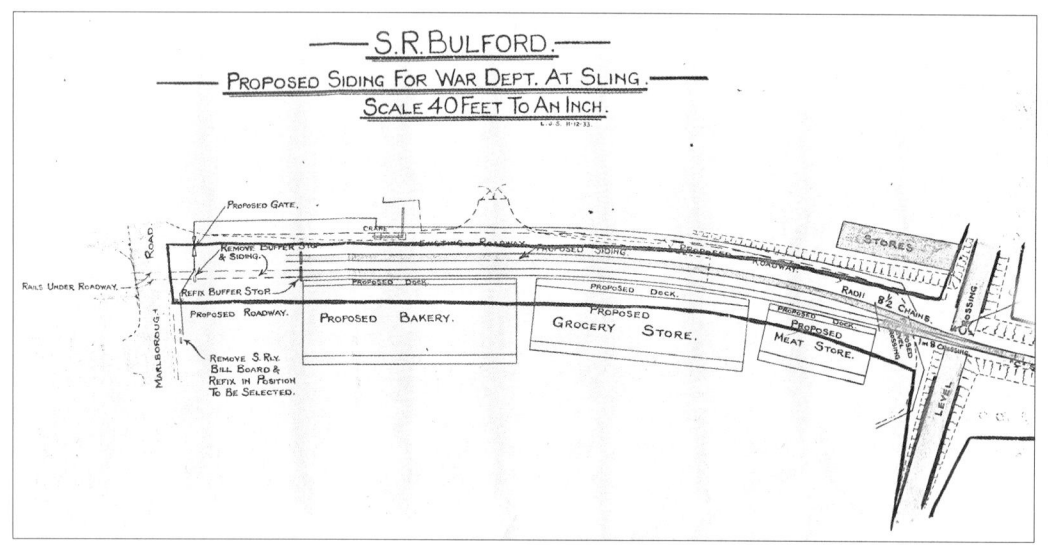

Proposed War Department siding at Sling, December 1933.

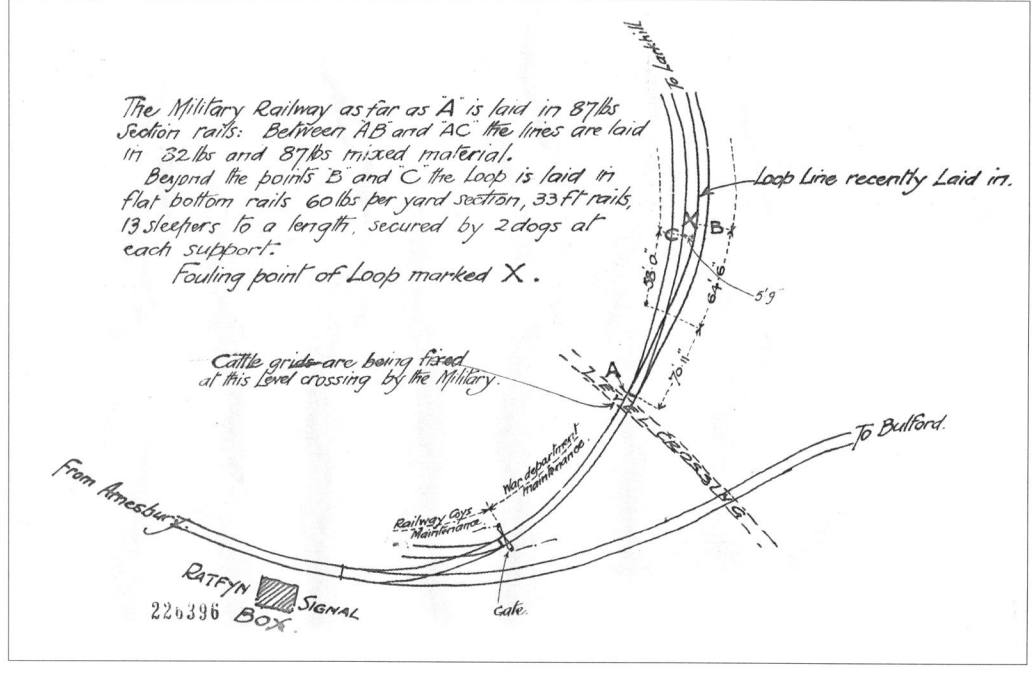

Junction and permanent way details for the Larkhill Military Railway from Ratfyn Junction, August 1917.

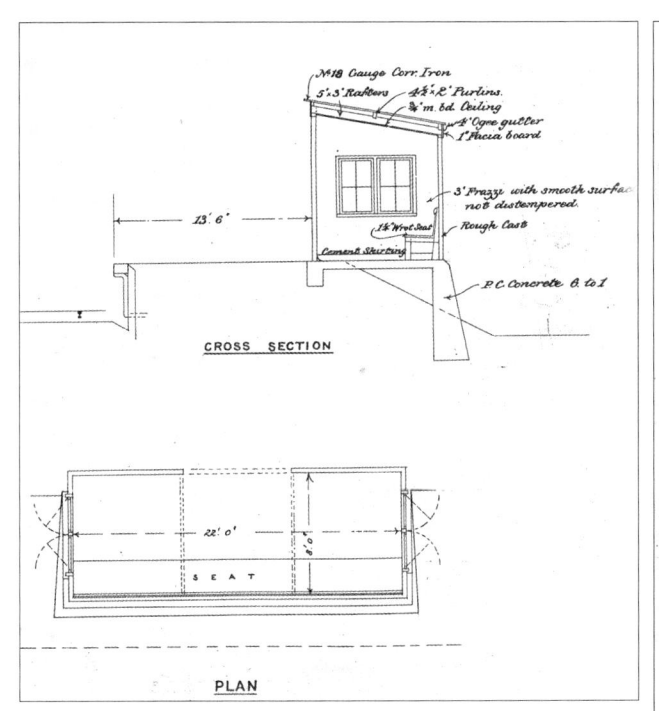

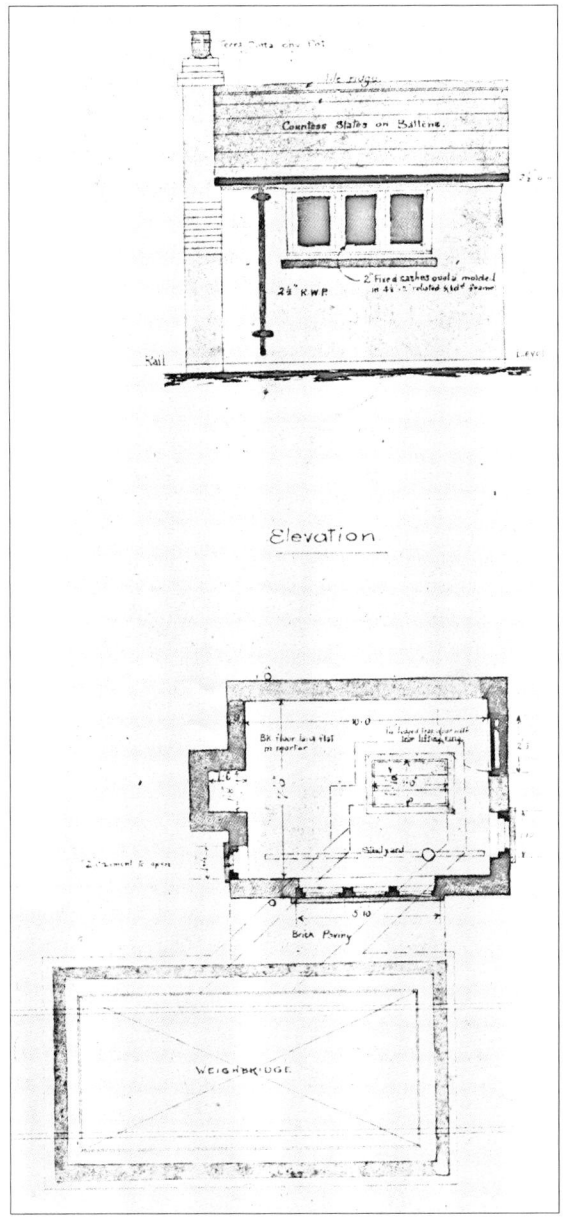

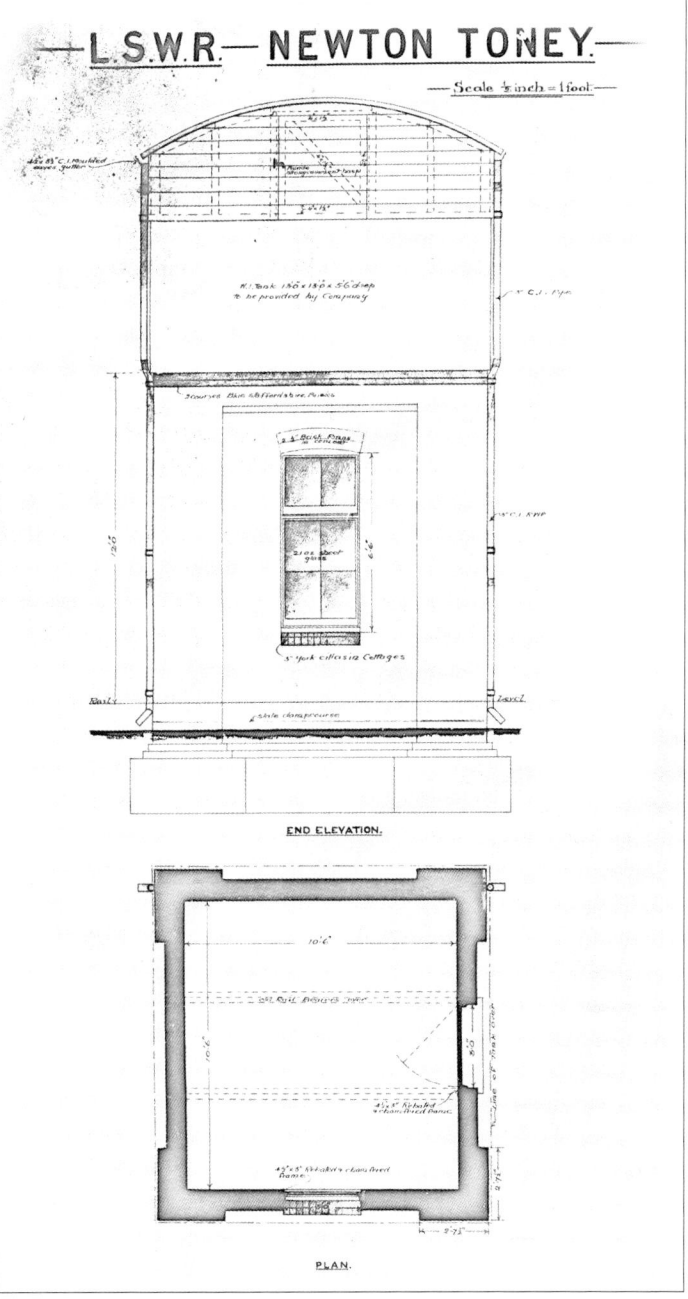

Top left - Shelter for Newton Tony down platform, undated.

Above - Newton Tony water tank, November 1900. Capacity not given.

Left - 20 ton weighbridge and office at Amesbury, October 1900

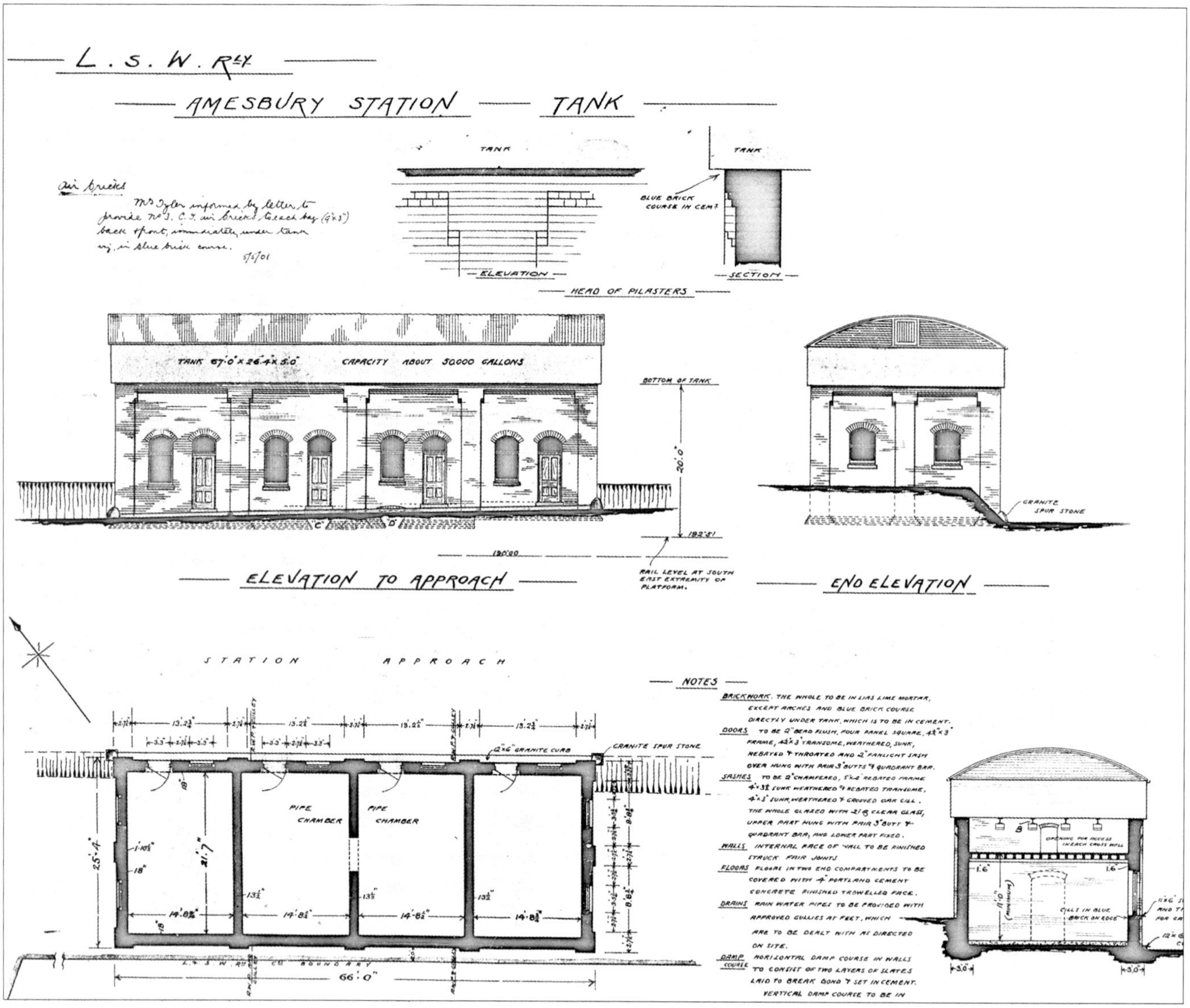
L. S. W. Rly
AMESBURY STATION — TANK
TANK
ELEVATION
BLUE BRICK COURSE IN CEMT
SECTION
HEAD OF PILASTERS
TANK 67'0" x 26'4" x 5'0" CAPACITY ABOUT 50,000 GALLONS
BOTTOM OF TANK
20'0"
192'81
190'20
RAIL LEVEL AT SOUTH EAST EXTREMITY OF PLATFORM.
ELEVATION TO APPROACH
GRANITE SPUR STONE
END ELEVATION
STATION APPROACH
NOTES
BRICKWORK. THE WHOLE TO BE IN LIAS LIME MORTAR, EXCEPT ARCHES AND BLUE BRICK COURSE DIRECTLY UNDER TANK, WHICH IS TO BE IN CEMENT.
DOORS TO BE 2" BEAD FLUSH, FOUR PANEL SQUARE, 4½" x 3" FRAME, 4½" x 3" TRANSOME, WEATHERED, SUNK, REBATED & THROATED AND 2" FANLIGHT SASH OVER HUNG WITH PAIR 3" BUTTS & QUADRANT BAR.
SASHES TO BE 2" CHAMFERED, 5" x 4" REBATED FRAME 4" x 3½" SUNK WEATHERED & REBATED TRANSOME, 4" x 3" SUNK, WEATHERED & GROOVED OAK CILL. THE WHOLE GLAZED WITH 21 oz CLEAR GLASS, UPPER PART HUNG WITH PAIR 3" BUTT & QUADRANT BAR, AND LOWER PART FIXED.
WALLS INTERNAL FACE OF WALL TO BE FINISHED STRUCK FAIR JOINTS
FLOORS FLOORS IN TWO END COMPARTMENTS TO BE COVERED WITH 4" PORTLAND CEMENT CONCRETE FINISHED TROWELLED FACE.
DRAINS RAIN WATER PIPES TO BE PROVIDED WITH APPROVED GULLIES AT FEET, WHICH ARE TO BE DEALT WITH AS DIRECTED ON SITE.
DAMP COURSE HORIZONTAL DAMP COURSE IN WALLS TO CONSIST OF TWO LAYERS OF SLATES LAID TO BREAK BOND & SET IN CEMENT. VERTICAL DAMP COURSE TO BE IN
PIPE CHAMBER
PIPE CHAMBER
12" x 6" GRANITE CURB
GRANITE SPUR STONE
25'4"
21'7"
66'0"
L. & S. W. RY CO BOUNDARY

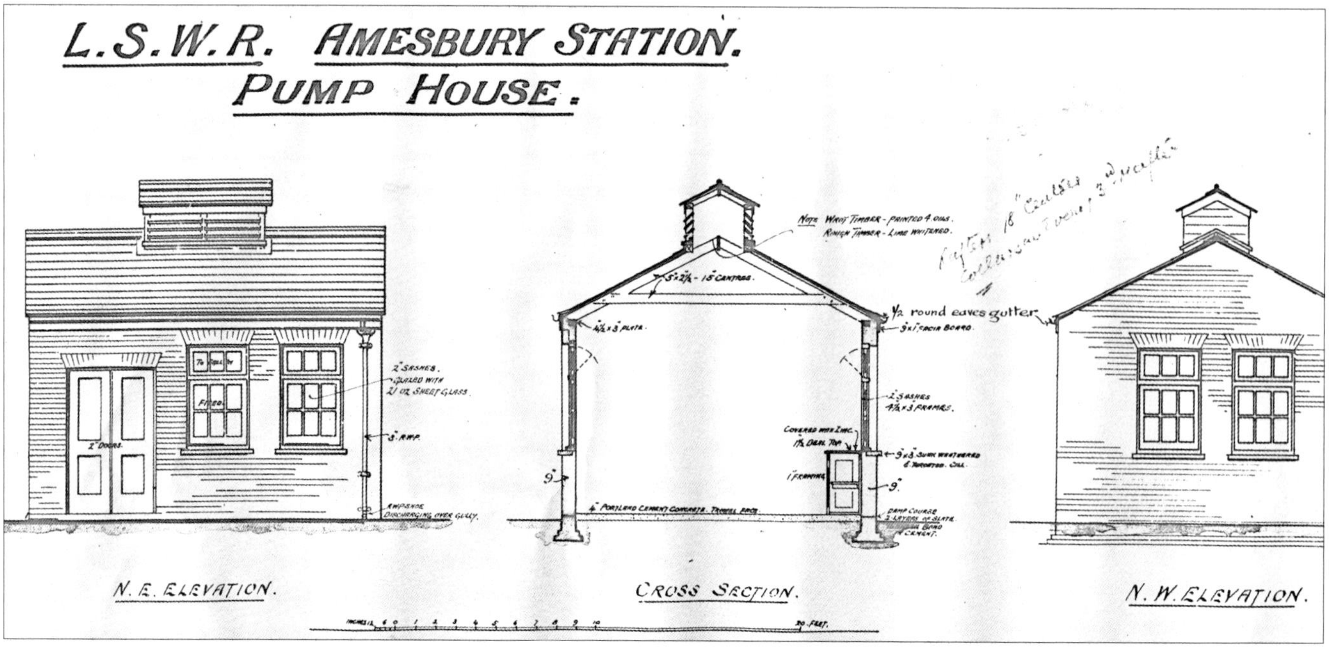
L.S.W.R. AMESBURY STATION.
PUMP HOUSE.
2" SASHES. GLAZED WITH 21 oz. SHEET GLASS.
2" DOORS.
3" R.W.P.
DISCHARGING OVER GULLY.
NOTE WROT TIMBER - PAINTED 4 OILS.
ROUGH TIMBER - LIME WHITENED.
½ round eaves gutter
9 x 1 FACIA BOARD.
2" SASHES
4½ x 3 FRAMES.
4½ x 3 PLATE.
4" PORTLAND CEMENT CONCRETE - TROWEL FACE.
DAMP COURSE 2 LAYERS OF SLATE IN CEMENT.
N. E. ELEVATION.
CROSS SECTION.
N. W. ELEVATION.

Opposite page - The Amesbury 50,000 (approx) gallon capacity water tank and associated pump house, 1901.

Right - Drawing for a pair of identical cottages for Amesbury, June 1910. Both pairs were of the 3-bedroom type having one bedroom at the front downstairs. The rear of the ground floor comprised a living room and built-on scullery. The cost for both pairs was estimated at £841 15s 2d.

This page, middle - Standard footbridge for Amesbury, dated February 1907.

This page, bottom - Additional goods storage, Amesbury, February 1919.

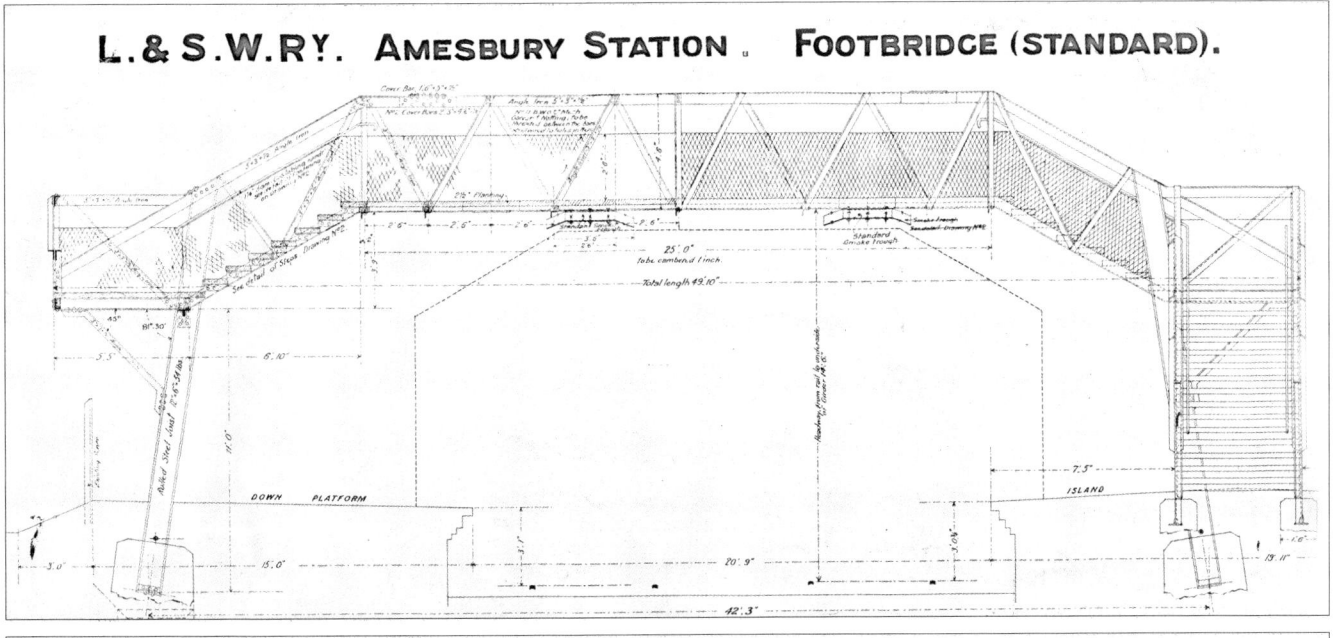

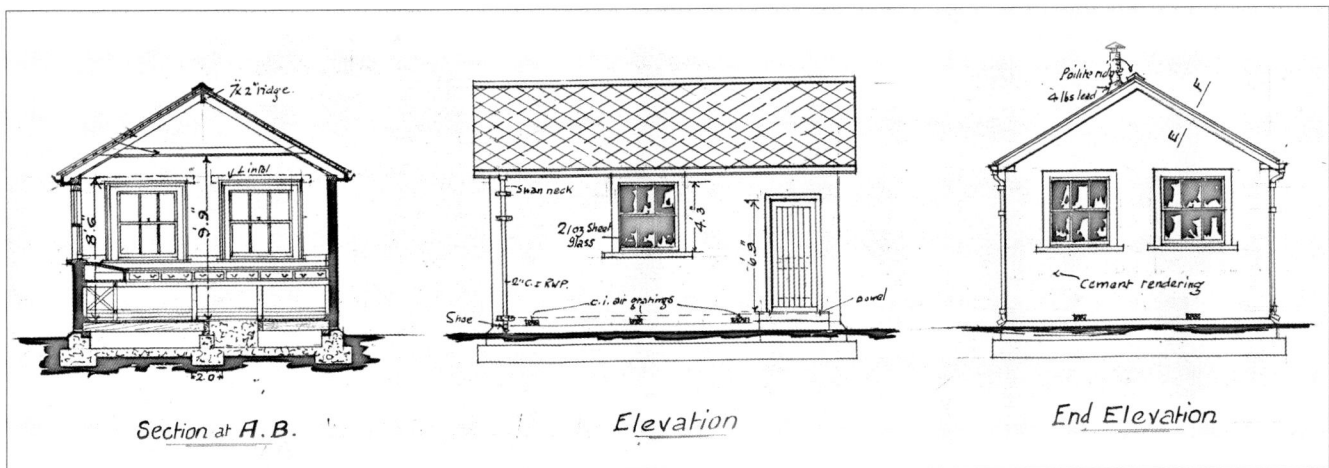

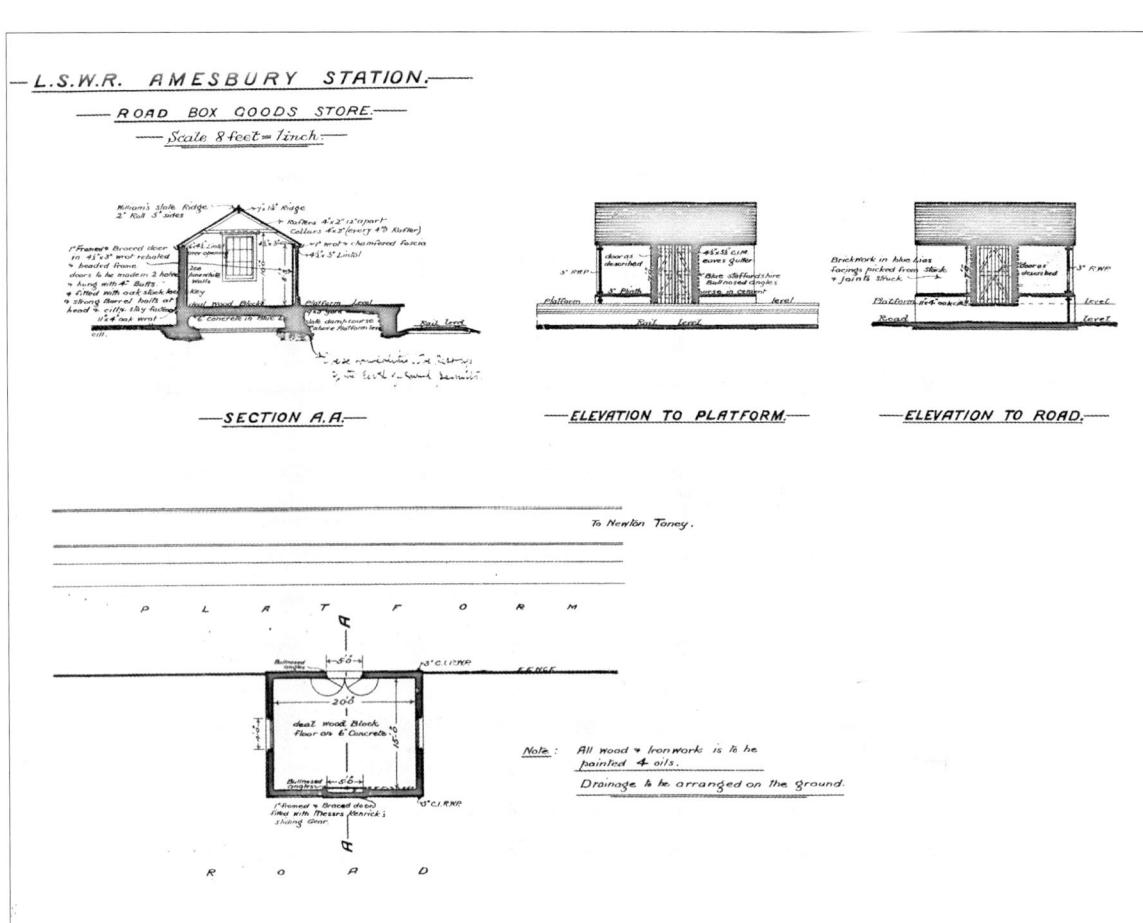

Left - *Amesbury Road Box Goods Store, June 1901.*

Bottom - *Bulford, extension of Goods Store, March 1915.*

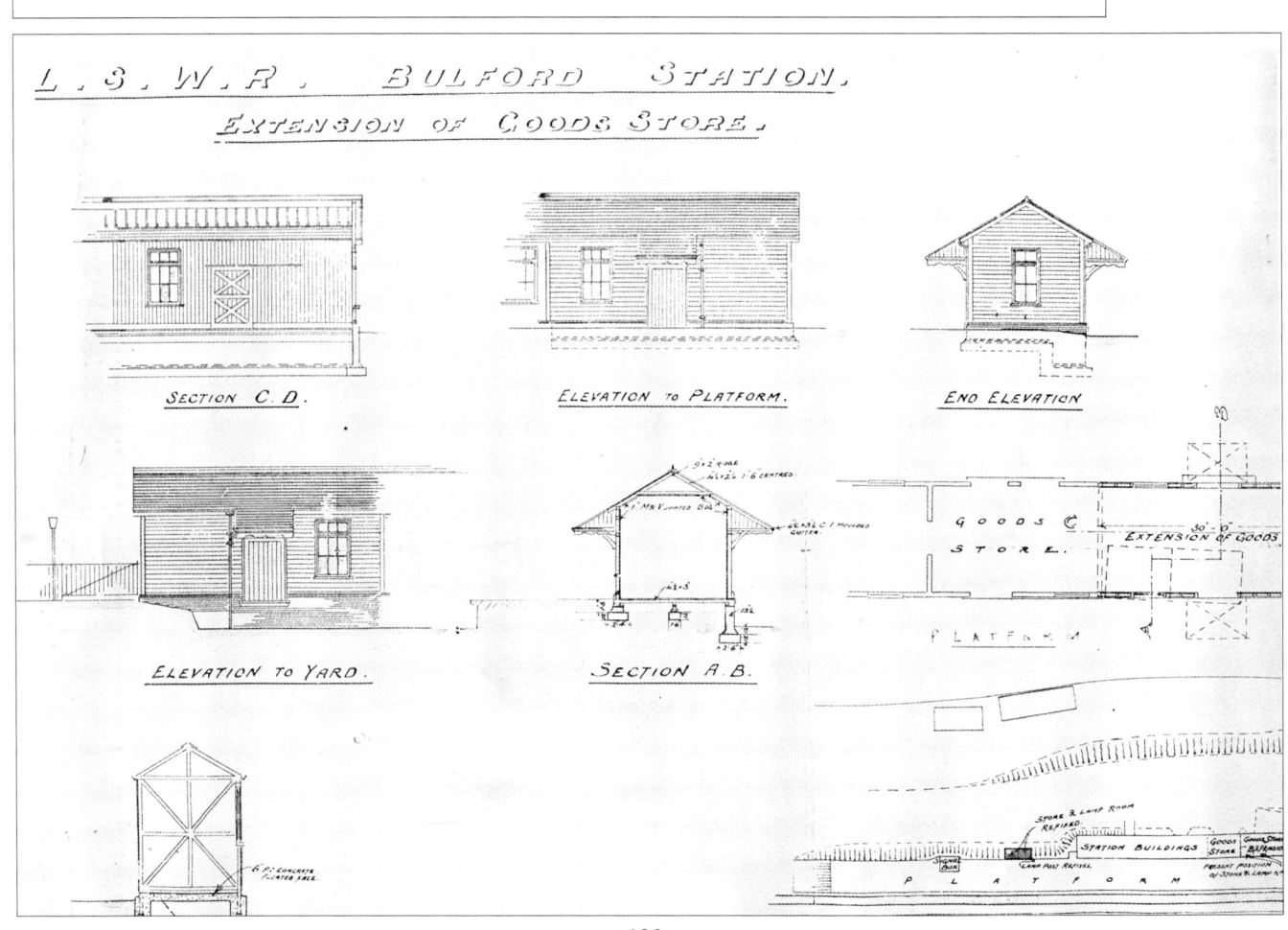

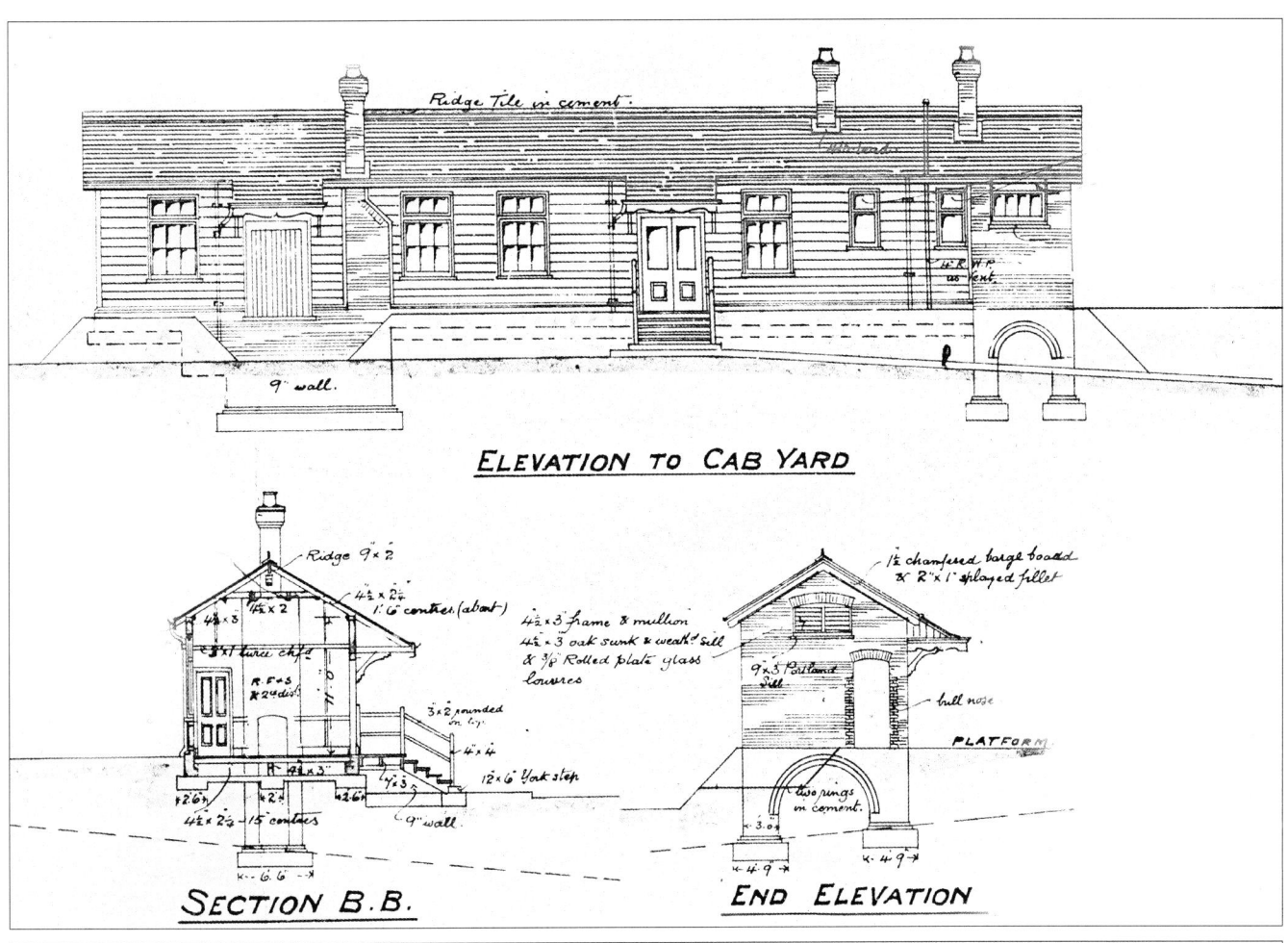

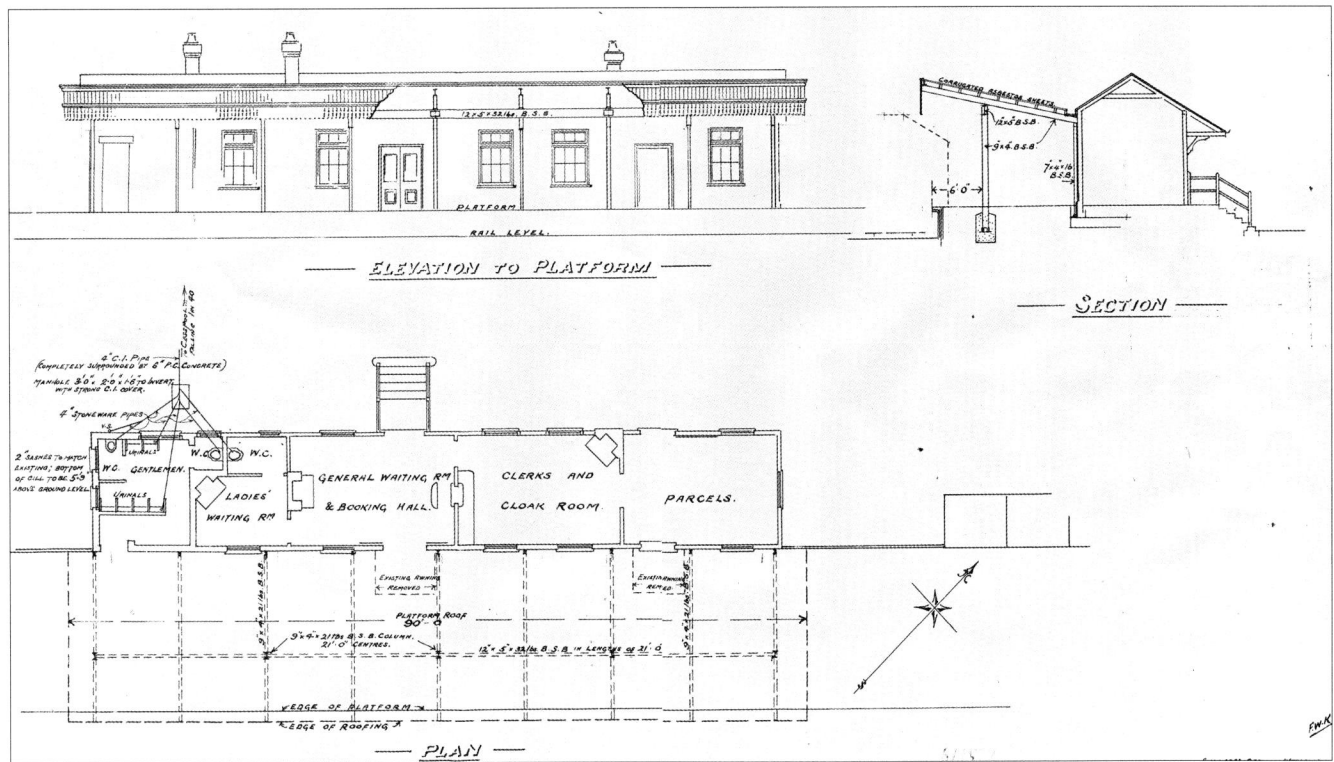

Top - *'Bulford Extension Line: Bulford Village Station' elevations, March 1904.*
Bottom - *The later canopy provision at Bulford.*

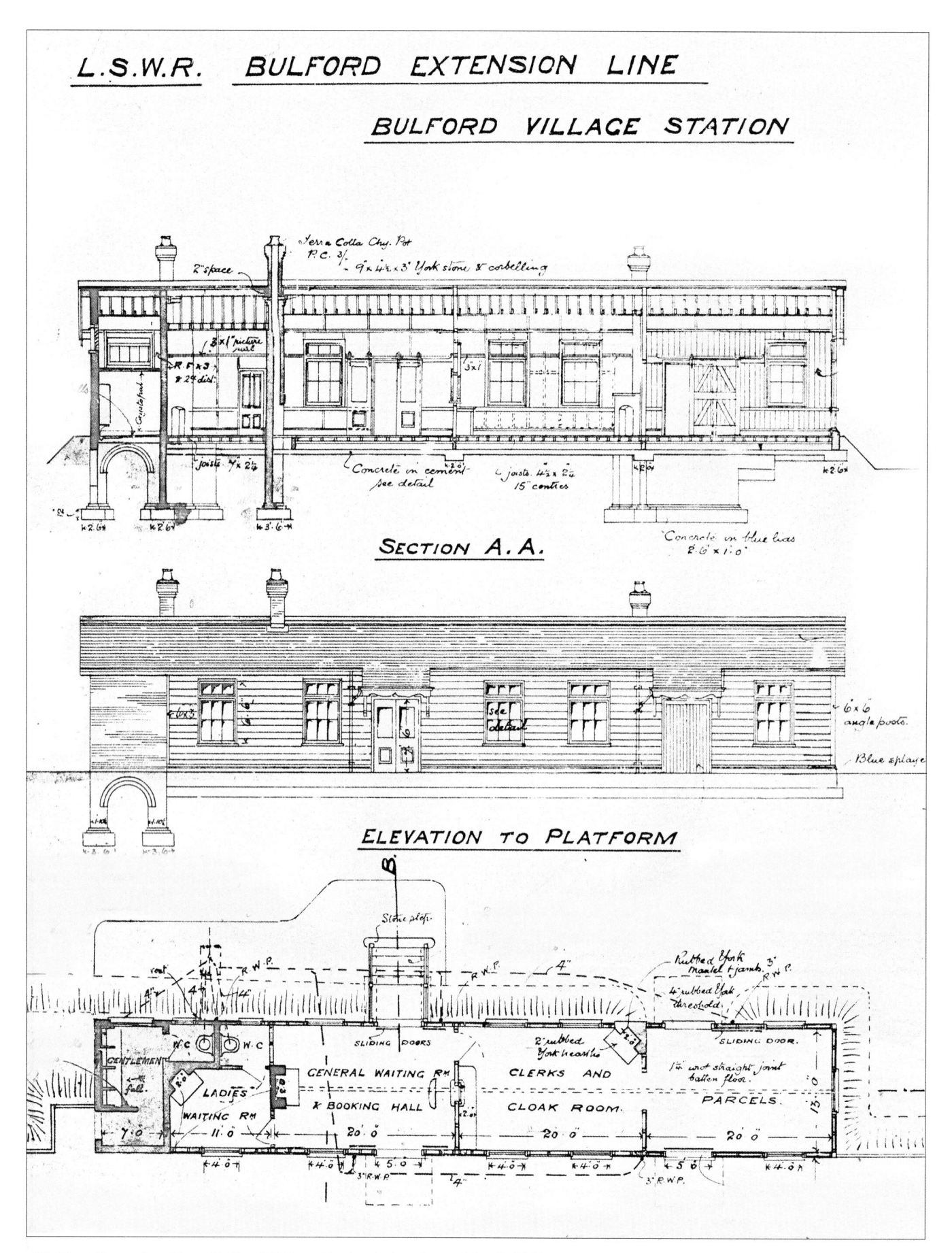

'Bulford Extension Line: Bulford Village Station' elevations, March 1904.

APPENDIX IV. TIMETABLES

1906

		WEEKDAYS AM				PM						SUNDAYS PM		
London Waterloo	dep:	5.50		b8.50	11.15		2.10	b3.30	5.50			: c5.40	10.00
Andover Junction	dep:	7.55		b10.38	1.05		3.58		7.35	c7.49		: c8.17	11.59
Salisbury	dep:	7.40	8.25	11.10	12.45	2.35	3.20	5.25		9.12		: 8.40	
Porton		: 7.51	8.35	11.20	12.56	2.45	3.32	5.35		9.22		: 8.50	
Grateley	arr:	8.02			1.08		3.45					:	
Grateley	dep:	8.08			1.18		4.15		7.48			:	
Newton Tony		: 8.17	8.45	11.30	1.27	2.55	4.24	5.45	7.57	9.32		: 9.00	
Amesbury		: 8.28	8.56	11.41	1.38	3.06	4.35	5.56	8.08	9.43		: 9.11	12.28
Bulford		: 8.35	9.07	11.50	1.45	3.17	4.45	6.03	8.15	9.50		: 9.17	12.35

		AM			PM								
Bulford		: 7.03	8.55	10.03	12.08	1.08	3.05	4.32	6.53	8.28		: NO	
Amesbury		7.10	9.05	10.10	12.15	1.15	3.20	4.43	7.00	8.35		: SUNDAY	
Newton Tony		: 7.21	9.16	10.21	12.26	1.26	3.31	4.54	7.11	8.46		: SERVICE	
Grateley	arr:	9.25		12.35		3.40						:	
Grateley	dep:			1.32		4.11						:	
Porton		: 7.31		10.31	1.42	1.36		5.04	7.21	8.56		:	
Salisbury		: 7.40		10.40	1.52	1.45	4.25	5.13	7.30	9.05		:	
Andover Junction		: c8.11	c9.36	c11.04	12.46		3.54	c5.32	b8.42	c9.36		:	
London Waterloo		:c10.09	c12.00	c1.35	2.35	3.30	6.15	c7.30	b10.02	c11.04		:	

b Via Salisbury   c Via Porton

1914

[Amesbury and Bulford Light Railway timetable — reproduced as printed image]

1924

		WEEKDAYS AM		PM					SUNDAYS PM
London Waterloo	:	c7.30	11.00	1.00	3.00	c5.00	c6.00		c6.00
Salisbury	: 8.25	10.15	12.30	3.13	4.45	7.22	9.05		8.30
Porton	: 8.37	10.27	1.01	3.23	4.56	7.33	9.17		8.42
Newton Tony	: 8.47	10.37	1.11	3.35	5.06	7.43	9.27		8.52
Amesbury	: 8.58	10.48	1.22	3.46	5.17	7.54	9.38		9.03
Bulford	: 9.05	10.55	1.29	3.53	5.24	8.01	9.46		9.12

	AM		PM					PM
Bulford	: 8.12	11.04	1.42	2.50	4.45	5.35	8.20	9.35
Amesbury	: 8.21	11.11	1.49	2.57	4.52	5.42	8.27	9.42
Newton Tony	: 8.32	11.22	2.00	3.08	5.03	5.53	8.38	9.53
Porton	: 8.42	11.32	2.10	3.18	5.13	6.03	8.49	
Salisbury	: 8.53	11.43	2.21	3.30	5.25	6.15	8.59	10.13
London Waterloo	c10.56	1.56	a4.30	5.50	c8.20	8.41	c11.20	:

c Via Porton   a Arrives 4.06 on Saturdays

1944

		WEEKDAYS AM			PM				SUNDAYS AM
London Waterloo	:	x5.40	9.00	10.50	12.50	x3.30	x5.35	x7.35	:	11.00
Salisbury	:	8.55	11.10	1.12	3.03	5.43	7.55	9.45	:	4.30
Porton	:	9.04	11.20	1.21	3.12	5.54	8.05	9.54	:	4.39
Idmiston Halt	:	9.06	11.22	1.23	3.14	5.56	8.07	9.56	:	4.41
Newton Tony	:	9.14	11.30	1.31	3.22	6.04	8.15	10.04	:	4.49
Amesbury	:	9.23	11.40	1.41	3.32	6.14	8.25	10.14	:	4.53
Bulford	:	9.28	11.45	1.46	3.37	6.19	8.30	10.19	:	5.03

			AM			PM				PM
Bulford	:	8.00	9.40	11.52	1.53	3.55	6.26	8.38	:	5.10
Amesbury	:	8.05	9.44	11.56	1.58	4.00	6.30	8.42	:	5.14
Newton Tony	:	8.14	9.53	12.05	2.07	4.09	6.39	8.51	:	5.24
Idmiston Halt	:	8.23	10.01	12.13	2.15	4.17	6.47	8.59	:	5.32
Porton	:	8.25	10.04	12.16	2.18	4.20	6.49	9.02	:	5.35
Salisbury	:	8.36	10.12	12.25	2.27	4.29	6.58	9.13	:	5.44
London Watcrloo	:	x11.09		2.42	5.12	6.32	10.30		:	x8.27

x Via Porton

1951

		WEEKDAYS ONLY AM
London Waterloo	:	11.00
Salisbury	:	1.00
Porton	:	1.09
Idmiston Halt	:	1.11
Newton Tony	:	1.19
Amesbury	:	1.28
Bulford	:	1.35

		AM
Bulford	:	9.40
Amesbury	:	9.44
Newton Tony	:	9.53
Idmiston Halt	:	10.01
Porton	:	10.04
Salisbury	:	10.13
London Waterloo	:	x12.20

x Via Porton

APPENDIX V. GRADIENT PROFILES

Gradient profiles for the Amesbury Branch and the Bulford Extension

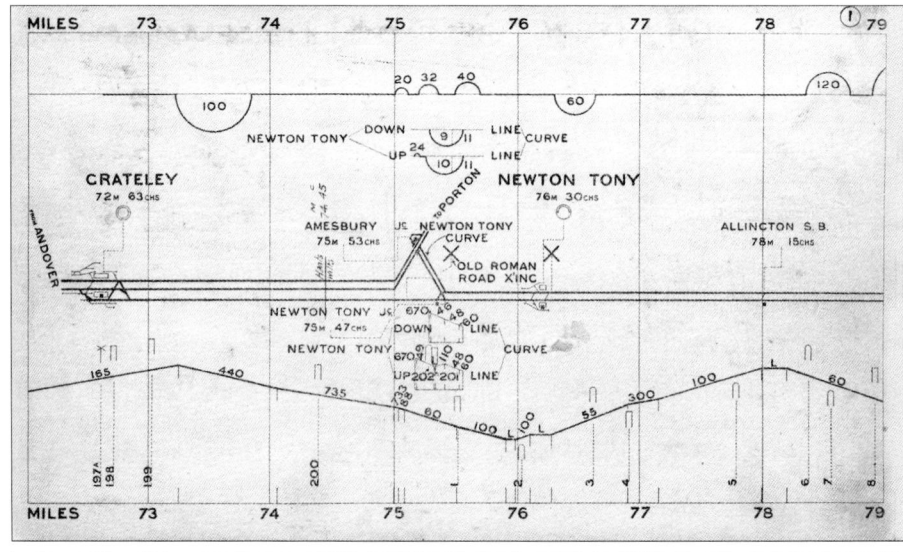

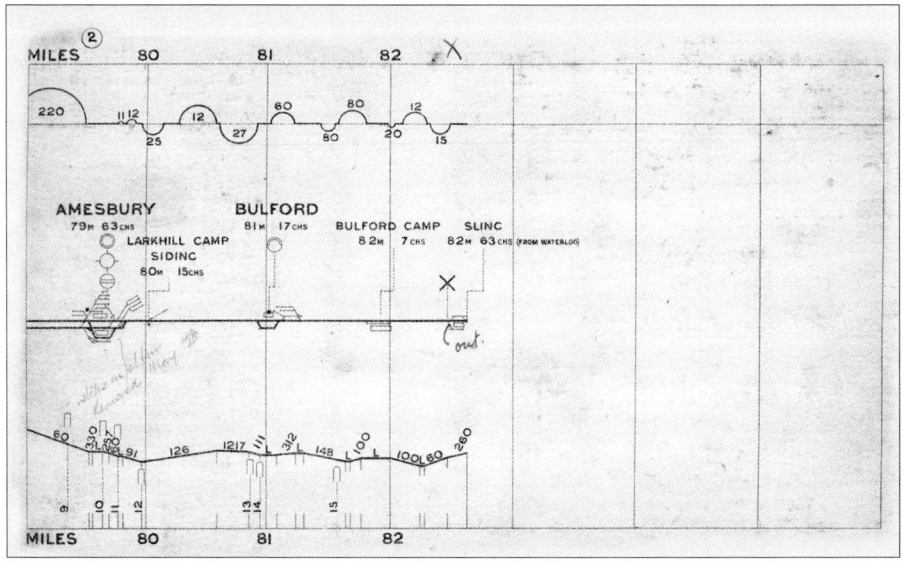

APPENDIX VI. WORKING TIMETABLE APPENDICES
Southern Railway Working Timetable Appendices for 1934

Goods trains may be made up to 40 wagons, with a heavy brake van at the rear, between Salisbury and Amesbury, and between Andover Junction and Amesbury, but an assisting engine must in such cases be attached at the rear of the trains between Newton Tony and Amesbury stations.

When an assisting engine is provided at the rear, and also when from the nature of the load of a train worked by one engine only, or the weather conditions, the men in charge consider it desirable, the train must, before descending the decline to Amesbury in the case of down trains, or to Newton Tony in the case of up trains, be brought to a stand before passing on to the falling gradient, and three-fourths of the total number of wagon brakes must be pinned down to ensure safe working of the train down the gradient.

The Guard will be responsible for seeing the wagon brakes are pinned down as before indicated, and also for seeing the brakes are released on arrival of the train at Amesbury or Newton Tony, as the case may be.
The assisting engine must, in every instance, run through from Newton Tony to Amesbury, or vice versa, attached to the train, and must not be uncoupled between those points.

One twenty-ton goods brake van must be attached at the rear of every goods train running over this line.

Ratfyn military siding. - Wagons for the siding must be propelled from Amesbury station. Upon completion of the work at the siding, outgoing traffic from the siding must be hauled to Amesbury station.

Working of traffic from Bulford station to Bultord Camp (Military) and Sling. - The layout at Bulford Camp station consists of a long loop in the single running line, with a crossover road about midway between the ends of the loop. The normal position of the points, which are worked by hand lever, is for the single running line.

The single line extends beyond Bulford Camp station for a distance of about half a mile and terminates at buffer stops immediately before reaching Marlborough Road at Sling.

The gradient of the single line at the facing connection to the loop at Bulford Camp is 1 in 100 rising towards Sling, changing to level through the station and falling 1 in 100 towards Sling thereafter, with a rise of 1 in 60 from the 82½ mile post to the buffer stops at Sling.

Traffic from Bulford station to the Camp station and Sling terminus is worked by a shunting trip in charge of a competent man. Wagons must be hauled from Bulford to Bulford Camp, and propelled from Bulford Camp to Sling, the latter movement being restricted to not more than five wagons on each occasion. In the reverse direction wagons must be hauled from Sling to Bulford Camp, and from Bulford Camp to Bulford.

Before movements are made between Bulford Camp and Sling, the Station Master at Bulford must make arrangements with the military authorities for a man, deputed by the latter, to be stationed at the level crossing situated approximately 500 feet from the buffer stops at Sling, to warn users of the roadway. The competent man must inform the watchman provided by the military authorities on each occasion when movements are completed.

A level crossing without gates passes over both roads of the loop at the Sling end of the connection nearest No. 15 bridge and the staff must keep a sharp look-out and safeguard this crossing when shunting operations are taking place through the adjacent connection or during the passage of trains over the Camp line at this spot.

Name	Location	Nearest station	Gradient	Shunting limit	Released by	Person in charge	How operated
Ratfyn Military	Down side between Amesbury and Bulford	Amesbury	125 falling towards Amesbury	Clearance point	Ground frame Train Tablet	Station Master	Special Service
Bulford Camp (Military)	Up side ¾ mile from Bulford station	Bulford			Hand points from single line		Special Service from Bulford

SOUTHERN RAILWAY - Signal Instruction No. 12, 2 April 1935

Introduction of Key Token system between Amesbury and Bulford.
To be carried out on Tuesday 9 April, commencing at 9.30 am.

The existing electric train tablet system of working will be abolished and in lieu thereof the line between Amesbury and Bulford will, in future, be worked under the key token system, instruments known as the 'No-Signalman' Key-token instruments being provided. The Signalman at Bulford will be withdrawn and the signal box worked as a ground frame.

The down home and up starting signals at Bulford will be abolished.

'No-Signalman' Key token instruments will be provided in the signal box at Amesbury and the ground frame at Bulford, these instruments being described and illustrated on page 101 of the Standard Regulations for Train Signalling and on page 29 of the Instructions for information of Drivers, Firemen and Guards.

The points connecting with the single line at Bulford will be worked from the ground frame, which will be released by the key token. The points at Ratfyn siding will also be released by the key token.

The Rules for working Single Lines by Train Staff and Ticket shown on pages 70 to 76 inclusive of the Standard Regulations for Train Signalling, and on pages 24 to 27 of the Instructions for information of Drivers, Firemen and Guards, will apply to the section of line between Amesbury and Bulford, except that tickets will not be used and trains will carry a key token instead of a staff, and as otherwise modified in these special instructions.

T9 No. 30719 waiting to leave Bulford for Amesbury with a solitary van 2 June 1952. Post 1935, the stop signal seen (of LSWR lower quadrant vintage) at the far end of the platform was the only remaining signal at the station, this was No 3 in the lever frame, and could be cleared provided the hand (scissor crossover) points providing access to and from the goods yard beyond the signal had been detected as 'normal'. Beyond the stop signal the line continued towards Bulford Camp and Sling. To indicate the location of the station for trains arriving from the direction of Amesbury, a marker light was provided a little distance before the station. As referred to in the official notice reproduced on these pages, the former signal box (the roof of which can just be seen above the tender) was not designated a Ground-frame, but it was from here that the loop points and signal were controlled. Lever No 7 in the frame unlocking these and which in return was released by the key token. No signal or other indicator was provided for departing trains. Notice the engine number appears in small letters on the rear of the tender. (S C Nash)

Trains will not be block signalled between Amesbury and Bulford, but the telephone communication provided between Amesbury signal box and Bulford ground frame must be used for advising the departure of trains in both directions.

The Guard of the train must, when and as required, receive the key token from, and deliver it to, the Driver of a train at Bulford, the Porter at Bulford being held similarly responsible in the case of a light engine. When it is necessary for a key token to be placed in or taken from the instrument at Bulford, this must be done only by the Guard of a train, or by the Porter in the case of a light engine.

Prior to despatch of a train from Amesbury, the Signalman there must, provided the indicator of the instrument shows 'Free', withdraw a key token from the instrument and hand it to the Driver. At the same time the Signalman must inform the Guard, or the Driver in the case of a light engine, whether a second train is to follow for Bulford and must also telephone this information to that station.

On arrival of the train at Bulford, the Driver may retain the key token for the return service to Amesbury, but for running round or shunting purposes he must deliver the key token to the Guard, who will hand it to the Porter to enable the ground frame to be released. After shunting operations have been completed, the key token must be handed back to the Driver by the Guard, but if a second train has to follow from Amesbury, the first train must be shunted clear of the platform line, in which case the Guard must, after satisfying himself that the train has been so shunted, place the key token in the instrument.

Whenever a second train has to follow from Amesbury to Bulford, the first train, with tail lamp attached, must always be shunted completely clear of the platform line BEFORE the Key token is -placed in the instrument by the Guard or Porter, as the case may be.

Prior to the despatch of a train from Bulford to Amesbury, the Guard in charge of the train, or the Porter in the case of a light engine, must, if the key token has previously been placed in the instrument, and the indicator shows 'Free', withdraw a key token and hand it to the Driver. On arrival at Amesbury the Signalman must satisfy himself that the train or engine is complete with tail lamp attached before replacing the key token in the instrument.

The Porter at Bulford will be held responsible for correctly setting the points for all running and shunt movements, and for securing the points by the facing point lock for such movements in the facing direction. The Guard of each train must be careful to see that the points are correctly set before authorising shunt movements over them, the Fireman being held similarly responsible in the case of a light engine.

The points in the running line at the Amesbury end of Bulford Station must be set normally for the platform line and correctly secured by the facing point lock. The points in the single line at the Camp end of Bulford station must be set normally for the loop line.

The key token must be withdrawn from the instrument for all shunting movements fouling the single line.
Drivers of trains from Bulford to Amesbury must understand that the line may be clear only to the Amesbury up home signal and must run cautiously prepared to bring their trains to a stand at that signal, if required.

S.D.S.O. SOUTHAMPTON CENTRAL. S.N.NO.S. 188. S.D. 28th January, 1944.

NEWTON TONY.

(1)   To be carried out on Tuesday, 1st. February, commencing at 9.30a.m.

Trailing points leading from a new siding will be provided in down line 1½ miles Amesbury side of signal box, with catch points in siding at clearance point of connection with down line. The trailing points and catch points will be worked from a new 2-lever ground frame which will be electrically controlled from Newton Tony signal box and worked in accordance with the instructions under the heading "Standard Electrical release lever control" appearing in Standard Block Regulations and Book of Instructions for information of Drivers, Firemen and Guards.
NOTE AND ADVISE ALL CONCERNED.
J.K.   11.20A.M. (S.N.NO.S. 188.S.D.)

APPENDIX VII. LINES AROUND STONEHENGE
Proposed and constructed railway lines within the vicinity of Stonehenge

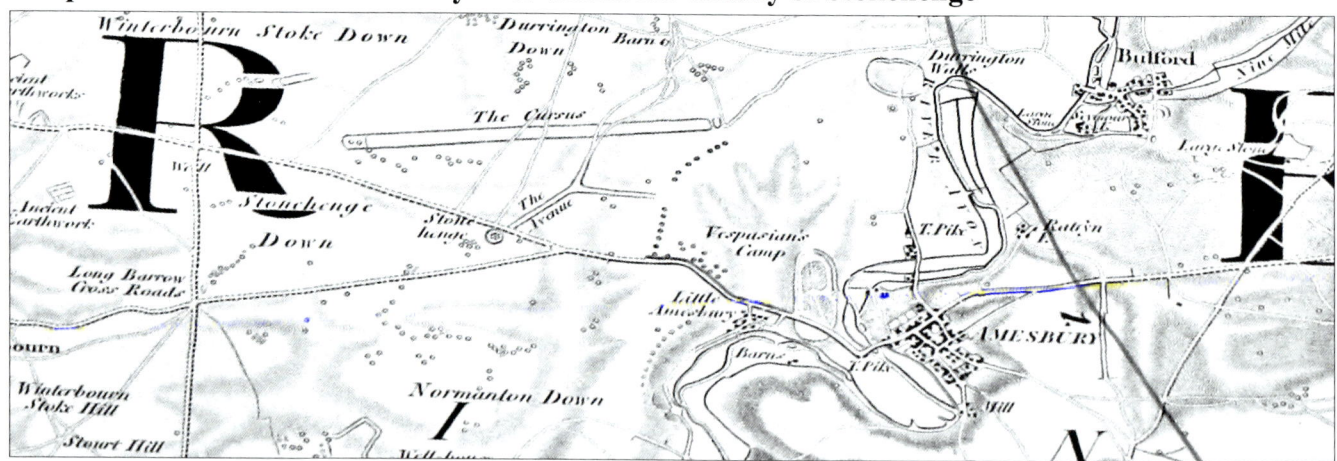

The Wiltshire Railway proposal of 1864.

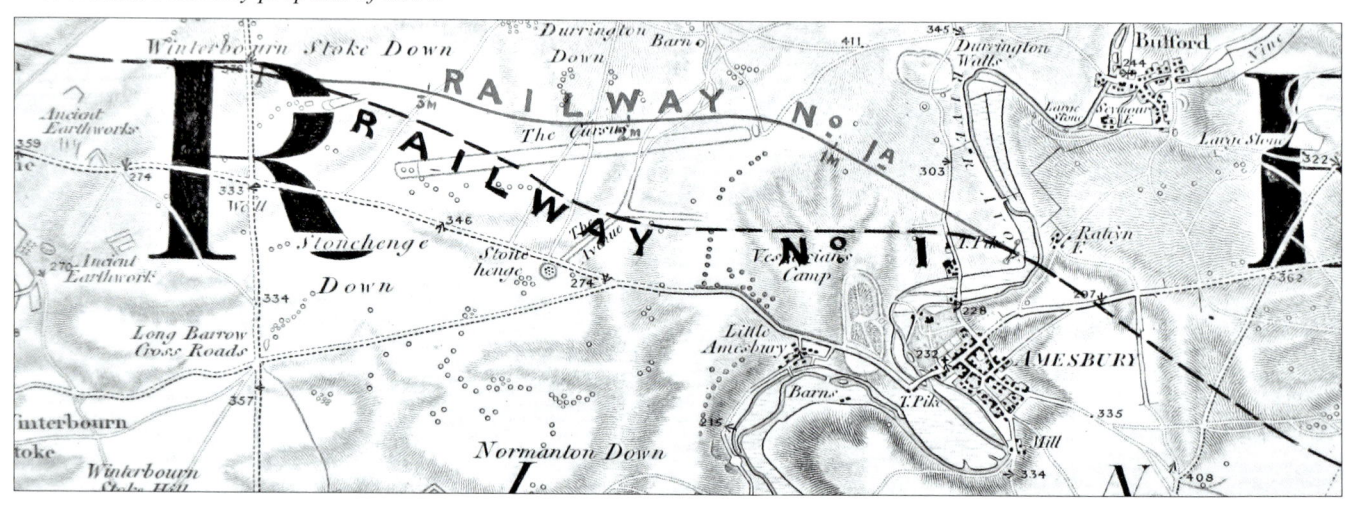

The Bristol & LSW Junction Railway proposal of 1882 showing the original line, 'Railway No 1', and the proposed 1883 deviation, 'Railway No 1A', to take the line further away from the Stones.

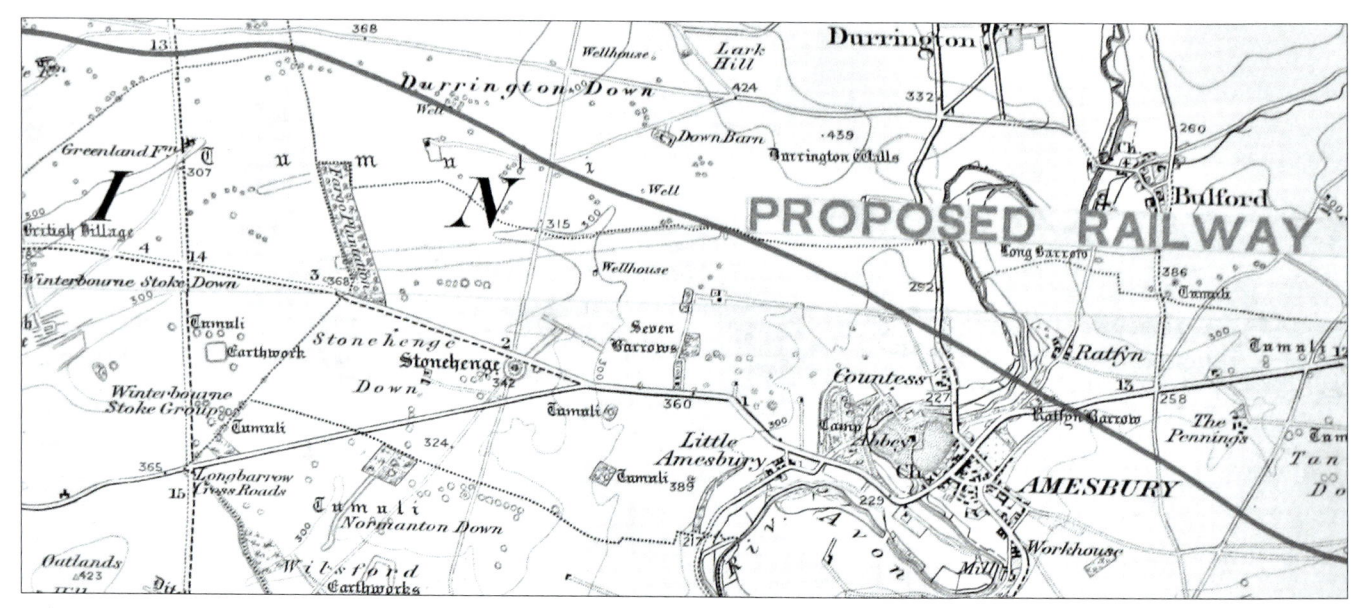

The LSWR Amesbury & Military Camp Light Railway of 1897, originally proposed to run to Shrewton.

Proposed and constructed railway lines within the vicinity of Stonehenge

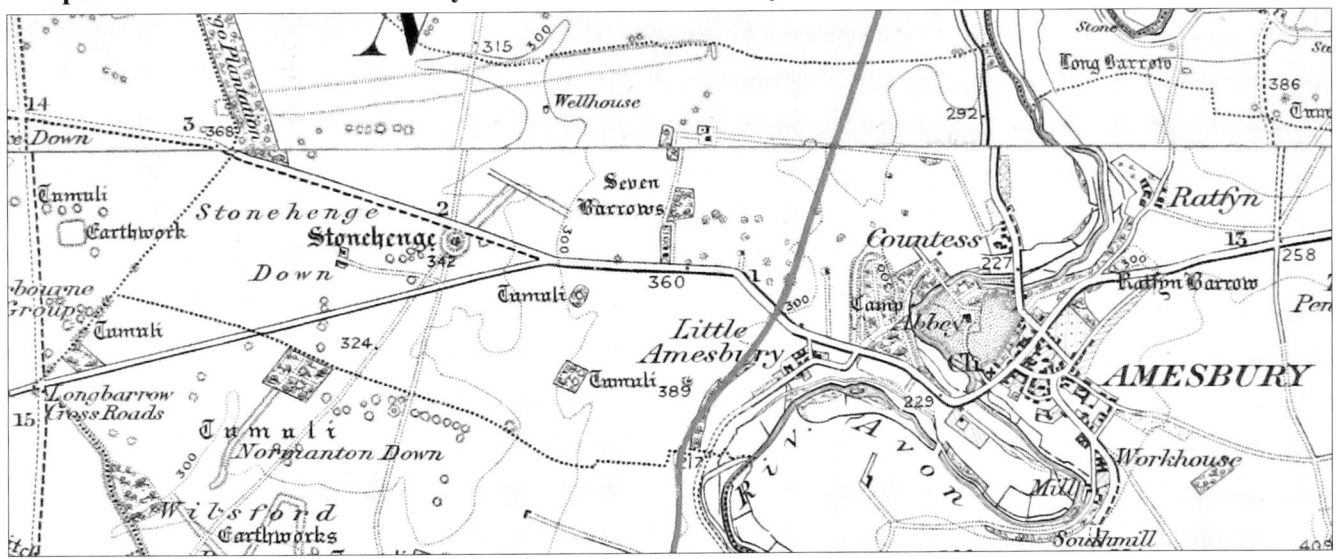

The GWR Pewsey & Salisbury Railway proposal of 1882, although authorised was never constructed.

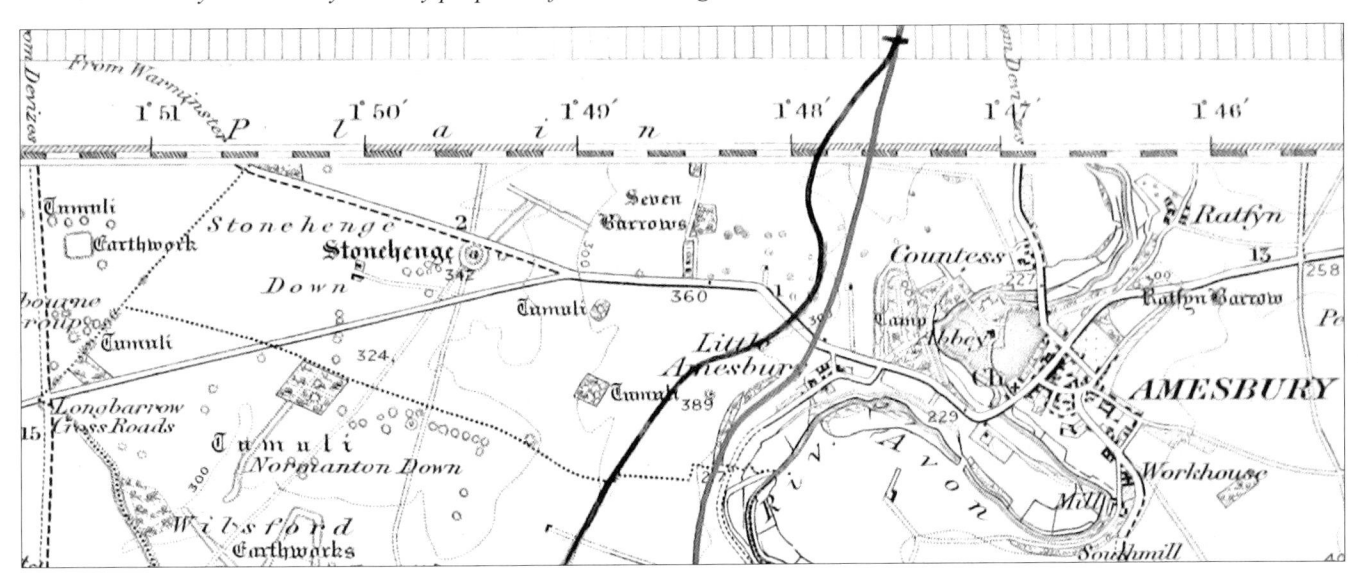

The GWR Pewsey & Salisbury Light Railway of 1898, showing the deviation from the 1883 proposal.

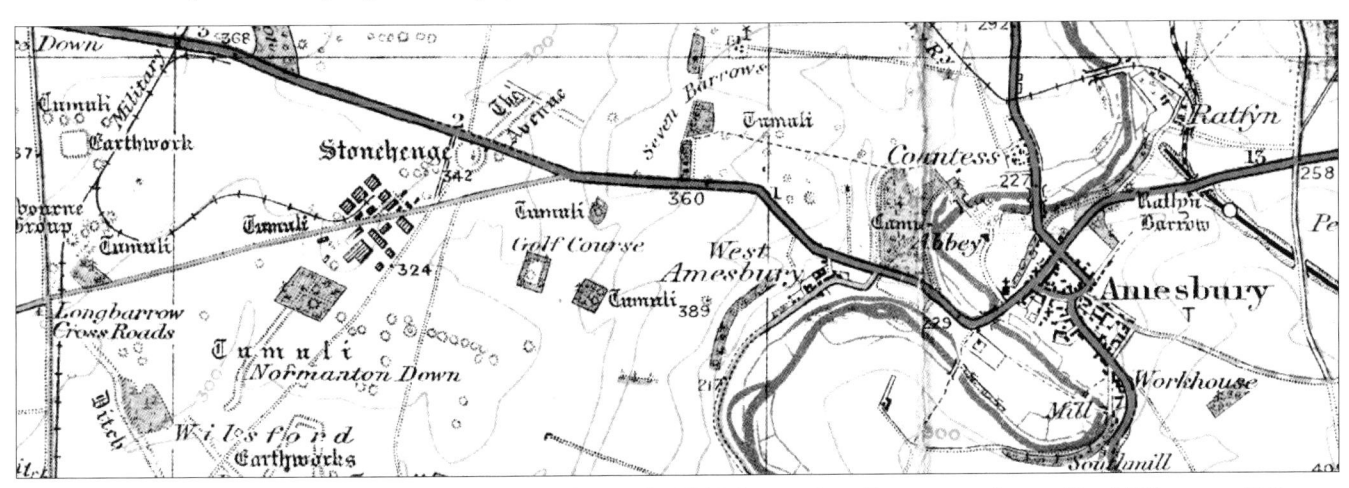

Rails finally arrive in the vicinity of the Stones in 1917 via the LMR line to the adjacent aerodrome. The LMR spurs off the 1906 Bulford extension from the LSWR Amesbury & Military Camps Branch of 1902.

APPENDIX VIII. RATEABLE VALUES 1930

Newton Tony Station

Assessment Area: - SALISBURY Rating Area: - AMESBURY RURAL

Occupier: - Southern Railway Company Plan Number: - LXI.N.W
Owners: - Themselves

Present Assessment: - £624 N.A.V. (To include Line of Railway).

Description	L.	W.	H.	Cubic Feet	Price	£	s	d
Concrete and eternite tiled building, containing: -	38'	12'	13'	5,928	6d	148	4	0
Booking Office 11' x 10' General Waiting Room 11' x 10' Ladies Waiting Room 11' x 10' inc. W.C. W.C. and 3 Stall urinal								
Corrugated Iron Lamp Room	10'	7'	9'	630	3d	7	17	6
Up Platform, gravel and wood	408'	10'						
Down Platform, gravel and wood	408'	10'						
Open Concrete and etenite slated Waiting Room	7'	15'	10'	1,050	4d	17	10	0
Cattle Pen and Loading Dock (One Pen)	19'	13'				10.	0	0
Siding - Up. Single	450'				30/- yd.	275.	0	0
Siding - Down. Single	360'				30/- yd.	180.	0	0
Platelayer's Hut, wood and felt roofed	15'	13'	8'	1,560	(Permanent Way)	-	-	-
Store, on brick foundation	12'	13'	12'	1,872	3d	23	8	0
Cast Iron Tank (6,825 gals)	13'	12'	7'	1,092	£22 per 1,000	135	0	0
Windmill (Supplies Station and three Cottages)						250	0	0
Sub Total						1046	19	6
£1,045 at 5%						52	0	0
Less 36% of £325.00.00						18	0	0
Estimated New Net Annual Value						**34**	**0**	**0**

Amesbury Station

No on Plan	Description	Condition	L.	W.	Area.	H	Cubic Feet	Price	£	s	d
1	"Let Off" Chaplins Ltd.		40'	8'	320'	9'	2,880	4d	48		
2	Timber and Iron roofed building on concrete piers. Small corrugated iron Oil Store on brick foundation thereto		8'	8'	64'	9'	576	4d	10		
3	Small building. - ditto - on wood piers Rough cast brick and slated Goods Shed, with part brick and part concrete floor Small partitioned office therein One ton Weighbridge by Pooley Platform set in floor		10½ 26' 52' 4'	10½ 8' 15' 4'	110' 208'	9' 10' 13'	990 2,080 10,140	4d 4d 4½d	17 35 190 2 10		

4	Corrugated Iron Shed Station Master's Room with tiled roof and concrete floor Wood Shed		12' 11' 11'	11' 11' 11'	132' 121' 121'	8' 12' 8'	1056 1,452 968	4½d 4d 4d	20 24 16	0 0	0 0
5	Brick and slated building (9" brickwork) Containing: - Ticket Office and Booking Hall Parcels and Cloak Room Goods Office Gents 4 Stall Urinal and 2 W.Cs. Ladies Waiting Room and W.C. Small Canopy Surround		60'	15'	900'	15'	13,500	7d	394 15	0 0	0 0
6	Open Platform Shelter with Corrugated Iron Roof carried by 6 steel uprights		34'	25'	850'	12'	10,200		65	0	0
7	Iron Frame Footbridge with wire sides - Very old pattern. Steps 5' wide								60	0	0
8	Turntable 45'								275	0	0
9	Wood, sleeper timber and Corrugated Iron roofed Gangers Shed (Not in)										
10	Wood and slated Signal Box (Not in)										
11	Porter's Cabin. Truck cover thereto - open		10'	7'	70'	8'	560		7 2	0 0	0 0
12	Rough cast and slated store with lean-to Coal Store thereto		25'	9'	225'	11'	2,475	4½d	46	0	0
13	Corrugated Iron Oil and Lamp Shed, with brick floor		11'	8'	88'	8'	704	3d	9	0	0
14	Double Iron Beam Crane on circular brick base. 5 ton. By R C Gibbins	Good							125	0	0
15	Brick built structure at entrance to Station, carrying Tank. Structure consists of 5 potato stores Tank - corrugated iron (1903)		65' 65'	26' 26'	1,690' 1,690'	17' 5'	28,730 at 8,450	5d	599 500	0	0
16	Brick and slated Engine House at entrance to Station. Containing: - 4 Plunger Pump, driven by a Dynamo		22'	17'	374'	14'	5,236	4½d	98 150	0 0	0 0
17	Small Water Crane								35	0	0
18	Island Platform - gravelled with brick facing								200	0	0
19	Unloading Platform - all Tarmac								50	0	0
20	Water Crane (Old Pattern)								20	0	0
	Approach Roads								50	0	0
Estimated Capital Value									2852	0	0

Bulford Station

No on Plan	Description	Condition	L.	W.	Area.	H	Cubic Feet	Price	£
1	Part brick, mainly timber and slated building, on brick wall foundation 4' deep Containing - Goods Office Parcels Office Waiting Room Ticket Office Ticket Hall Gents W.C. & Urinal (Size of last named - glazed walls 15' x 14')		135'	16'	2,160'	14'	30,240	5d	630
2	Canopy thereto over Platform - Carried by five stanchions Four Small Canopies to road for loading purposes		90'	22'	1,980'		19.8 squares at £5 each £5 each		100 20
1a	Lamp Store on Concrete Foundation		20'	7'	140'	10'	1,400	5d	30
1b	Signal Box (Not in)								
3	Part asphalt and part sleeper platform on concrete columns	Fair	390'	18'	7,020'		780 sq.yds at 15/-		585
4	Rough cast and tiled Office in Goods Yard		20'	16'	320'	12'	3,840	5d	80
5	"Let Off" - E B Maton								
6	"Let Off" - Cullen and Allen								
7	Small Cattle Surround Small Loading Platform thereto								5 40
8	Small Building - Permanent Way - Out								
9	Demolished								
10	Demolished								
11	"Let Off" - Chaplins Ltd.								
12	Tracks								
13	Gangers Shed - wood with sleeper floor - Permanent Way - Out								
14	Porters' Room opposite to platform. Wood and iron with brick foundations	Good	15'	15'					15
15	Iron Tank carried on stanchions, with Wind Pump, - serves Stations and Houses.								250
16	Station Master's House								
17a	Railway Cottage								
17b	Railway Cottage								
Estimated Capital Value									1755

APPENDIX IX. ESTIMATE OF EXPENSES, AMESBURY & MILITARY CAMP RAILWAY

LIGHT RAILWAY COMMISSIONERS - NOVEMBER 1897

ESTIMATE OF EXPENSE of the proposed LONDON AND SOUTH WESTERN RALWAY (AMESBURY AND MILITARY CAMP LIGHT RAILWAY)

Railway		Miles	F	Ch	Whether Single or Double
Length of Line		10	6	2.1	Single
Gauge		4 feet	8½ inches		
		Cubic Yards	Price per Yard	£ s d	£ s d
Earthworks			s. d.		
Cuttings	Rock				
	Chalk and Soft Soil	273,000	1.0	13,650	
	Roads	2,600	1 0	130	
Total		275,600		13,780	13,780 0 0
Embankments, including Roads		281,000 cu.yds			
Bridges - Public Roads		No. 9			5,850 0 0
Accommodation Bridges and Works					2,750 0 0
Viaduct					4,000 0 0
Culverts and Drains					2,100 0 0
Metallings and Fencings of Roads and Level Crossings					
Gatekeepers' Houses at Level Crossings					900 0 0
Permanent Way, including Fencing					
10 Miles 6 Furlongs 2.10 Chains at £1,900 per mile					20,474 17 6
Permanent Way for Sidings, and Cost of Junctions					1,500 0 0
Stations					3,000 0 0
					55,254 17 6
Contingencies, 5 per cent					2,762 14 10
Land and Buildings 90 Acres					4,500 0 0
Total					62,517 12 4

NEWTON TONY CURVE - ESTIMATE OF EXPENSE

Railway No. 1		Miles	F	Ch	Whether Single or Double
Length of Line			2	4.15	Single with land for a double line
Gauge		4 feet	8½ inches		
		Cubic Yards	Price per Yard	£ s d	£ s d
Earthworks			s. d.		
Cuttings	Rock				
	Chalk and Soft Soil	2,337	1.6	175 5 6	
	Roads				
Total		2,337	1.6	175 5 6	175 5 6
Embankments, including Roads		13,780 cu yds			
Bridges - Public Roads		No. 1			1,000 0 0
Accommodation Bridges and Works					100 0 0
Viaduct					
Culverts and Drains					50 0 0
Metallings and Fencings of Roads and Level Crossings					200 0 0
Gatekeepers' Houses at Level Crossings					
Permanent Way, including Fencing					
0 Miles 2 Furlongs 4.15 Chains at £3,630 per mile					1,095 16 2
Permanent Way for Sidings, and Cost of Junctions					1,200 0 0
Stations					
					3,821 1 8
Contingencies, 5 per cent					191 1 1
Land and Buildings 2 Acres 1 Rod 37 Perches					75 0 0
Total					4,087 2 9

Notice in connection with the provision of Allington Signal box and associated crossover. See top plan, page 116.

APPENDIX X. ENVOI, BIBLIOGRAPHY AND ACKNOWLEDGEMENTS

A final farewell as troops, believed to be from the Royal Artillery, prepare to depart from Salisbury Plain c.1914. (Fuller of Amesbury)

BIBLIOGRAPHY

The Bulford Branch Line	Peter Harding
Main Line to the West Vol.1 Basingstoke – Salisbury	Nicholas & Reeve
Basingstoke – Salisbury : Including the Bulford Branch	Mitchell & Smith
Gunners at Larkhill	N D G James
Plain Soldiering	N D G James
Narrow Gauge Railways on Salisbury Plain	Donald A E Cross
Railways: A History of the County of Wiltshire, Volume 4	Edited by Elizabeth Crittall

ACKNOWLEDGEMENTS

John Alsop, Colin Chivers, The South Western Circle, Peter Daniels, Ian Duckett, Derek Fear, John Fairman, Vic Freemantle, Peter Goodhugh, Jim Fuller, Bruce Murray, Kevin Potts, Roger Simmonds.

"....a few years later....the Royal Flying Corps, then occupying Stonehenge airfield, wrote to the MOD requesting that the ancient monument be moved as it was interfering with flying activities !"

OTHER ALL-COLOUR TITLES BY JEFFERY GRAYER PUBLISHED BY NOODLE BOOKS

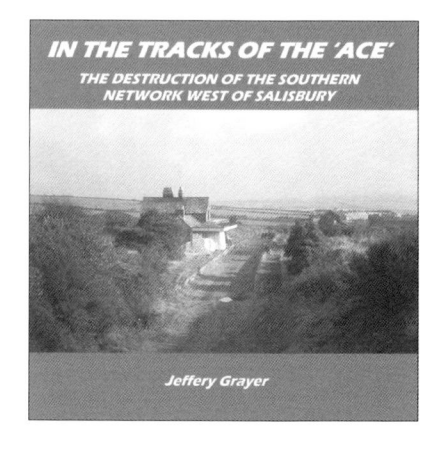

Further

'IMPERMANENT WAYS' and

'SOMERSET & DORSET'

VOLUMES ARE IN PREPARATION